Education Policy & Social Inequality

Volume 3

Series Editor

Trevor Gale, University of Glasgow, Glasgow, UK

This series publishes monographs and edited collections that investigate relations between education policy and social inequality. Submissions that provoke new and generative ways of thinking about and acting on relations between education policy and social inequality are particularly invited from early career, emerging and established scholars.

While education policy has often been understood as having a normative function and is proposed as the solution to social inequality, the series is interested in how education policy frames, creates and at times exacerbates social inequality. It adopts a critical orientation, encompassing (1) innovative and interdisciplinary theoretical and conceptual studies—including but not exclusively drawing on sociology, cultural studies, social and cultural geography, history—and (2) original empirical work that examines a range of educational contexts, including early years education, vocational and further education, informal education, K-12 schooling and higher education.

The series sees critique and policy studies as having a transformative function. It publishes books that seek to re-articulate policy discourses, the realm of research, or which posit (1) new dimensions to understanding the role of education policy in connection with enduring social problems and (2) the amelioration of social inequality in ways that challenge the possibility of equity in the liberal democratic state, as well as in other forms of governance and government.

Education Policy and Social Inequality is edited by Professor Trevor Gale.

Please contact the publishing editor, Nick Melchior (email: nick.melchior@ springer.com) if you are interested in submitting a proposal to this series.

More information about this series at http://www.springer.com/series/13427

Claudia Matus
Editor

Ethnography and Education Policy

A Critical Analysis of Normalcy
and Difference in Schools

 Springer

Editor
Claudia Matus
Center for Educational Justice
Pontificia Universidad Católica de Chile
Macul, Santiago (RM), Chile

ISSN 2520-1476   ISSN 2520-1484   (electronic)
Education Policy & Social Inequality
ISBN 978-981-13-8447-9   ISBN 978-981-13-8445-5   (eBook)
https://doi.org/10.1007/978-981-13-8445-5

This Springer imprint is published by the registered company Springer Nature Singapore Pte Ltd.
The registered company address is: 152 Beach Road, #21-01/04 Gateway East, Singapore 189721, Singapore

Contents

Chapter 1
Introduction: Schools Are Being Produced Right *Now*

Claudia Matus

Abstract This chapter introduces the major theoretical frames that delineate the object of study for researching the production of normalcy in school contexts. The major intellectual exercise in this work is to trouble the discursive, material, and affective paths that define how and why we should study the intertwined relation between policy, research practice, and inequality. In this introduction, major theoretical concepts and articulations will be laid out. It will also provide a critical contextualization of where this research is developed, with a specific focus on how neoliberal economic cultures and liberal ways of understanding policy reproduce inequality. The introduction also offers a description of the coming chapters, their foci, and articulations.

1.1 Introduction

Ethnography and Education Policy—A Critical Analysis of Normalcy and Difference in Schools is a book addressing the relationship between the production of social problems in educational policy, those research practices required to inform policy, and the daily production of normalcies and differences in school contexts. Considering the ways inequalities and their productions are still a problem to be addressed, I firmly believe in the critical moment this represents for research on social sciences (World Social Sciences Report 2016). The current scenario of increasing inequalities demands that we deepen our knowledge and understanding of inequalities to document why and how inequalities persist. Therefore, social sciences research studies are asked to question how they are implicated in the very production of research questions and objects of study that perpetuate power asymmetries, stabilize identities, and give causal explanations on how inequalities are produced.

Along with this, the prevalence of education policies understood as directed to specific identities; therefore, as partial and segmented (e.g., policies for women, policies for migrant populations, policies for the disadvantaged communities, policies

C. Matus (✉)
Center for Educational Justice, Pontificia Universidad Católica de Chile, Santiago, Chile
e-mail: cmatusc@uc.cl

© Springer Nature Singapore Pte Ltd. 2019
C. Matus (ed.), *Ethnography and Education Policy*, Education Policy
& Social Inequality 3, https://doi.org/10.1007/978-981-13-8445-5_1

for disabled people, etc.), and the dominant colonialist understanding of difference as deficit or problems to be solved in school contexts, it is critical to question the ways policies produce social problems and the kinds of research we are using to transform the unescapable circuit of inequality. The research and data that inform policies need to be critically analyzed and understood as important factors in reproducing inequalities, segregation, and enduring systems of differentiation (Dixon-Román 2017; Weheliye 2014). This book intends to advance a critical questioning of policy and the research that informs policy decisions particularly on issues of diversity and inclusion.

We are in urgent need of new research practices to document practices, discourses, materialities, and their relations to question the production of inequalities. This is a claim for those possibilities we as researchers have to open up new methodological horizons when imagining different objects of study. I believe we are facing a major moment for research in social sciences to rethink inequalities because social sciences research has proven not to have solved these issues. Moreover, inequalities have come to be more pressing to contemporary research and policies in which a shift is being asked for (World Social Sciences Report 2016). For instance, one way to approach this contemporary concern might be to ask what inequality is today and in what ways it relates to imaginaries of equality. One way to start questioning the very production of inequalities in our own research might take the shape of asking the nature of those categories we use to identify specific identities and communities as well as to ask ourselves "how this classification [of populations or groups] was achieved" (Roberts 2011, p. 72). To continue studying social class, ethnic groups, sexual minorities, women, and children as disadvantaged communities with no reference to how and why they have been constructed this way is a manner to persist in the production of a normative order to identify, differentiate, and hierarchize different identities. Therefore, the only possibilities we have to advance transformation and change for these communities get framed under the concept of compensation, which has not been proven to be enough.

Ethnography and Education Policy—A Critical Analysis of Normalcy and Difference in Schools achieves five main purposes. First, it presents theoretical frames for the study of the production of normalcy and difference in school settings. Second, it theorizes and documents ethnographic practices used that produce insights into the discursive and material entanglements of normalcy and difference. Third, it reports contradictions and silences in education policy design and content. Fourth, it provides examples of ethnographic fieldwork and intervention work with in-service teachers. Finally, it rehearses ways of presenting ethnographic knowledge, including the compositions of texts produced through the ethnographic work. In short, this book reports the possibilities and consequences for policy, research, and practice when normalcy (whiteness, western, male, heteronormative practices, common sense femininities and masculinities, adult, abled bodies) is stigmatized at the same level as difference (black, poor, disabled, child, woman, girl, homo). When normalcy is stigmatized and put into question, new possibilities to rethink issues of inequality and justice become visible (Davis 2013; O'Connell 2015). It is this focus this book intends to address. *Ethnography and Education Policy—A Critical Analysis of*

Normalcy and Difference in Schools offers a critical analysis using queer, feminist, and post-representational theories to understand the implications of dominant ways of understanding the division between normal and different subjectivities and how they reiterate structures of inequality in schools.

The major intellectual exercise in this work has been to trouble the discursive, material, and affective paths that define how and why we should study the intertwined relation between policy, research practice, and inequality. It is our belief that they do not proceed on their own path. They exist in a very complex and intertwined relation. In this introduction, major theoretical concepts and articulations will be laid out. It will also provide a critical contextualization of where this research reported in this book is developed, with a specific focus on how neoliberal economic cultures and liberal ways of understanding policy reproduce inequality. The introduction also offers a description of the coming chapters, their foci, and articulations.

1.2   The Evolving Research Project

Ethnography and Education Policy—A Critical Analysis of Normalcy and Difference in Schools is the result of a major research project in Chile, funded by Conicyt, National Commission for Scientific and Technological Research (SOC1103). The research team worked for 3 years (2013–2015) in five different Chilean schools producing ethnographic information on the ways normalcy (whiteness, western culture, male, heteronormative practices, common sense femininities and masculinities, adulthood, abled bodies); or "male/white/heterosexual/owning wives and children/urbanized/speaking a standard language" (Braidotti 2018, p. 6) are produced in school settings. Our main objective was to challenge the idea of social and cultural differences as something we *need to know more about*. Instead, we focused on observing, documenting, and describing the active production of dominant values regarding issues of normative understandings of gender, race, sexuality, age, ability, class, ethnicity, and nationality. As a result, our very ethnographic processes challenged traditional ideas on how to think of subjects, fields, notes, reports, the researcher, and the researched. Along with the production of ethnographies, we produced a professional development model for in-service teachers as well as for state professionals who are designing policies in regard to diversity and inclusion in Chile.

A book to report 3 years of producing non-normative research questions, constantly questioning the meanings of working at five schools at the same time, attention to the articulation among senior and junior researchers coming from different disciplines, academic trajectories, and particular ways to understand and live *normalcy* is an intense practice, indeed. As I will show, this book presents different layers of the process of producing a way to research on issues of normalcy and difference in educational institutions in Chile. This project started as an idea that became more complex as the research team became involved and affected by the topic and the ways we were producing the research practice.

Some of the more rewarding qualities of this research process were the creative disposition toward thinking differently about every aspect of the study. The project in itself starts as a major national grant, blindly evaluated by international reviewers. I mention this because, 1 year previous to this call, I presented the same idea, in a shorter version, to a funding call with national evaluators. My proposal was rejected. I always understood that this proposal was problematic in some ways since it was defying the conservative way of understanding and researching issues of difference in Chile. Therefore, the possibility to present the same research idea, to expand its scope, and be read and evaluated blindly was a political chance for this project.

From March 2013 to December 2015, members of the Normalcy, Difference, and Education interdisciplinary research team explored ways in which different power regimes operate to maintain the idea that there is a body, a behavior, an attitude, an emotion that is normal. We decided to stop researching on those who have been labeled as different, marginal or minority subjects and communities, assuming that we know enough about them. We wanted to expand our research interests on the articulations of what is called *normal* and *different*, stating that it is only in this relationship that power and commonsense operate. In order to do this, we had to create a new problem, something that usually is not seen as such. What we deem as normal had to be put into question and imagined in a way so that it could be researched. The most suitable research practice to accomplish these purposes was ethnography. Thus, ethnography could not be understood in the traditional fashion; therefore, the research team was pushed to think of new ways to name the field, name what we observe, train other professionals working in schools, and the like. By traditional ethnography, I mean the usual idea that persistent time and presence in the field will accomplish a detailed description to get the ethnographer closer to the lived experience of participants in school settings. In other words, "time in the field is needed to discern both the depth and complexity of social structures and relations" (Jeffrey and Troman 2004, p. 535). In this project, we stated that a post-representational ethnography was critical to research on those dominant values that produce the idea of normalcy as something obvious and intelligible (Matus and Haye 2015; Matus and Rojas 2015). (I will discuss this issue in detail in chapter three.) As the project started growing and evolving, we became a research team of 40 people assigned to different roles: senior researchers, junior researchers, ethnographers in the field, monitors working with teachers in service, scientific journalists, and research assistants, among others.

In the first year of the project (2013), we organized the research team to produce post-representational ethnographic accounts about the production of normalcy and its articulations with ideas and discourses of difference. We worked collaboratively with five schools in Santiago (Chile) for 2 years. These schools were eager to participate and their only incentive was to learn and help us complicate what usually is seen as natural within school spaces. These five schools represented a whole variety of types of schools in terms of money resources, composition of the population (only girls, only boys, co-ed), confessional and non-confessional, public and private schools, etc. One important note on how we recruited these schools was the fact that those participating schools had to make this decision with no incentive in advance.

The premise was we had to be sufficiently attractive to them to capture their attention because the topic in itself was critical, important, and useful enough to them. After we concluded the visits to recruit schools and finally got our five schools, we communicated to them that we had arranged an official participation certificate (by the Ministry of Education) for participating teachers. As their participation in this project involved using a significant portion of their time to work with us, we strongly believed that this recognition was important for the purposes of our work with them. Therefore, the commitment to this project was more than relevant to our purposes.

As part of the ethnographic planning, we decided to work in pairs in each school. This meant that we had to train 10 professionals from different disciplinary backgrounds, who have had experience in producing school ethnographies before, on the ideas on how to research and produce field notes on the production of normalcy. The decision to have two trained people working at each school came from the idea that to research on the production of normalcy and its articulation of normative notions of difference, we needed more than one eye to register and produce the field. The training period lasted 2 months where we read, analyzed, and exercised ways of registering the production of normalcy. The ethnographic production itself lasted 8 months in each school. The most pressing and challenging question of this process was how to train other professionals to research on those commonsense values and make them problematic enough to become part of an observation, a field note, etc. The process of producing the field was accompanied by the second process in which we gathered together every other week to discuss and reorient questions and problems encountered in the fields. Five senior researchers, four junior researchers, and the ten ethnographers participated in these meetings. During these meetings, we shared field notes, and we discussed particular issues from each school and reoriented questions to go back to the field. Thus, it became the second level of ethnography.

During the second year (2014), we continued working with the same five schools through something we called "accompanying process." As part of the ethnographic process, we designed this moment to work with participating teachers in which we challenged ourselves to work with those more salient issues we had produced in the field. Therefore, our effort during the second year was to understand or produce something we named as a "cultural profile" of each school which contained those more relevant issues in relation to the production of normalcy through processes of racialization, sexualization, genderization, classing, among others.

During the third year (2015), we dedicated ourselves to look back at those processes involved in the research and the accompanying process, as a way to be critical about our own potentialities and to give us time to theorize on those *failures* while we were immersed in this process as an important part of the research study. Most of the complicated issues we had to deal with were related to the changes participating teachers were experimenting because of the work and conversations they had with the research team. Particularly relevant was the experience we went through at one particular school, a girls-only school, where the issues we worked around were focused on gender. Teachers were affected by *knowing* gender other than the normative understanding of the binary between men/women. At some point, we had to make arrangements to have a specialist (member of the research team) in charge in case any conflicting situation may arise. For instance, one of the participating teachers of this school realized her own gendered position in her marriage and decided to get divorced. These were part of the unexpected situations working around issues of the production of normalcy of gender we had to face. As these processes were evolving, our project became nationally well known and we started being asked by the Ministry of Education to support the implementation of the education reform particularly on issues of inclusion and diversity. We started a series of workshops with different professionals of the Ministry of Education focusing on the production of normalcies in schools, presenting the information we had produced in the previous 2 years of ethnographic work, and questioning the very social problems they proposed for their policies. This was a rewarding and exhausting process. I have to say that we only encounter good disposition of our work.

Over the 3-year lifespan of the project, beginning with contacting potential schools at the beginning of 2013 through the school-based post-representational inquiry ethnographies, the articulations with the Ministry of Education to change policies to the final editing of this book, the idea of the project has grown, shifted, and complexified in ways we could not have imagined when I wrote the initial funding bid. Now, we continue our work in one of the research lines at the Center for Educational Justice at the Pontificia Universidad Católica de Chile under the name of BioSocioCultural Inclusion: challenging homogeneity in contemporary schools in Chile. The purpose of this continuation line is to advance a field of discussion that problematizes and updates the complex relationships between the biological, social, and cultural dimensions that define who we are or might be and the effects their relations have for the production of subjects, objects, and effects. One of the main focuses of our interdisciplinary research group is to problematize the ways in which humanist assumptions (e.g., causality, linearity, and representation) embedded in the naturalized separation among biological, social, and cultural domains actively operate in daily life decisions. Our research orientations are mostly located in contemporary theoretical perspectives that seek to rethink not only objects of research and methodological practices but also their relationships, thus allowing the production of new problems and the exploration of their potential for change. Posthumanist and post-representational approaches provide us with a political frame to question the natural separation of the subject who knows from what she knows as a problematic *habit* for the production of what we have come to believe as bits of truths. We continue to ask the question and rehearse news ways to research-oriented toward change.

Drawing upon a methodological framework of post-representational perspectives, we insisted from the beginning that our research on the production of normalcy and difference has to be developed based on the research team's own going back and forth about the topic. In so many ways, we had to expose ourselves to the possibilities of being more traditional and conservative than we would have expected and the challenge was to expand our own ways of pushing ourselves to the production of a different type of knowledge. For instance, some of the assumptions we had to face as a research group were (1) to accept that we were all implicated in the production of normalcy through dominant understandings of sexuality, gender, race, etc.; (2) that given the hierarchical biological, cultural, and social orders, we have been socialized to produce subjects and reproduce specific, always evolving racist, homophobic, sexist discourses, and materialities; (3) that when all these processes are naturalized, commonsense operates to makes us believe we have something in common to agree on. With all these assumptions in mind, we had to communicate what we were doing to different audiences and make them understand why it is relevant to question these frames, to undo unequal practices. We had to stop (for a moment) to believe in concepts such as compensation, inclusion, exclusion, and minorities to start thinking about the very production of these concepts either as solutions or ways of framing research questions. If we would have framed our research within these concepts, we would have chosen to approach the problem of difference as isolated from the concept of normalcy and, as a consequence, we would have continued repeating the explanation of discrimination as a product of individual biases or as a consequence of unequal biological, social, and cultural dispositions of subjects.

All these thoughts led us to create a community of reflexive (in the posthuman fashion) (Barad 2003, 2007; Koro-Ljungberg 2016) and critical practice where change was conceptualized as complex and possible. Change, for us, had to be built on a strong political stand to critically examine any biological, social, and cultural order to sustain whatever linear, causal, and stable relation between people and places, people and behaviors, people, and objects. Change was a political and intellectual exercise that happens in individual bodies.

The way in which Parker et al. (2017) have proposed inequalities, or new inequalities take unpredictable shapes. Under the commonsense language we have available, such as *gaps* and *biases* we strongly believe that we perpetuate the production of marginalized and privileged groups but with little chance to advance justice. When this is the only available language we have to talk about these productions, I believe we are facing the result of a problematic assemblage that allows us to continue talking and thinking in such a way that inequality itself becomes inescapable. To achieve our purpose, we had to start against the idea that there is a normal experience for those defined as minorities, which usually involves pain, suffering, shame, and pity. We had to stop thinking this way and search for those discourses, objects, and effects that allow the reproduction of this thinking as the only way to provide other answers to the problems of inequalities.

Therefore, we were oriented to produce information on how inequalities are embodied and expressed in the articulation of normalcy and difference. Our way to enter into the conversation on how to fight against inequality is based on the political project to maintain normalcy as an untouched category that organizes and gives life to racism, genderism, and sexualization processes. We sustain that it is only through the maintenance of ideas of normal behavior, normal attitudes, and normal emotions that inequalities come to life. Inequalities are not outside of the systems that reproduce racist, gendered, and sexual orders.

To study and report the production of normalcy, we had to play with the ambiguity involved in the production of the normal. This means that, as a special category, normalcy shapes itself in different ways, to appear as something desirable and expected. The language of the desirable, aspirational normalcy silences the active production of inequalities.

1.3   How Normalcy Became a Research Problem

Over the last decades, a significant emphasis on cultural politics of difference in educational institutions in Chile has been posited. The active production of diversity and inclusion discourses in Chile since 2012 represents an effort to undo the effects of privatization practices of schooling driven by the neoliberal agenda. Since educational privatization is related to broader neoliberal and neoconservative ideologies, policies, and political projects, there are opportunities to discuss the possibilities and challenges new reforms offer for public education (Gillborn 2006, 2008, 2010, 2016). We question the economic, cultural, and political practices ingrained in the privatized model in Chile and question: how *public* can the Chilean educational system be after a long and tenacious story of privatization? How might a deeply segregated school system need to be transformed to produce public education? Chile as a successful and well-recognized experimental site and testing ground for neoliberal policies in education provides a rich context to explore the possibilities and challenges for the reinstallation of the notion of public education. For instance, the ongoing implementation of the Law for School Inclusion (Mineduc 2016), explicitly aims at achieving two main goals: (1) free access to school (no payment) and (2) no discrimination. As expected, the passing of this law has brought different reactions into view. On one hand, this law promises an advancement in the ideal of public education through the mixing of students (this is facilitated through universal access to free education). On the other hand, this law regulates discriminatory practices in school contexts. Expected reactions particularly from parents when asked about the benefits of public education for their children were mostly oriented toward being worried for their kids being mixed with "other kids in schools." This might be understood as to how neoliberal and neoconservative agendas have engrained the idea of high- and low-status cultures that now come to be mixed in school contexts (Matus 2015). In other words, this law is being implemented in a highly segregated context that needs to be problematized.

Having said this, I have to recognize that it is true that we have moved from meanings of difference or diversity in schools only related to categories of disabilities and special learning needs (Infante and Matus 2009; Matus and Infante 2011). Nonetheless, this way of associating diversity with disabilities has left an important imprint on the way we reason diversity as the grouping of all those people and communities that are *different* for some reason (social class, gender, sexuality, nation, race, etc.). Popular knowledge replicates practices, representations, and valuations of difference as something real independent from ideas of normalcy. In other words, the weight given to disability and special learning needs, as the obvious way to frame diversity in educational policies has caused an important common sense idea about normalcy. This has had important consequences for the ways we intend to approach issues of inequalities and injustices in schools. It has secured a limited idea for how to imagine and organize difference in educational spaces. For instance, a usual practice in those institutional imaginations to address issues of diversity in schools is through the design and implementation of methodologies to either better organize the classroom, evaluate students paying special attention to their particular differences, or being more sensitive to those students who are defined for any reason as different. This is relevant because people have come to understand and act on diversity as a deficit, and as such, those labeled groups are in need of compensatory practices for the problem to be *solved*. This way of reasoning diversity in research creates the idea that policy initiatives are possible through a compensatory approach, which is not sufficient for the promotion of changes in cultural, social, and educational processes and practices.

It is important to highlight that an inclusive education approach is part of a global strategy to promote equality in society. Without a doubt, efforts to infuse educational policies with inclusive approaches are a way to advance ideas of equity and democracy in Chilean school systems. Although these initiatives are valued, educational policies and the Chilean educational discourse continues to neutralize the idea of normalcy with corresponding consequences in the ways students, teachers, and administrative staff imagine difference. When we speak of normalcy, we are talking about particular ways to position people in institutions (Matus and Haye 2015; Matus and Rojas 2015, 2018). This is why we contend that we should not only question how normalcy is rationed, policed, limited, and reproduced, but also how it organizes and assigns values to bodies. In other words, a commitment to question the production of normalcy transforms the ways in which knowledge is sought and transmitted. This might help us to trouble the dominant way to understand the constitution of differences as genetic, biological, social, or cultural. Normalcy should not be a comfortable site, because it stigmatizes ideas of *differences* as something to be identifiable, measured, and in need to be repaired. We believe that the insistence on neutralizing knowledge about normalcy threatens the development of an education that equalizes just futures for everyone.

In Matus and Infante (2011), for instance, issues of diversity are revealed to be strictly connected to special educational needs, where the tendency is to medicalize students' learning differences. How discourses of the normal take different shapes today include the proliferation of diagnoses in schools where teachers play an important role in defining what behaviors, attitudes, and emotions are deemed to be at risk and in need of the initiation of the circle of treatment with specialists (psychologist, psychiatry, neurologist). For instance, among those problems teachers consider worth a diagnosis today, we find that if a student is not being attentive in a class, if the student does not follow instructions, if the student gets easily frustrated, or if the student is restless, the initial thought at that moment is to initiate the medicalization path (Baker 2002; Harwood and Allan 2014). To make this issue more problematic, it is important to ask: how did it happen that these social ways of expressing something in a classroom became a problem?

For instance, the naturalization of the ways a teacher interprets her/his students' capacities is presented in the following ethnographic scene:

This situation happened when the ethnographer was observing a language class in first grade. It was the beginning of April 2018 (and the beginning of the school year), which is the time of year when those school professionals in charge of the Integration Educational Program start their processes of evaluation and re-evaluation of students:

Carolina, the person in charge of the Integration Project, gives some notices to the teacher and asks her if she has identified any students with learning difficulties and whom she thinks should be evaluated. The teacher nods and silently observes the students. She then approaches the teaching assistant and asks which students could be referred to the Integration School Project. The teaching assistant stands next to the board and observes the students.

The teacher walks around the room, touches a student on the shoulder and looks at the teaching assistant, [but] does not say a word; however, the assistant says aloud: "Yes, she could possibly [be referred to the program], since she struggles at times. Then the teacher continues walking and approaches another student and looks at the teaching assistant again. She asks her: "How about her?" The assistant responds aloud: "No, not her. She can stay because she does well." Finally, the teacher indicates another student with her hand and the assistant says: "Yes, there is a deficit problem there, because she gets easily distracted.

While the teachers were identifying which student had learning problems, the students talked and did the class activity.

Teachers making diagnoses based on the observation of externally visible traits takes us back to ideas of old eugenics where the idea of quality control of the population appears as an everyday activity in schools today. The common experience of identifying, sorting, tracking, and classifying students' practices performed by teachers, as presented in the excerpt above, reconfigures a complex rationality of identification and differentiation. It becomes more complex when diagnosed at schools in Chile have become a way to obtain financial resources for schools under the new prescriptions of the Law for School Inclusion, gradually implemented since 2016. As this law states: schools, as they have to be free of payment for every student, they do not receive money from the State anymore. Nonetheless, every diagnosed child allows the school to receive a certain amount of money (Matus et al. 2018), which relates to the increase of hiring of psychology specialists in schools. As Gulson and Webb (2017, p. 25) note: "… education has long been associated with various forms of biological rationality, notably forms of eugenics," and this law is an example of how policies are bringing these practices to schools.

These processes of defining students to undergo medicalization have at least two problematic assumptions. First, the notion of essentialism reinforces the imagination of correspondences between identities and meanings, practices, and experiences lived by people. Second, by insisting on differences among groups, and not problematizing the idea of *normalcy* against how these differences are constructed, the notion of *normal* is naturalized. Repetition and the circulation of discourses of essential differences under the rhetoric of medicalization preserve an unproblematized regulatory order and hierarchical organization of normalcies and differences that need to be analyzed within the context of schools responding to the requirements for equity and democracy proposed by international institutions.

This is why our orientation to train in-service teachers about racism, sexism, classism, etc. was important to our project. To talk about processes of genderization, sexualization, and racialization with in-service teachers meant to transform practices at school because our intention was to move beyond the explanation that discriminatory practices are mainly biased individual actions. Actually, in order for teachers to make sense of and to escape the psychological frame of stereotypes and prejudices, we instead referred to ways of knowing about gender, class, sexuality, race, etc., we have learnt, and they can be problematic particularly when making pedagogical decisions. With this framing, we had the chance to prevent the conversation on values to produce change on gender, race, and social class issues. For instance, several studies in the U.S. have shown the problems that occur when in-service teachers sustain a perspective of color-blindness when referring to issues of race (Sleeter 2001). For these teachers, "students are students." These ways of approaching issues of racism in school contexts critically reproduce liberal discourses of equality but with no recognition of how differences and inequality are created, expressed, and sustain. When teachers profess to be color-blind or gender neutral when trying to suppress negative images they attach to students, this has important consequences for students and how they interpret discriminatory practices and how these practices might be addressed. In this project, we worked on the assumption that social categories of difference, namely, race, gender, social class, and sexuality matter because teachers bring ways of knowing about these categories that require the identification, differentiation, and placement of students in relation to other categories. These interpretations that teachers bring to the classroom are heavily informed by normative understandings of race, gender, social class, sexuality, etc. We believe that not interrupting those ideas teachers bring to the classroom is a way to reproduce racism, sexism, classism, rather than reverse these practices at school.

1.4 Assemblages

To research on the production of normalcy in schools, we had to rethink schools as merely the context or the field where human actions occur. We had to redefine the field as the heterogenous and unpredictable encounter of bodies, objects, discourses, and effects within a broad network of enabling and constraining factors that had to put into question their relations. At the same time, we understood those five participating schools had a complex relation to each other. Those five schools acted as an assemblage in such a way that our mangling work with them helped us to enter the problem of thinking structure as well as multiplicity and indeterminacy as a critical moment of our production of meaning within social formations (Youdell and McGimpsey 2015). It was hard not to see those five schools operating under principles of multiplicity and indeterminacy. For instance, while one school was well known for its high number of disadvantaged students, the other one was recognized for its production of elite students. They both worked at the same time in the production of vulnerability and elite. While one school was only girls, where girls were educated under patriarchal practices (even though there were no men around), the only boys' school was reproducing the idea of women as objects. None of the five schools acted as isolated fields to produce normalcy. They intra-acted in unpredictable and in unnoticeable ways; they reciprocally worked on one another (Barad 2007; Frost 2016). This led us to understand that,

A performative understanding of discursive practices challenges the representationalist belief in the power of words to represent preexisting things. Performativity, properly construed, is not an invitation to turn everything (including material bodies) into words; on the contrary, performativity is precisely a contestation of the excessive power granted to language to determine what is real. Hence, in ironic contrast to the monism that takes language to be the stuff of reality, performativity is actually a contestation of the unexamined habits of mind that grant language and other forms of representation more power in determining our ontologies than they deserve. (Barad 2003, p. 802)

Our humanist habits lead us to think of schools as clearly differentiated, one from another. They are not ontologically independent. Race, class, gender, and sexuality systems operate in dynamic ways. They take different shapes even when teachers think they have overcome these systems' harmful consequences. As Rosiek (2018, p. 415) states, "The material-semiotic assemblages that produce racialized social hierarchies and people as racialized subjects have proven resilient and have transformed over the last century in response to our inquiry and interventions." It also brings the impossibility for us to *represent* schools in a final and totalizing manner. As the ethnographic practices were taking shape, we had to start questioning the place given to the way language or discourse defined the possibilities of the ethnographer encountering the schools' world. "The world [school] plays a role in responding to the design of our inquiries and always retains latent potentialities that exceed our ability to capture it in a single representation or inquiry" (Rosiek 2018, p. 408).

The *normal*, as a material and discursive assemblage, manifests itself in multiple ways. As an active ordering activity, it cannot be defined by a single or specific mechanism, such as values or ethics, knowledge, or common sense. Instead, it involves several mechanisms to allow its appearance and seductive attribute. Our focus was to register the adaptability of this concept. This is why the ethnography plan had to be revisited constantly. As soon as we started our fieldwork, we understood that we could not have just one place to produce the ethnographic accounts. As a condition of the concept of normal, we considered that because of its evasive meaning, we had to extend the field. This is why I state that to research the production of normalcy we need to have at least two places from where to produce information. As normalcy is an ontological agent (Barad 2003, 2007), we had to find the way to follow the dynamic, complex, and moving attributes of it. In so many ways, we had to consider producing an ethnographic account of those producing the ethnographies in schools. We had to prevent the co-opting of ethnographers by the operations of the *normal*. We had to track the agency of the concept of normal. As Peirce (1992) notes: "ideas are not all mere creations of this or that mind, but on the contrary have a power of finding or creating their vehicles, and having found them, of conferring upon them the ability to transform the face of the earth" (cited in Rosiek 2018, p. 417).

When studying systems of oppression like genderism, racism, classing, the concept of normal (the normal body, normal femininity, the normal child, the normal brain, normal behavior) has proven its ability to co-opt researchers' progressive thinking. This is why we had to reorganize our ways to work and those interactions among researchers were critical to advance our research questions. Ethnographers as the "agencies of observation" (Barad 2007) could not be subtracted from the world they were documenting. They were not independent in those terms. Thus, we were not taken-for-granted entities toward words and things. As we were producing meaning and explaining boundaries to produce subjectivities, we were using the same concepts to live our everyday lives. To do that, we had to problematize those core words that give life to narratives of the production of normalcy: structure, relation, space, time, knowing, intentionality, representation, causality, and set them in an unstable position to produce something different, something we did not know yet. School could not be thought as *inside* and researchers as located *outside*. We were part of the very idea or problem we were addressing: the production of normalcy. To escape or leave out the representationalist habit, we have been trained for in research had to do with understanding the failure representationalist ethnographies entail. The world is not at a distance anymore, and we had to face the fact that we were documenting the very practices that make the relations among objects, people, and words look natural and evident. As Barad (2007) beautifully states, "[...] the point is not merely that knowledge practices have material consequences but that practices of knowing are specific material engagements that participate in (re)configuring the world" (p. 91). To trace the limitation of what we can know was permanent in our research process. For this reason, feelings like disturbance and uncomfortable moments were part of the intensities that played out in our meetings. We as researchers were emerging from, rather than preceding those school fields. To move from static notions of process and risk our stability to work on how concepts move and take different shapes was a matter of study in itself. Leaving out the idea of correspondence between the words I have available to describe and the thing I am describing is always a matter of anxiety. This, from the beginning, was a political stance. Meaning "is not a property of individual words or groups of words but an ongoing performance of the world in its differential dance of intelligibility and unintelligibility" (Barad 2007, p. 149). How embodied was the concept of normal in our research group? Were we outside of the practice of producing the normal subject, practice, object, effect? Could we tell we were on the outside looking in? These were the kinds of questions we had to keep asking ourselves. In so many different ways, we had to press ourselves to make normalcy embodied as a political place to research on these issues. This was how the normal body, the normal effect, the normal brain became not a natural state of being but a specific form of embodiment produced through organizing practices that identify, differentiate, and give statuses to people and communities. Normalcy has to be lived as an active force (not as a trajectory) that separates and locate subjects in differentiated places. It creates ontological boundaries to locate subjects and make them look stable and natural. We approached participating schools as living entities giving us different possibilities for the becoming of subjects, materialities, and effects and those different configuring were part of our initial assumptions about the relational aspects of *separate* schools involved in our study.

In the following chapters, we will be exploring these issues from different perspectives. The eight authors invited to this collection come from different disciplinary backgrounds among them psychology, philosophy, social work, sociology, anthropology, cultural studies, and education. They also represent different geopolitical scholarships (France, the United States, UK, Chile). These researchers were part of the research team in different moments of its implementation and participated in different activities and statuses. Their academic trajectories also reflect movement and change in their approaches and orientations to write their chapters. They have considered different pieces of information from the ethnographic studies to write their particular chapters.

Pablo Herraz and Andrés Haye in chapter two, titled the "Shot and Fragment: The Place of Researchers in Ethnography", provide a critical self-description of the position of the researcher as key to understanding how knowledge is constructed from the field to fuel both further steps of fieldwork and knowledge communications. They specifically discuss the production conditions of ethnographic writing, about the ways in which images of the field that the researcher elaborates on by means of notes, descriptions, and narratives are generated and transformed into the context of the folding and unfolding of the fieldwork. Drawing on the comparison with cinematographic composition of moving images, they argue that the position of the researcher is not reduced to the abstract point of view entailed by any image, but is part of a technical assemblage of operations, such as framing, cutting fieldwork into fragments, juxtaposition of these fragments, and projection of a continuous movement of the field. From the disposition involved in ethnographic field notes, to the composition of an ethnography, the authors stress how the place of the researcher is crossed by the technical and the aesthetical. They conclude that writing intermediates between the always exceeding field and the position of the reader that surpasses the authoritative narrative of the researcher, displacing or suspending the problems of both the representation of reality and the authorship and authority of ethnographic knowledge, thus projecting the fieldwork to increasingly wider and open distancing positions that enable analysis, criticism, and thinking.

In Chap. 3, "Queering Habits and Entanglements of the *Normal* and *Deviant* Subjectivities in Ethnographies," Claudia Matus critically analyzes the production of normal and deviant identities in schools through the production of ethnographic texts. In this chapter, she advances the argument that dominant notions of time and space facilitate an apolitical stability of subjects' cultural and social positionalities as presented in five school ethnographies. Studying the political, material, epistemological, and effective production of identities considered *normal* in school settings requires questioning the representational habits we (researchers) maintain when producing knowledge using ethnographic methods. She argues that there is a "habit of mind" (Barad 2007) that presses the replication of dominant representational templates of the biological, social, cultural, and effective compositions of those we observe, the spaces they inhabit, and the temporal stages defining how they behave.

Carolina Rojas, in Chap. 4, "Discomfort—Affects, Actors, and Objects in Ethnographic Intervention", discusses the development of a productive circuit of observation and transformation of discursive practices regarding normalcy and difference in educational institutions. In addition, a conceptual and methodological analysis of the complex relationships between ethnography and intervention are presented. In working with educational institutions, both processes were nominally raised and sequentially planned as different processes. However, the boundaries between the ethnography and the intervention proved to be difficult to establish. This may be due to the fact that the study of the production of normalcy and difference is based on a political and transformational positioning that makes determining the limits of each impossible. Ethnography is a mode of intervention, and this intervention is nurtured, facilitated, and acquires meaning through ethnographic observation. In this chapter, the author focuses specifically on interventions associated with a professional development process for practicing teachers, but also on a more general understanding of the process of creating public policy that considers difference. The chapter discusses the instruments used for documenting the ethnographies and intervention such that they may be used or replicated in future research studies.

In Chap. 5, "The Production of the Problem of Difference in Neoliberal Educational Policies", Marcela Apablaza responds to questions related to how educational policy produce and circulate discourses of *difference* and how such discourses play out in schools. She poses her research questions within the framework of an educational system based on administrative and financial neoliberal principles. Her aim is to problematize Chilean educational policies of inclusion focusing specifically on mechanisms of production, operation, and articulation, as well as the ways educational actors circulate discourses of difference. To do this, she analyzes three components: (1) policy documents, (2) the administering body, and (3) the school by unpacking discourses related to the policy of school community life and the inclusion of students with special needs. These discourses are tied to government rationality that develops the problem as a depoliticized matter of identity, linked to the deficit or lack of particular student subjectivities and therein, points to the objectification and management of, and intervention on social and cultural differences in a neoliberalized educational system.

In Chap. 6 "Normalizing Identities: The Disciplining of School Subjects", Anita Sanyal aims at describing the ways normal and deviant school identities are ordered and put into place. She draws from two ethnographic studies to describe two different schools and the ways these two schools place students along hierarchies of value. She focuses her analysis on all-girls schools which brings a significant contribution to the production of systems of difference regarding gender, sexuality, and race analysis which are usually based on male school practices. The chapter responds to two principal questions: How is normally produced within specific school settings? How does normal frame the construction of school identities of teachers and students? In the analysis that follows, she emphasizes the ways in which normal and its deviants are ordered. The author also argues that these orders serve a productive function in that they permit the sustenance of the school and its mission. The identities ascribed to types of students help a constant mechanism of production of the school through locally and institutionally meaningful processes.

Laura Luna and Alfredo Gaete, in Chap. 7, "*Diversity* and the Failure of the Civilizing Project in Two Chilean Public Schools", show how the diversification of the school population in two Chilean public schools has turned into a crucial means for survival and an awkward problem at the same time. Coigue School and Alerce School, despite many contradictions between their discourses and their practices, seem to have embraced diversity as a value by making it the core of their educational projects. The ethnographies carried out in these two schools illustrate the deep discomfort caused by the presence of children who are "different" because of their nationalities, their cognitive abilities, their conduct, or other aspects. They also make evident that another, older agenda, which they call *the civilizing project*, still prevails in school daily practice and resists against discourses on diversity. The authors argue that attempts at student homogenization, inspired by the ancient values of nationalism and progress, have undermined the diversity project, but without making school members truly engage with the civilizing project either.

Claudia Matus, in Chap. 8 "Unpredictable Meanings", presents excerpts produced in the field arranged around themes with no "analytic intervention" from the writer. She organizes this chapter rhizomatically rather than linearly. The act of interpreting and getting *something* out of the field notes interrupts the narrow idea of *expertise* through understanding field notes as already analyzed pieces of data. Therefore, the process promotes a more political, chaotic, and unpredictable usage of this material and forces the reader to question her/his own ways of perpetuating dominant understandings in the production of normal and deviant school identities.

In Chap. 9, entitled "Disentanglements", Claudia Matus argues that the production of ethnographies can be a critical source for informing policy design on issues of diversity and inclusion. Ethnography from a post-representational perspective and the implications for the ways we conceptualize and represent issues of difference in school contexts and policy-making are explored. By making sense of the possibilities ethnographic research practices afford for informing policy design, the chapter engages in the exploration of new ways of thinking and researching *inequalities*, and the possibilities of change and transformation that they might bring. She contends that the regulation of subjectivities through specific meanings of normalcy and difference leaves no opening for active politics. This last chapter intends to advance on more creative ways to achieve social transformation.

After all these years of intense research, the conviction that new ways to imagine data, to go against descriptive and representationalist explanations on how inequalities are produced and the chances we have to overcome them are more intense.

Data, as well as those research processes to produce it, humanizes and dehumanizes. We may choose those that are more suitable to give equal dignity for all of us who inhabit institutions and expect to live in a just world.

References

Baker, B. (2002). The hunt for disability: The new eugenics and the normalization of school children. *Teachers College Record, 104*(4), 663–703.

Barad, K. (2003). Posthumanist performativity: Toward an understanding of how matter comes to matter. *Signs, 28*(3), 801–831.

Barad, K. (2007). *Meeting the universe halfway: Quantum physics and the entanglement of matter and meaning*. Durham: Duke University Press.

Braidotti, R. (2018). A theoretical framework for the critical humanities. *Theory, Culture & Society, 0*(0), 1–31.

Davies, L. (2013). *The end of normal identity in a biocultural era*. Ann Arbor: The University of Michigan Press.

Dixon-Román, E. (2017). *Inheriting possibility. Social reproduction & quantification in education*. Minneapolis: University of Minnesotta.

Frost, S. (2016). *Biocultural creatures. Toward a new theory of the human*. Durham: Duke University Press.

Gillborn, D. (2006). Citizenship education as placebo: 'standards', institutional racism, and education. *Policy education, citizenship and social justice, 1*(1), 83–104.

Gillborn, D. (2008). Coincidence or conspiracy? Whiteness, policy and the persistence of the black/white achievement gap. *Educational Review, 60*(3), 229–248.

Gillborn, D. (2010). Reform, racism and the centrality of whiteness: Assessment, ability and the 'new eugenics'. *Irish Educational Studies, 29*(3), 231–252.

Gillborn, D. (2016). Softly, softly: Genetics, intelligence and the hidden racism of the new geneism. *Journal of Education Policy, 31*(4), 365–388. https://doi.org/10.1080/02680939.2016.1139189.

Gulson, K., & Webb, T. (2017). Emerging biological rationalities for policy: (Molecular) biopolitics and the new authorities in education. In S. Parker, K. Gulson, & T. Gale (Eds.), *Policy and inequality in education* (pp. 23–39). Singapore: Springer.

Harwood, V., & Allan, J. (2014). *Psychopathology at school. Theorizing mental disorders in education*. New York: Routledge.

Infante, M., & Matus, C. (2009). Policies and practices on diversity: Possibilities to reimagine new discourses. *Disability and Society, 24*(4), 437–445.

ISSC, IDS, & UNESCO. (2016). World social sciences report. Challenging inequalities: Pathways to a just world. Paris: UNESCO Publishing.

Jeffrey, B., & Troman, G. (2004). Time for ethnography. *British Educational Research Journal, 30*(4), 535–548.

Koro-Ljungberg, M. (2016). *Reconceptualizing qualitative research. Methodologies without methodologies*. London: Sage.

Matus, C. (2015). The uses of affect in education: Chilean government policies. *Discourse: Studies in the Cultural Politics of Education, 38*(2), 235–248. https://doi.org/10.1080/01596306.2015.1087678.

Matus, C., & Haye, A. (2015). Normalidad y diferencia en la escuela: diseño de un proyecto de investigación social desde el dilema político-epistemológico. *Estudios Pedagógicos, 41*(2), 135–146.

Matus, C., & Infante, M. (2011). Undoing diversity: Knowledge and neoliberal discourses in colleges of education. *Discourse: Studies in Cultural Politics of Education, 32*(3), 293–307.

Matus, C., & Rojas, C. (2015). Normalidad y diferencia en nuestras escuelas: a propósito de la Ley de Inclusión Escolar. *Revista Docencia, 56,* 47–56.

Matus, C., & Rojas, C. (2018). Ethnography of the normal. In J. Assael & A. Valdivia (Eds.), *Lo cotidiano en la escuela. 40 años de etnografía escolar en Chile* (pp. 254–290). Santiago: Editorial Universitaria.

Matus, C., Rojas, C., & Luna, L. (2018). ¿"Inclusión con filtro"?: Aprendizajes y recomendaciones para la implementación de la Ley de Inclusión. (CEPPE Policy Briefs, N° 21). Santiago: Centro UC de Estudios de Políticas y Prácticas en Educación. Retrieved from http://ceppe.uc.cl/images/contenido/policy-briefs/ceppe-policy-brief-n21.pdf.

Ministerio de Educación. (2016). Ley de Inclusión Escolar. Retrieved from https://www.mineduc.cl/wp-content/uploads/sites/19/2018/03/libro_Inclusión_final.pdf.

O'Connell, K. (2015). Bad boys brains: Law, neuroscience, and the gender of 'aggressive' behaviour. *Gendered neurocultures: Feminist and queer perspectives on current brain discourses.* Zaglossus: UTS: Law Research Paper No. 2015/1. Retrieved from https://ssrn.com/abstract=2581322.

Parker, S., Kalervo, N. G., & Trevor, G. (2017). Introduction to policy and inequality in education. In S. Parker, K. Gulson, & T. Gale (Eds.), *Policy and inequality in education* (pp. 1–5). Singapore: Springer.

Peirce, C. S. (1992). *The Essential Peirce: Selected Philosophical Writings*. Edited by N. Houser, & C. Kloesel (Eds.), Bloomington: Indiana University Press.

Roberts, D. (2011). *Fatal invention: How science, politics, and big business re-create race in the twenty-first century*. New York: New Press.

Rosiek, J. L. (2018). Agential realism and educational ethnography. Guidance for application from Karen Barad's new materialism and Charles Sanders Peirce's material semiotics. In D. Beach, C. Bagley, & S. Marques da Silva (Eds.), *The Wiley handbook of ethnography in education* (pp. 403–421). New Jersey: Wiley Blackwell.

Sleeter, C. (2001). Preparing teachers for culturally diverse schools: Research and the overwhelming presence of whitenes. *Journal of Teacher Education, 52*(2), 94–106.

Weheliye, A. (2014). *Habeas viscus. Racializing assemblages, biopolitics, and black feminist theories of the human*. Durham: Duke University Press.

Youdell, D., & McGimpsey, I. (2015). Assembling, disassembling and reassembling 'youth services' in austerity Britain. *Critical Studies in Education, 56*(1), 116–130. https://doi.org/10.1080/17508487.2015.975734.

Chapter 2
Shot and Fragment: The Place of Researchers in Ethnography

Pablo Herraz Mardones and Andrés Haye Molina

Abstract The critical self-description of the researcher's position is key to understanding how knowledge is constructed from the field to fuel fieldwork and knowledge communications. We specifically discuss the production conditions of ethnographic writing, focusing on the ways in which images of the field that the researchers elaborate by means of notes, descriptions, pictures, videos, and narratives, are generated and transformed in the context of the folding and unfolding of the fieldwork, and particularly through the intertwinement of writing and reading. Drawing on the comparison with cinematographic composition of moving images, we argue that the position of the researcher is not reduced to the abstract point of view entailed by any image, a particular view, or selective angle of the field, but is part of a technical assemblage of operations, such as framing, cutting fieldwork into fragments, juxtaposition of these fragments, and projection of a continuous movement of the field. From the disposition involved in ethnographic field notes, to the composition of an ethnography, we stress how the place of the researcher is crossed by the technical and the aesthetical. We discuss methodological and epistemological implications concerning the role that reading ethnographic texts plays across the assemblage of ethnographic writing. We argue that the critical account of this intermediate place of the researchers has the potential to displace and suspend the problems of both the representation of reality and the authorship and authority of ethnographic knowledge, thus projecting the fieldwork to increasingly wider and open distancing positions that enable analysis, criticism, and thinking.

2.1 Introduction

In this chapter, we discuss a singularity of our research about difference in schools. We reflect on the implications concerning knowledge production that derive from an anomalous methodological structuration of the research process, at least regarding one of the basic assumptions about ethnographic research. Our research involved a

P. Herraz Mardones (✉) · A. Haye Molina
Pontificia Universidad Católica de Chile, Santiago, Chile
e-mail: pcherraz@uc.cl

© Springer Nature Singapore Pte Ltd. 2019
C. Matus (ed.), *Ethnography and Education Policy*, Education Policy
& Social Inequality 3, https://doi.org/10.1007/978-981-13-8445-5_2

multiplicity of fieldworks, both in parallel at different schools and in a longitudinal drift within each evolving field, by a number of ethnographers working in sub-teams that produced and gave the first organization to an extensive set of written fragments, mostly field notes and interview accounts over 8 months. Another team took these fragments, during and after fieldwork, as research material for several analytical studies (reported in the chapters of this book). Therefore, the fieldwork and the associated writing mediation of the fieldwork experience are open to be partially or totally separated from the finalizing writing/reading work of knowledge production. As a result, the design opens for the generation of research reports (as this one) by researchers who did not participate in the fieldwork. Among the questions and controversies that such a division of research work may arise, the present chapter focuses on the problem of the ethnographic text, of how it is possible to read an ethnographic fragment, analyzing the abovementioned conditions of knowledge production. Our goal is to offer a reflection concerning ethnographic writing by way of a critical analysis of its modes of production.

The relationships between ethnography and writing have long been addressed, especially from the point of view of the place of the text in the form and value of ethnographic knowledge. *Writing culture* (Clifford and Marcus 1986) has probably been the most important reference of this topic within contemporary ethnography, as can be verified in *The composition of anthropology: How anthropological texts are written* (see Rapport and Nielsen 2018). In this chapter, we focus on this theme, specifically reflecting on the problematic conditions of the production of texts as both are a product of research practice and at the same time an object of study, an expression, as we will argue, of the unfinishable condition of writing. The texts that are the knowledge product from the perspective of the ethnographers can be taken as material for interrogation and analysis from the displaced perspective of researchers outside the field, extending the research process and surviving the fieldwork beyond the abyss.

To contextualize our approach to this problem, consider what Marcus and Cushman (1982) say about the way in which social scientists take ethnography outside anthropology:

> Readerships from the other sciences treat fieldwork simplistically as a method like any other and ethnography as description. Anthropology's achievement from this perspective is thus to provide facts about marginal societies to be marginally used by Western social sciences. As noted, any revision of what an ethnography is or offers through a reflection on how it is written is potentially subversive to positivist methodologies and goals. Thus, with ethnography respectfully marginalized as a medium for providing trivial information, the general social science readership is probably the least sensitive among these categories to variation in ethnographic writing and the most puzzled by the significance of the theoretical and epistemological problems the current experiments pose. (p. 52)

In contrast to the authors, we argue that the position of the researcher who reads the ethnographic texts as method, renders possible a sensible and complex approach to ethnography, if developed as a reflection about the ways in which they are written. This is because from this perspective the text shows its twofold, as a product and an object of knowledge. That is, by displacing the position of the ethnographer, the critical analysis of ethnographic texts entails a privileged perspective on texts as planes of two faces, one oriented to the field from which they are an expression, and the other to the research process within which they are objects of analysis. Without such a displacement, these two faces of field and writing fuse into a single process. This notion of *plane* is important to our research design because the ethnographic text does not take the form of a monograph, or an ethnography proper, that is, as a text accounting for the experience and interpretations of the researcher about a social group with whom the fieldwork was done. Rather, the ethnographic text takes the form of a vast series of fragments, that is, fieldwork notes, descriptions, and interpretations organized, archived, and compiled by date, as well as thematized by reports where the ethnographers offer, to specific readers anticipated in writing, one or more particular ways of approaching a set of fragments. When accessed without the text that locates them in an anthropological plot and rhetorics, the isolated notes offer an amplified perspective concerning key features of ethnographic writing that have attracted attention in the literature since *Writing culture* to our days, namely, the operation of a selective and partial cutting, the fragment-like nature of texts, and in a more general sense, the relationship of ethnographic writing with the notions of composition and montage (Bertelsen 2018; Marcus 2012; Nielsen 2013; Rapport and Nielsen 2018; Suhr and Willerslev 2013; Tyler 1986). The displacement of the ethnographic text in its field and writing moments opens a broader reflection scope about *ethnography*, a scope that has progressively included the cinematographic language to account for writing operations. In this way, the questions of how to read an ethnographic fragment from its conditions of productions lead us to interrogate the relationships between writing and the cinematograph, and more generally between text and image, between the written and the visual.

Isn't each ethnographic fragment or fieldwork note a set of images? If this is the case, then, isn't there a visual operation in ethnography, beyond the montage, in operations of the framing and shot? Wouldn't a written fragment be a shot composing a set of images at the moment of reading?

2.2 Written Image

There seems to be nothing especially problematic in the idea that an author presents an image, or constructs or creates an image through an ethnographic text. In this line, an interesting contribution to the literature is a co-authored work where Kathy Charmaz develops a critical commentary of the field notes taken by Richard Mitchell, reflecting precisely on how ethnographic writing *tell tales* and *write stories*. Charmaz points out that ethnographic writers share some writing strategies with writers of other genres, and among these common strategies she stresses "reconstructing the experience through written images" (Mitchell and Charmaz 1995, p. 144). Regarding these "written images" she says:

I contend the writer's presented images must resemble the experience... Readers will compare their experiences to the ethnographer's portrayed images. ... How can we reconstruct and present lived experience through our written images of it? We must show our readers what we want them to know. We cannot simply tell them. Nor can we persuade through mere assertion. (Mitchell and Charmaz 1995, p. 156)

Here, written images are addressed in the dimension of being a representation of the experience of the ethnographer, and at the same time situates these texts within the context of a persuasion effort, that is, as part of the rhetorics of ethnography. The extracts of interviews by Mitchell are analyzed as product of a selective operation that "distill the experience" (p. 156) as part of a creative composition work aimed at representing experience in a convincing picture. This form is thought of by Charmaz as a painting, rather than a photograph. It is important to consider the difference between photography and painting in terms of the fixed capture produced by the former, and the imaginal demands and freedom characterizing the latter. "Writers need to give us the shape, color, tone, order, and form of their stories; they do not need to provide the entire experience. Instead, they stress some events, minimize others, and ignore still others" (Mitchell and Charmaz 1995, pp. 156–157). Written images are taken as distilled experiences of the ethnographer, organized as a painting, and used as a persuasive representation for a reader. Therefore, the initially simple idea of the text as image discloses the work of ethnographic writing as a creative work of selection and composition of images, thus opening deep aspects of the production of texts and their productive effects.

There is another aspect of written images that are of interest. Consider the reflections of the anthropologist Bjørn Bertelsen about his own ethnographic writing, on the bases of his fieldwork taking place in the context of the popular revolts in Mozambique between 2008 and 2010. The author argues that an ethnographic text is an *anthropological composition*, giving to the notion of composition a different meaning. According to Bertelsen (2018), the main feature of written images is that they fix a changing and moving reality, so that the text "will necessarily eclipse the nonlinearity of its making, the stochastics of its becoming and, if you will, its congealing into a stable form" (p. 64). Here, the text is an image as far as it carries out a capture or a seizure; that is, it takes a shot: "A text is but a freeze-frame and, paradoxically, becomes an image, an anthropological composition" (Bertelsen 2018, p. 64). The author does not compare the written image with a painting but with a photogram, a freeze frame, promoting a twist of reference from the language of plastic art to the cinematographic language, thus giving ethnographic writing a new semblance that is absent in Charmaz's account. If written images imply the fixation of time–space frames, then what is emphasized in text composition is not the selective combination of elements but the operation of framing.

Bertelsen states that ethnographic writing implies the fixation of a frame, but in the sense of an open cut, capturing the image from moving multiplicity: "writing in its anthropological and academic guise is multiple rather than singular, is sedimentary rather than segmented and sequenced. It is an open-ended freeze-frame cut out from multiple temporal flows" (Bertelsen 2018, p. 71). That is to say that the ethnographer, in writing, frames, cuts out frozen shots from the continuity of movement. Therefore, writing resembles more the camera than the painter's technique. However, the frame or image produced by writing, although a fixation, is open to the outside of the image. There seems to be something in the composition of an image that escapes the limits of their frames, which exceeds the very image. In this sense, writing is understood as anthropological composition, besides the cut and capture of a continuum, because of this *excedent* of the frame that enables new ways for thinking:

> The composition of anthropology thereby mimics or, better, doubles, reflects and emerges from the event in an attempt to not only capture temporal dimensions of field events but also to generate novel configurations of thought about what it means to be, for instance, a post-colonial subject. (Bertelsen 2018, p. 70)

In contrast to the idea of the scientist working to represent reality, and to the painter who distils it in a plastic image, the ethnographer is more similar to the cinematograph, capturing sediments to provoke thinking on the part of the reader through a visual experience.

Some common elements across the formulations of Charmaz and Bertelsen are worth noting. First is the element of extraction. Both authors emphasize that written images are not a copy or simple representation of the real, but the result of selective cutting. Second, the authors coincide in understanding ethnographic writing as a compositional work that, if not artistic, is essentially aesthetic. Writing is a work that provokes a visual experience. The notion of the *written image* acquires all its importance in this connection of these conceptual elements, namely, extraction and visuality. However, the imaginal dimension of writing is understood in different terms, because Charmaz and Bertelsen hold a different idea of composition. From the first point of view, the composition of images come from the creative work of the writer, who draws and paints her own lived experience, from which particular places and relations are turned into life. From the second, composition derives from the frame with which the writer extracts a shot, fixing, in the space–time of the image, those places and relations that are in continuous flow. The contrast seems to depend on the comparison to painting, in the first case, and the photogram, in the second. Both points of view seem to us limited to specific aspects of ethnographic writing, failing to show the full theoretical relevance of the comparison with art and cinema in understanding compositional work. Overall, the analysis of the imaginal dimension of ethnographic texts leads to a more radical question about the craft and devices of ethnographic writing.

2.3 Montage and Fragment

Although the notion of montage has been widely addressed in anthropology in general and in visual anthropology in particular (see MacDougall 2006; Pink 2007; Suhr and Willerslev 2013), the specific problem of the relations of ethnographic writing and montage has scarcely been developed. Among the exceptions is the work of Marcus between 1993 and 1994, where the relation of text and image is reworked from the point of view of the historical influence of cinema on ethnographic writing that can be properly called modernist:

> Montage is of course the key theoretical concept of cinema, and I began to examine the influence of cinema after its appearance in the late nineteenth century upon classic literary modernism. This development seems to me to offer the originary precedent for the emergence of a kind of modernist sensibility in ethnography. Reference to how cinema establishes narrative through montage is the way this writerly sensibility explicitly advertises itself. (Marcus 1994, p. 40)

Thus, the author aims to show the potential of a modernist ethnography in writing, sensitive to its own cinematic basis, as if montage were the technical support of narrative composition in ethnographic writing. To this end, Marcus (1994) explores a particular problem, namely, how the notion of cinematographic montage helps to understand how the sequentiality of writing can account for ethnographic space and the construction of simultaneity effects (p. 41). This is a problem for ethnography especially when the place or the field ceases to be the space–time unit that contains that which the ethnographer observes, that is, when the issue is to write a transcultural and deterritorialized ethnography:

> I came to focus upon the increasingly deterritorialized nature of cultural process and the implications of this for the practice of ethnography. If ethnographic description can no longer be circumscribed by the situated locale or community, the place where cultural process manifests itself and can be captured in the ethnographic present, what then? How to render a description of cultural process that occurs in transcultural space, in different locales at once, in parallel, separate, but simultaneous worlds? (Marcus 1994, p. 40)

It is in the cinematographic operation of *parallel editing* or *cross-cutting* that the authors find a solution to the problem of the linearity of writing, making possible the construction of an effect of simultaneity in ethnographic writing. The successive juxtaposition of ethnographic descriptions can be read as a simultaneous totality by means of the composition of certain ways of choosing, combining, and ordering written pieces. Therefore, with the cinematographic model, the author offers an interesting critical interrogation about the forms in which ethnography is written and in which ethnographic writing becomes an ethnography.

> Objectification in ethnographic representation has been effectively critiqued, but the need for setting the scene objectively even in the most radical attempts to use a montage of consciousness requires some revision, but also a preservation, of an objectifying discourse about process and structure. This is what the use of montage technique in the service of representing the simultaneity and spatial dispersion of the contemporary production of cultural identity achieves. (Marcus 1994, p. 48)

The discussion elaborated by Marcus leads to think of montage as the (at least modernist) ethnographic operation that, by means of the cross-cutting of fragmentary images, sets the scene of a convincing and truthful narrative. One critical issue is the conception of the images or fragments that are the materials in ethnographic writing. Are they to be understood as paintings or as photograms? Are the ethnographic images compared to loose perceptions upon which knowledge is built by associative and narrative composition? Are ethnographic fragments analogous to photographic shots, static abstractions extracted from the social process? What does the notion of montage imply, and what does it dispose us to think about in this connection?

In the epilogue to *The composition of anthropology*, Rapport and Nielsen (2018) work out further the simile of the image movement in cinema, focusing on the fragmentary condition of ethnographic written images. "Not unlike a cinematic montage that is composed by juxtaposing different framed images-in-movements cut off from their narrative structure (Nielsen 2013, p. 49), the fragment is liberated, as it were, from a pre-given whole and presented alongside others without assuming an implicit order" (Rapport and Nielsen 2018, p. 197). Image movement understood here as the paradoxical effect of a twofold operation of extraction and liberation in reference to a previous set. On the one hand, these units become enclosed wholes as fragmentary individual pieces and, on the other, montage makes them open units or incomplete wholes as a fragment only in relation to the other fragments and to the surpassing totality or the exceeding concreteness of the field. As soon as photograms and shots enter in juxtaposition with other units, they render possible the composition of untold relationships with unanticipated effects. How is this trick possible? What does the model of the cinema imply understanding ethnographic writing?

Rapport and Nielsen (2018) argue that the ethnographic text is always oriented toward a representation of social life, in line with our discussion of Marcus (1994). Because it is oriented to a concrete social field, ethnographic texts always articulate an extraction, a fragment, in line with our discussion of Bertelsen (2018), and as such are oriented toward the field from which they are extracted. The key aspect for Rapport and Nielsen (2018) of ethnographic writing as an image movement is the paradoxical orientation of the text in the opposite direction: toward an open disposition to composing new texts decoupled from the origin. According to the authors, ethnographic texts are fragmentary because they are written. It is as texts that ethnographic fragments involve "processes of 'entextualisation'—turning experience into written text—that seem to transcend the particular circumstances of their composition" (Rapport and Nielsen 2018, p. 197).

Of particular relevance to our research discussion is the idea that an ethnographic text always puts into operation, as an unpredicted effect or as a counterface of the extractions out of which it is composed, a virtual field of intertextuality that makes possible new compositions, new texts, critical texts, analytical texts, commentaries, and replies. As soon as it is extracted from the field, the text transcends itself, exceeded by its own conditions of production.

As ethnographical material is turned into text – entextualised – it undergoes a series of irreversible transformations that are crucial for the making of a meaningful account. While it may not be completely detached from its previous form, the relationship between the two becomes increasingly blurred. Indeed, to paraphrase Maurice Blanchot from his reflections on textual fragments, we may argue that ethnographic material is written up as a series of "unfinished separations" (Blanchot 1995, p. 58). But it is precisely by way of these dynamic and always pulsating intervals between ethnographic data and anthropological account that texts come to point beyond themselves. (Rapport and Nielsen 2018, pp. 197–198)

The surplus of ethnographic texts is understood as the impossibility of avoiding the readers' own compositional work, and the connection of a fragment with other conceptual domains that make ethnography an unfinished work. Following these authors, we find that ethnographic texts considered as fragments are indeed an extraction, as suggested by Bertelsen, although not a fixation comparable to the photographic shot but to the photogram. If texts are images, the cinematographic model implies that these images are fragments of a movement, pieces of a sequential montage, a temporal composition, and as such they are moving fragments. Unlike photographic pieces, photograms are fragments of a dynamic juxtaposition. In this way, we get the idea that the ethnographic text, similar to the image movement, is an open unity, a unity in relation, because it is already a relation with other fragments. The unity of a cinematographic fragment radically depends on the setting of relations with another fragment, because this unity or completeness of a fragment is differed, as if containing in itself a movement that leads to another fragment. The fragmentary nature of images in cinema is determined by montage. In order to understand this, and to make sense of any comparison with ethnographic writing, we need to better understand what is cinema.

2.4   Moving Shot

Deleuze argues that the specificity of cinema is to make the shot a temporal category. The technical transformations through which cinema reached its essence were the separation of the apparatus for shooting and the apparatus for projection, the mobile camera, and the techniques of montage. The cinematographic image is thus liberated from the spatial anchor that fixated the image to reproducing natural perception, and opened to the possibility of creating new images, ever yet unknown to sensorial perception, from unexpected angles and combining different temporalities that, through montage, enter in the temporality of projection.

> What *was* cinema's position at the outset? On the one hand, the view point [*prise de vue*] was fixed, the shot was therefore spatial and strictly immobile; on the other hand, the apparatus for shooting [*appareil de prise de vue*] was combined with the apparatus for projection, endowed with a uniform abstract time. The evolution of the cinema, the conquest of its own essence or novelty, was to take place through montage, the mobile camera and the emancipation of the view point, which became separate from projection. The shot would then stop being a spatial category and become a temporal one, and the section would no longer be immobile, but mobile. (Deleuze 1986, p. 3)

The full implications of the cinematographic model of montage cannot be recognized until realizing that compositional fragments presuppose an apparatus for projection liberated from perception. The cinematograph is the device by means of which photograms are disposed to produce the cinematic experience, thus transposed into an image movement.

> Cinema proceeds with photogrammes – that is, with immobile sections – twenty-four images per second (or eighteen at the outset). But it has often been noted that what it gives us is

not the photogramme: it is an intermediate image, to which movement is not appended or added; the movement on the contrary belongs to the intermediate image as immediate given. (Deleuze 1986, p. 2)

By analogy, each ethnographic text, like a photogram, is in part a piece of the field to be transposed to the order of the reader, and in part an *intermediate image* produced in line with the conditions of reception. The analogy is possible if we further realize that the cinematograph is part of an assemblage of elements involved in the processes of cinematic writing, and as such is only an example of the variety of devices for the technical transduction of fragments into readable wholes. Ethnographic writing, regarded from this cinematographic model, involves an art of transduction, including devices, practices, methods, and policies employed by ethnographers to compose, with fragmentary texts, a comprehensive narrative in line with the rhythm of the reader. Ethnographic texts become moving fragments, in the sense of open units of unfinished separations, as soon as the diachrony of reading is introduced in the work of writing.

How then can we read an ethnographic text? The text can be taken as an image if we take it as a read text, as an image for a reader, whose narrative temporality makes the text a moving fragment. To read it means to follow its movement and to attend to the compositional and rhetorical texturization of its movement. Moreover, if we think that the position of the reader is both that of the researchers and that of the wider potential readership, then the cinematographic model of ethnographic writing has important methodological and analytical implications. It suggests that the notion of montage, taken from the arts, is relevant for understanding the technical support of knowledge production, not reduced to but including in advance the eventual delivery of an ethnography among ethnographers, and radically open perspectives of knowledge dissemination. Therefore, texts are fragmentary not only in relation to the concrete field from which they are extracted but also in relation to the exteriority of virtual points of view or positions of reading toward which they are addressed.

The main consequence we follow from the previous considerations is that a fragment as such has two faces, one turned toward the field from which it is an extraction and the other toward the researchers and to readers in general. In this connection, a further implication of the cinematographic account of this twofold structure of ethnographic texts is worth noting. According to Deleuze, the decisive category of cinema, of the cinematographic image, is not the photogram but the moving shot. The shot is the basic unit of a film. Each shot is the result of the framing and extracting operations, but the shot must not be confused with these operations. The shot is the continuous moving fragment that is seen on screen, which corresponds to a complete frame shot, part of it, or one of the several moving shots constructed through montage on the basis of one frame. In this way, the shot comes from both the frame and the montage but is not reducible to either. Following Deleuze, we focus on the intermediate place and transductive function of the cinematographic shot:

The shot, of whatever kind, has as it were two poles: in relation to the sets in space where it introduces relative modifications between elements or sub-sets; in relation to a whole whose absolute change in duration it expresses. This whole is never content to be elliptical, nor narrative, though it can be. But the shot, of whatever kind, always has these two aspects: it presents modifications of relative position in a set or some sets. It expresses absolute changes in a whole or in the whole. The shot in general has one face turned towards the set, the modifications of whose parts it translates, and another face turned towards the whole, of which it expresses the -or at least a- change. Hence the situation of the shot, which can be defined abstractly as the intermediary between the framing of the set and the montage of the whole, sometimes tending towards the pole of framing, sometimes tending towards the pole of montage. The shot is movement considered from this dual point of view: the translation of the parts of a set which spreads out in space, the change of a whole which is transformed in duration. (Deleuze 1986, pp. 19–20)

As we see, the shot is a twofold image, with one face oriented toward the frame and the elements, and the other toward montage and the whole. The temporal shot expresses the movement going from one frame to the other, such that what is seen is one frame that is changing. What is projected is an image always already becoming another. Deleuze notes that what we see is the modification of the elements composed in the frame. At the same time and in an opposite direction, the shot is turned to the whole in relation to which it expresses a change. The shot is always the signal of a difference. From the side of montage, the shot shows the changing nature of the narrative totality, the duration of the whole. Deleuze argues that the montage of any narrative totality is a composition of lapsing elements and as such an open totality, crafted from the potentiality of changes.

How, in conclusion, should we read an ethnographic text? Following the Deleuzian conceptualization, we note that when reading an ethnographic text we not only have a frame, that is, a composition or relationships among elements delimited in the way of photography, but also a moving picture in which these elements get related. Something happens in a fragment and, in this sense, something goes on, there is a change. The diachrony that characterizes reading makes that the content described in ethnographic notes is the image of an event, a fragment of duration, and expression of a modification of the field. In other words, ethnographic descriptions, before representing elements in space, can be taken as articulating a movement in time and thus talking to the researcher, as well as to potential readers, about a change taking place in the becoming of everyday life under research. Ethnographic texts, regarded with the lenses of the cinematographic metaphor, can be compared to image movements and as such they should be read as a double-sided image: as a limited frame and a fragmentary cut in relation to the field, but also as an open and incomplete narrative in relation to the researchers' multiple, conflictive, problematic, or at least unlimited readings of the event or, in other words, the ongoing social change that is taking place even beyond the time frames of the any researcher or reader. The ethnographic text would then be at the same time a capture and a liberation. The concept of montage enables us to open this second dimension for critical analyses. We suggest that any ethnographic description, as soon as it is written, is always already an emancipation from its own conditions of production and exceeding the field under description, for any ethnographic fragment calls for its continuation in multiple and unlimited texts overstepping the temporality of the fieldwork. In this sense, we argue that texts, thus writing, are constituted in relation to their outside. The content, concrete social referent that is the inside of the text, has a backside from which the content is produced: The back of ethnography is the relation of the text with the montage of the whole narrative, a research project, a published ethnography, or the thoughts of the reader, by which any ethnographic image movement is already projected outside and continued by another writing. Moreover, this backstage of ethnography is disclosed, with the help of the cinematographic model of montage, as a second fold, layer or coat of the fieldwork articulating technical, hence, political, options to shape knowledge production. We claim that it is in this relation to the readable whole, to the outside of the field, that ethnographic fragments, at least read from their back, always (must) present an open event, an ongoing and still undetermined change. Put in different words, when a fragment is read as image movement, something changes.

2.5 Reading Ethnographic Image Movements

Let us illustrate our point with examples to show how it grounds in our ethnographic practice, and to glimpse at some analytical and methodological orientations derived from the conceptualization of ethnographic texts in terms of cinematographic fragments as image movements. We selected three fragments written by one ethnographer as field notes at the middle and the ending phases of an 8-month fieldwork.

Fragment 1. Other older kids, dressed in black, cross by running and hiding outside the principal's corridor. The principal comes out. She shouts to the older boys that are walking towards her: "Hey, you, why did you run out?" One of them walks directly towards her with a challenging attitude, walks directly only twisting to the side the moment before clashing. The principal pushes his shoulder at this moment. He looks at her and then pushes one of his schoolmates with a slap. The girl pushes him back. The principal stops and looks at him. He keeps looking at her while clapping his hands. (August 1, 2013)

Fragment 2. There was a conflict in the school cafeteria between a first grade boy and an older boy. I don't know the motive. When the younger boy rushes away crying and screaming through the door, a schoolmate (also from the first grade but still older) helps him, asking him what happened. He gives him a side hug and leads him to the cafeteria again. At the same time one of the lunch ladies comes out from the kitchen with a reproaching and disapproving attitude, and asks for the teacher of those fighting. She then asks the kids to go get the teacher, and at that moment one teacher comes in and the lunch lady, with a slight change of tone, making it more gentle, asks the teacher to take care of the kids saying that ALL of them are fighting. (August 5, 2013)

Fragment 3. Victor comes out of the first grade classroom. After a while, the door opens again. Gabriel peeps out and shouts "Victor, what are you doing outside?" The boy does not answer. Gabriel leaves the door open and then pops out, standing outside the classroom. Another boy comes out. The religion teacher shows up. He shouts at them to enter. Before the indifference of the boys, the teacher tries to close the classroom door, but Gabriel slides his foot between the door and the frame. The teacher shouts "Remove your foot! Remove your foot!" The boy looks at him without moving. "Remove your foot, please!" The teacher shouts louder. Finally, the teacher removes the kid's foot and tries to close the door again, but before he can do it, Gabriel puts his foot in the door again. "Remove your foot, I said!" Gabriel shouts back at him "No, no, no, no!" The teacher struggles with him, but Gabriel does not move. The teacher insists on closing the door with more strength, hitting the boy's foot with the door, and then tells him, "Do you see what happens, hu? See what happens?" But the boy does not remove his foot. The teacher then grabs the boy from his apron, looks around at the offices and shouts "Janet! Janeeet!" but nobody answers. The boy shakes, managing to get away. The teacher tries to catch him again and Gabriel tries to kick him but fails to do so. Gabriel runs towards the door again, but the teacher strongly hangs him in the air and pushes him away. The boy shouts at him "Fuckin' old man!" The teacher closes the door with a strong bang leaving the two boys – Gabriel and Victor – out of the classroom. (October, 2013)

To begin with a general observation, note that the three fragments are composed in a different way, even if they describe one or more actions within one and the same fieldwork process. In Fragment 1, the description seems to follow the action, as if the researcher's or the reader's position moved along with the kids, achieving a sequence shot that is interrupted only by a cut by which the focus leaves the kids to show us the principal coming out of the office. Then, it returns to the kids until the close encounter with her takes place, and finally shows the back of the boy who keeps walking until the sequence is cut off. Instead, in Fragment 2 we see how action jumps or shifts from one frame to another, producing for the reader a simultaneity effect, as shown by Marcus when discussing parallel editing. While the boy is crying outside of the cafeteria and another boy hugs him, one of the kitchen workers is crying out for a teacher to take care of the children. In contrast to these fragments, in Fragment 3, the narrative describes actions occurring in one place. We see a fix framing, focused on the classroom door, where the struggle between the boy and the teacher takes place. In this way, the actions inside the classroom remain out of the field, only announced by the teacher at the border. Everything else we see through the narrative takes place from the door outward, without any change of perspective, cut, or juxtaposition with other frames.

When we read an ethnographic text attending to its visual operations, the narrative acquires a completely new relief, because immediately the work of capture and composition by the ethnographer shows up, including the perspective, the changes in the angle from which the shot is taken, its approaching and distancing movements, the frames chosen, in sum the cinematographic resources and the observation technologies employed. At the same time, we see how the compositional work of writing, of organizing the different frames and cuts into a unitary fragment, projects them as a whole while we read.

At one level of analysis, each fragment refracts the perspective of the ethnographer, for instance, in the insistence on showing a challenging action from the students to which teachers, to variables degrees, are manifested as incapable of containing the situation or even reacting with violence. Each fragment cuts out, frames, and composes a diverse and unique aspect of conflict and power relations between students and teachers. Now, what interests us is how the relations of power and the perspective of the ethnographer are produced as ethnographic writing; and how we, then, should read them. In this sense, the fragments show us a cutout of an event that takes place at school, but since it is extracted from its original preceding and following movements, it appears in reading as a moving shot, a fragment of the living movement of the school, a moving cut, that is, as an image movement. As a shot, each fragment expresses a singular event or change, taking place in an unrepeatable moment of school life, only determined as such event or change as soon as we arrive at the end of the fragment, at its final but arbitrary cut. When reading, the selected action must happen as it occurred at the school; this is the way in which we are used to reading image movements. However, the moving cut is achieved in writing on the basis of an arbitrary cut on the part of the ethnographer, thus setting the bounds and limits to the continuous becoming of school life and then fixing this cut in a descriptive record.

At another level, consider the relationships among fragments. It seems that all of these fragments offer the same structure of relationships between boys and teachers, in which there are a challenging attitude and an aggressive move that adults in general are unable to stop, to press back, and to normalize at play; a common structure of social relations that is actualized in different and singular forms in each written image movement. However, the connection among the fragments is not a necessary one. They were not written by the ethnographer as part of a continuum. Only later, during analysis, some fragments and their connections were extracted from a vast set cuts, and then juxtaposed in contiguity as a series for the sake of a reflection of descriptions. Despite the arbitrariness of the cuts made by the ethnographer at the time of fieldwork, the montage achieved later with the juxtaposition of the three fragments, lastly after reading, produces the effect of a contestable totality, particularly around the issue of power relations, that is, the place from which the ethnographer seems to be recording the daily life of the school.

Thus, across these three field notes, we see in actions how the challenging attitude of the boys and the violence with teachers, as well as the difficulties they experience in maintaining social order, appear only as one issue or theme of the school fieldwork after the juxtaposition of separated records. Each note, in its own, speaks much beyond the theme of power relations between students and teachers, and offers diverse ways of asking about power relations in schools, or about the production of differences of age groups, gender, roles, class, and so on. At one level, we can see how the unity of each of the three images of the field, in spite of having a start and an end, is incomplete. Each contains in itself, as an arbitrary extraction, a centrifugal movement, that is, an active tendency to be continued, prolonged, and projected out of itself. Ethnographic field notes are, in this sense, both fragments and image movements: The finalizing cut of a fragment is, at once, its temporal opening. At the other level, we see that the whole compositional work entails a creative element not only in each mobile shot but also in relation to other fragments, and that their juxtaposition performs a possible drift, a projection of the whole. The montage of fragments opens up alternative analytic and theoretical drifts, engendering different interpretations and knowledge production processes. The exercise with the three fragments demonstrates that the montage of fragments is enough for enacting a selective question about the movement of the concrete everyday life at the school as a whole.

This illustrates how in our research process the position of the researcher was thought of as part of a dynamic emplacement of a field, coproduced with others within a social process or everyday life world. The field was thought of as an intermediate reality both joining and distributing research practices and everyday practices. As we understood this during the research process, ethnographers and local participants interact by means of raising and reshaping facades that connect and separate them, generating different faces and hidden sides as well; the complex and changing field that they share was thought of as an open intermediation process in which ethnographic writing took place. Ethnographic texts could only generate new layers of intermediation between the fieldwork and ever new positioning moves of the researchers. The present reflection on the cinematic conditions of production of written descriptions of the field suggests that texts emerge as a montage effect within the dynamic emplacement of a field, playing the role of intermediate images within a larger process of intermediation. Our discussion leads us to reason that, if the field itself is an effect of the assemblage of different movements, and if the images of the field must have a transductive potential within it, then the work of ethnographic fragments can be regarded as elaborating intermediations between the fieldwork and the anticipated point of view of researchers and readers less and less close to the field, projecting the fieldwork to increasingly wider and open distancing positions that enable analysis, criticism, and thinking beyond the geological center of the assembled field.

The analysis of the compositional work of researchers has been a critical consideration all along the research process and in particular for any analysis of the material produced in the fieldwork. Field notes, as the fragments above, were taken and kept in a diary by the ethnographer but regularly shared with a second ethnographer who worked at the same school, in order to progressively ensemble a reasoned and discussed selection and organization of the notes, and generate new descriptions along with the shared elaboration of the ongoing fieldwork experience. Notes and descriptions were also regularly shared with the wider research group, including ethnographers working in the other four schools, opening the opportunity to practice writing, description, reading, and critical discussion in group. These exercises were designed not only to trouble each fieldwork experience in order to promote critical reflexivity and to sharpen observation practices but also to problematize written registration and the position of the researcher. Hence, our research process unfolded with the question about the position of the researcher not only in relation to observation practices but especially in relation to the work of writing.

2.6 Discussion: About the Place of Researchers

In this chapter, we addressed the question about the position of the researcher, with a specific focus on the craft of writing ethnographic texts. This question has been usually taken as an epistemological issue, concerning the limits and biases of knowledge and its conditions of validity. In contrast, we oriented this question toward a critical reflection of the conditions of knowledge production, specifically of the conditions of ethnographic writing. We explored the production conditions of the images that the researcher elaborates and communicates by means of writing notes, descriptions, and narratives in the context of the folding and unfolding of an ethnographic fieldwork. A comparison with the cinematographic composition of moving images enabled us to suggest that the position of the researcher in ethnography is not reduced to the abstract *point of view* entailed by any image, but is part of a technical assemblage of operations, such as framing, cutting fieldwork intro fragments, juxtaposing these fragments, and projecting a continuous movement. The notion of montage emerged as a clue. We discussed theoretical and methodological implications of this notion, exemplifying them with our own research. We can now conclude from the discussion that the position of the researcher must be recognized and reviewed within the coordinates of aesthetic work and imaginal production.

This chapter traveled from the relationships of writing with the concept of image in ethnography, then to the notion of fragment to approach text, and finally the idea of montage, through the analysis of the cinematic basis of ethnographic writing. Considering the fragmentary nature of ethnographic notes and field descriptions, and their mode of production as fragments, we noted that they consist of a complex relation, for the fragment is a shot or cut off two sides, one pertaining to the field and the other to the reader. Ethnographic work seems to display this same twofold complexity. On the one hand, it includes a visual technology applied to the extraction and registration of movements in the field: framing, capture, a point of view projected from the frame, with a given angle, certain degree of movement, and a specific focus. Ethnographic work could be thought of as similar to cinematographic production. This already opens the question about the aesthetic dimensions of ethnographic research, the variety of aesthetics, their techniques and politics, stylization, and critique in ethnographic knowledge production. We argue that ethnographic writing entails, even beyond the specific visual or scopic domain, an aesthetic ambit of production in relation with images, involving techniques and an elaborated treatment of images.

From these conceptions, the craft of ethnographic writing appears as a technical work of editing, more properly, of composition. We argue that ethnographic fragments such as field notes and descriptions of the fieldwork can be thought of as a composition of elements or parts in a moving shot, realized as a written image movement in the act of reading; and that in another fold or phase, the montage of these fragments can be regarded as a composition that enables the projection of an image of the whole that exceeds each fragment, although being as open and as incomplete as the very fragment. In sum, from the cinematic disposition involved in ethnographic notes to the cinematic composition of an ethnography, we see how the place of the researcher is crossed by the aesthetical and the imaginal. Indeed, we can learn about ethnographic research from the ever new forms of composition and montage of different creative arts, in music, in painting, in dance, and in the novel, beyond film arts. Although we focus here on the latter because of its specific compositional formal unit, the image movement, several art practices offer much to learn about the technical dimension of composition. Therefore, our argument highlights the generative and creative aspects of ethnographic writing, and in this sense stresses the aesthetical dimensions of its modes of production as well as the political and scientific implications of compositional work.

As a consequence, the discussion offered in this chapter entails a displacement of the axis of the ethnographic research process. If traditional anthropological research was centered on the power to represent a social reality in a truthful form (image), resting on the ideal of the first person experience to which writing should serve, then from critical anthropology the gravity of the research process seems to shift toward ethnography as the written image in itself, whereby the researcher communicates ethnographic knowledge to a more or less specialized and open readership. The position of the researcher is thus mainly determined by the perspective of the reader, already anticipated in the process of descriptive and conceptual elaboration of a particular fieldwork experience. Instead, our discussion shifts our attention to the intermediate process between these two poles, namely, to the writing of ethnographic fragments, displacing or suspending the problems of both the representation of reality and the authorship and authority of ethnographic knowledge, enabling an approach to writing in which moving images intermediate between the always exceeding field and the position of the reader that surpasses the authoritative narrative of the researcher. It is in this mediational process that the fragmentary nature of ethnographic texts reveals its full importance and potential.

References

Bertelsen, B. (2018). Composing texts and the composition of uprisings. Notes on writing the postcolonial political. In N. Rapport & M. Nielsen (Eds.), *The composition of anthropology. How anthropological texts are written* (pp. 56–72). New York: Routledge.

Blanchot, M. (1995). *The writing of the disaster*. Lincoln: University of Minnesota Press.

Clifford, J., & Marcus, G. E. (Eds.). (1986). *Writing culture: The poetics and politics of ethnography*. Berkeley: University of California Press.

Deleuze, G. (1986). *Cinema 1: The movement-image* (H. Tomlinson & B. Habberjam, Trans.). Minneapolis: University of Minnesota Press. (Original work published in 1983).

MacDougall, D. (2006). *The corporeal image. Film, ethnography, and the senses*. New Jersey: Princeton University Press.

Marcus, G. E. (1994). The modernist sensibility in recent ethnographic writing and the cinematic metaphor of montage. In L. Taylor (Ed.), *Visualizing theory. Selected essays from V.A.R. 1990–1994* (pp. 37–53). New York: Routledge.

Marcus, G. E. (2012). The legacies of writing culture and the near future of the ethnographic form: A sketch. *Cultural Anthropology, 27*(3), 427–445.

Marcus, G. E., & Cushman, D. (1982). Ethnographies as texts. *Annual Review of Anthropology, 11*, 25–69.

Mitchell, R., & Charmaz, K. (1995). Telling tales, writing stories. Postmodernist vision and realist images in ethnographic writing. *Journal of Contemporary Ethnography*, 25(1), 144–166.

Nielsen, M. (2013). Temporal aesthetics: On Deleuzian montage in anthropology. In C. Suhr & R. Willerslev (Eds.), *Transcultural montage* (pp. 40–57). New York: Berghahn Books.

Pink, S. (2007). *Doing visual ethnography*. Los Angeles: Sage.

Rapport, N., & Nielsen, M. (2018). Writing the human. Anthropological accounts as generic fragments. In N. Rapport & M. Nielsen (Eds.), *The Composition of anthropology. How anthropological texts are written* (pp. 195–200). New York: Routledge.

Suhr, C., & Willerslev, R. (Eds.). (2013). *Transcultural montage*. New York: Berghahn Books.

Tyler, S. (1986). Post-modern ethnography: From document of the occult to occult document. In J. Clifford & G. E. Marcus (Eds.), *Writing culture: The poetics and politics of ethnography* (pp. 122–140). Berkeley: University of California Press.

Chapter 3
Queering Habits and Entanglements of the *Normal* and *Deviant* Subjectivities in Ethnographies

Claudia Matus

Abstract This chapter critically analyses the production of normal and deviant identities in schools through the production of ethnographic texts. The chapter advances the argument that dominant notions of time and space facilitate an apolitical stability of subjects' cultural and social positionalities as presented in five school ethnographies. Studying the political, material, epistemological, and affective production of identities considered *normal* in school settings requires questioning the representational habits we (researchers) maintain when producing knowledge using ethnographic methods. I argue that there is a "habit of mind" that presses the replication of dominant representational templates of the biological, social, cultural, and affective compositions of those we observe, the spaces they inhabit, and the temporal stages defining how they behave.

3.1 Introduction

In this chapter, I present a critical analysis of the production of normal and deviant identities in schools through the production of ethnographic knowledge. The chapter advances the argument that dominant notions of time and space facilitate an apolitical stability of subjects' cultural and social positionalities as presented in five school ethnographies. I question the traditional ways in which educational ethnography creates threads of social lives, experiences, cultural hierarchies, identities, and power relations and, in so doing, reorganizes and authorizes the asymmetrical relation between notions of *normal* and *deviant* identities in school contexts. Studying the political, material, epistemological, and affective production of the status of normal identity in relation to an essentialized difference in school settings requires questioning the representational habits we maintain when producing knowledge through ethnographic practices. I argue that there is a "habit of mind" (Barad 2003) pressing us to replicate dominant representational templates of the biological, social, cultural, and affective compositions of those we see, the spaces they inhabit, and the temporal

C. Matus (✉)
Center for Educational Justice, Pontificia Universidad Católica de Chile, Santiago, Chile
e-mail: cmatusc@uc.cl

© Springer Nature Singapore Pte Ltd. 2019
C. Matus (ed.), *Ethnography and Education Policy*, Education Policy
& Social Inequality 3, https://doi.org/10.1007/978-981-13-8445-5_3

stages defining how they (should) behave. These habits shape the process of documenting and representing, therefore shaping the production of racialized, gendered, classed, sexualized, nationed, and aged identities in schools. They are sustained by specific notions of time and space, which hold up recognizable meaning for us. Paying attention to the ways we understand and use ideas of time and space is a way to problematize the habituated knowledge paths we follow to produce descriptions of specific practices, sites, and social relations as ethnographic texts.

The arguments presented in this chapter are the result of one year of working with a group of 12 professionals (anthropologists, psychologists, teachers, sociologists, and occupational therapists) conducting ethnographic research in five schools in Chile. The purpose of these ethnographic studies was to document the ways in which schools produce, reproduce, and circulate discourses of the normal (heterosexual, abled, white, upper middle-class subjects) and deviant (disabled, gay, poor communities) identities in situated daily practices. One main assumption underlying these ethnographies is that normalcy and difference, as co-constitutive and situated in social practices, are heavily organized in terms of broader dominant cultural discourses around the production of the *other* or deviant and the *normal*. This is particularly relevant to my argument since, to sustain this particular power relation, hegemonic cultural productions of normal and deviant identities must be produced in invisible, unnoticeable practices of daily lives (Stewart 1996, 2007). The study I am narrating here was oriented to describe the operations of power that produce the field of normalization rather than simply to document practices of intolerance, discrimination, violence, and marginalization in schools. To accomplish this, it was necessary for me to pay critical attention to the assumptions embedded in the questions we, as ethnographers, employ to continue imagining straightforward associations between spaces, times, and subjectivities that repeat normativities and other power relations in schools.

In this chapter, I track my own process of planning ethnographic research (2013–2014), as well as, my own questions about how the group of professionals producing the ethnographies conceptualize notions related to who, what, how, and where are co-constituted among themselves, as they conduct research in schools. The ethnographies were constructed through two linked processes. First, a group of 12 ethnographers conducted field visits to schools and documented their observations in field notes. These field notes were discussed in biweekly meetings where this group along with five additional researchers met. Thus, there was a two-layer organization of the research field that produced the ethnographies: ethnographers in schools producing field notes and a group of researchers producing field notes on discussions of the experience of producing the *original* field notes. Focusing on the ways school ethnographers see, register, and document school practices helped me explore the limits of documenting the unknown. In different ways, the research practice itself became a constitutive practice of what I was trying to understand (Schneider 2002). As such, my questions were oriented around the understanding that those field notes produced by the ethnographers were not a list of *real* identities, practices, and relations instead, their very production (Youdell 2006).

It is in here where I consider theories of time and space to expand my analysis. I sustain that the notions of time and space we hold onto when producing ethnographic accounts are critical to explaining the obviousness of our narratives of stability and neutrality when reporting the field. It is my belief that traditional notions of time (as linear and sequential) and space (as an empty container) incite researchers to rely upon recognizable and stable identities and relations. As such, time and space authorize the perpetuation of binaries of gender, sex, race, social class, ability, and age as real structures to organize social lives (Britzman 2000; Pillow 2015; Tsolidis 2008; Weems 2006). Finally, power relations (gender, sexuality, social class, age, etc.) become naturalized and understood as unquestioned knowledge to position identities to get to know the school, which later becomes *ethnographic knowledge.* For instance, the already popularized knowledge that disadvantaged students are less successful in schools than non-disadvantaged students is produced through the repetition of several other knowledges, including economic gap, compensatory policies, neuroscientific knowledge, hegemonic notions of families, body able-ness, affective dispositions, etc. Therefore, racialized and classed notions of school success, learning, access, motivation, and cognitive development are enabled. The naturalized idea of correspondence between disposition to learn and specific social and cultural attributes reproduces particular conceptualizations of the ideal student, the ideal family, the ideal brain, the ideal moral life, etc. (Béhague 2015; Gillborn 2008, 2010a, b, 2016; Harwood and Allan 2014; Karping and O'Connell 2015; Katz 2013; O'Connell 2015, 2016). Assumptions of time as intelligible sequences, differentiated segments, and recognizable units, along with notions of space as containing identifiable and distinctive identities and practices, provide us with more elements to explain the workings of power when producing ethnographic accounts. Since these ideas are based on dominant notions of time as succession (Grosz 1995, 1999) and space as a container (Massey 2005), we can explore how shaking traditional notions of time and space might help us in re-thinking ethnographic descriptions.

If we question the embedded assumptions about time and space we hold onto when describing and documenting the production of normalized identities in schools, then what are the kinds of questions we should have in mind to uncover those hegemonic meanings presented above? Furthermore, questioning assumptions inherently means that I, as the researcher, need to understand and challenge my own personal humanist assumptions underlying traditional ways of understanding schools (Barad 2003; Britzman 2000; Lather 2013; Lather and St. Pierre 2013; Pillow 2015; Youdell 2010). For instance, when describing gendering practices in schools, how do traditional performances of gender operate to reinforce the very practice of normalizing gender? How can the static positions for girls and boys called for by the knowledge of developmental stages give an ethnographic account on gender? How can ethnography escape the idea that subject relations and practices are rooted in strict and recognizable divisions and relations, such as student–teacher relationships, learning–teaching dynamics, adult–child hierarchies, school–family associations, etc.? If not questioned, these established constructs function as preexisting lenses through which subjects become intelligible and recognizable in ethnographic accounts (Youdell 2010). The production of ethnographic accounts without the problematization of how dominant notions of time and space work to normalize what inquirers *see* and *name* reinscribes exclusionary practices and recirculates the idea of the subject and the site as someone and a place unproblematically ready and available to be described (Stewart 2007).

Therefore, my intent is to direct the focus of attention to the effects of dominant notions of time and space as preexisting ways that researchers perform power relations (Weems 2006) when producing ethnographic texts. This might be included in what has been studied and reported as the limits of the researcher's knowledge. If so, reflexivity is the concept that best responds to the problem I intend to address here. Within the varied ways to talk about reflexivity (see Pillow 2015), I lean on the idea that reflexivity can be used to problematize who is representing who while accepting the fact that the researcher is always embedded in that representation (Campbell and Lassiter 2015; Korthagen and Valsalos 2010). Although this notion may provide an interesting site to question the researcher's knowledge, reflexivity still gets caught in a humanistic frame in that the belief is that the researcher acts under certain assumptions of rationality, presenting herself as a rational, autonomous knowing subject (St. Pierre 1997, 2000). As Chambers (1994), presenting Nietzches' ideas, noted, "… we imagine ourselves to be the author rather than the object of the narratives that constitute our lives" (p. 25). In this case, I want to move my questionings to the workings of naturalized frames of reference we, as researchers, use when issues of the normal body, hegemonic femininities/masculinities, whiteness, and privilege, among other features, are at the center of inquiry. In other words, how and through what ideas and assumptions doing school ethnography—even as a critical project aimed at challenging hegemonic practices—continue to reiterate oppressive accounts of identities, experiences, relations, and practices (Tsolidis 2008; Weems 2006, 2010). If the challenge is to produce ethnographic accounts that defy power relations and those taken-for-granted notions of normal and deviant identities, then how what I see and how I report it can or should be problematized. Is it possible to reflect on the *content* of naturalized frames of reference? Are they the limits of social change and transformation? With these questions in mind, I make the argument that time and space may help us move away from reflexivity to something else, to "escape reflexivity as the stabilizing of identity across time and space" (Puar 2009, cited in Kafer 2013, p. 17).

To achieve this purpose, I will provide a contextual description of the ethnographic research conducted in five schools in Chile, and the problem constructed there. Then, I will present some key ideas about time, space, and ethnographic research to problematize the ways they inform the production of ethnographic subjects and sites. Later, I will refer to some examples from the research project to show the main concerns I address in this chapter. I will conclude with some final comments and ideas.

3.2 The Project

Since 2002, there has been an increasing interest in designing and implementing policies addressing issues of diversity and inclusion in Chile. Most of these policies over the last 10 years have emphasized administrative and pedagogical dimensions to address particular conceptualizations of diversity issues being disabilities and special educational needs as the main foci of these policies. As part of my concern, I contend that they have relied on reductionist and essentialist claims about difference mostly related to ideas of deficit, sickness, and lacking, and as a result, school agents have been encouraged to modify their pedagogical practices *new strategies and tools to work with those students defined as different* to respond to these claims (Ahmed 2012; Matus and Haye 2015; Matus and Infante 2011; Matus and Rojas 2015; Youdell 2010). The underlying narrative in these policies is that individuals are different (because of race, gender, social class, and so forth) from some norm, and after accepting that fact, researchers and policymakers can figure out how to measure, monitor, and repair that difference (Baez 2004). This way of reasoning diversity in policymaking sustains an idea of *difference* that is partial and requires segmentation (poor people, gay people, disadvantage people, etc.)—as in Haraway's (1992, p. 300) words, "difference as apartheid." To think of difference this way is to equate difference with *problems to be solved*. These *problems* usually are thought of as possibly to be solved through the implementation of compensatory practices that, as Yoshino (2007) argues have not been enough to allow meaningful changes in cultural, social, and educational structures and practices. Furthermore, as disabilities and special needs have been constituted as the most common or evident problem in educational policies, they have inscribed an aggressive culture of medicalization and diagnosis in school settings (Harwood and Allan 2014; Harwood and McMahon 2014) as the natural way to work with students labeled as problematic (either because of behavior, attitudes, or emotions) for teachers (Gillborn 2010a; Harwood and Allan 2014).

When we speak of diversity, whatever our position is in these debates, we all know that we are not speaking of just plurality or difference. *Diversity* is a particular organization of difference (Ahmed 2012; Matus and Infante 2011; Matus and McCarthy 2003; Youdell 2006, 2011). Thus, the question is, when we speak of a difference in schools, to what kind of organization of difference are we referring? The issue, then, is not only how difference is conceptualized, policed, limited, and reproduced, but also how it should be organized and for what purposes.

Dominant ways of deploying policy discourses of diversity in Chilean schools suggest that it is impossible to question the ways differences have been constituted as such. Difference is presented as a totalizing dimension, leaving no room to question how subjects have come to be constituted as *lacking* something. Thus, difference is constructed as a source for what people need to be compensated for, but it does not question why they have been produced as in need, lacking privilege, and why they have not been granted the status of *normal* (Davis 2013; Skliar 2007). For instance, dominant ideas that produce notions of diversity in educational policies do several things: first, they perpetuate the imagination of *cultural diversity* or the *arrival of new school subjects* as a new phenomenon, as if policymakers can claim a point of origin in history when diverse people came to exist (Matus and Infante 2011; Matus and McCarthy 2003). Second, the idea of commonalities around issues of differences (*lack or deficient of maternal care, dysfunctional families*) are identified and constituted as *problems* the educational system needs *to solve*. Thirdly, in teacher education, the question of *appropriate* preparation for solving such problems is particularly in need of reflection and discussion. They tend to orient their programs around new strategies and pedagogical tools to work with the new students. New students meaning the immigrants (who speak Spanish as well), the poor student, female students, etc. These institutional orientations that deal with issues of difference speak for themselves.

The ideas that frame the problem this project addressed include: (a) the notion of difference as essential and a problem to be solved; (b) that *normal identities* are made invisible when reporting *different identities*; (c) that educational policy favors the notion of disability and special education needs to address the *problem of diversity*; and (d) that school cultures link difference to sickness, deficit, or lacking, and therefore, structure the need for teachers to manage specific pedagogical tools for students labeled as different.

The project (2013–2015) that frames these analyses investigated the ways normalcy (hegemonic femininity, white privilege, abled body, etc.) is produced and maintained in daily school practices. As some authors have argued (Kumashiro 2002, 2008; Youdell 2006, 2010, 2011), the neutral and apolitical production of normalcy is only possible in relation to the active production of naturalized differences (the poor, the gay, the female student) and deviant features of the subject. To trace the articulation and coproduction of normalized and deviant gendered, racialized, sexualized, classed, aged, and abled subjects through the educational apparatus, required an emphasis on the registration of more than single interpretations of specific school agents. Instead, it required registering the workings of power relations in particular. This was particularly challenging since each member of the group involved in producing ethnographic fields brought their own ways of understanding and performing normative notions of gender, sexuality, race, ethnicity, social class, ability, and age. What I mean is, that the researcher makes assumptions based on common sense knowledge and as such he/she mobilizes stereotypes on the basis of ascribed characteristics (such as gender, race, class, age) that the researcher cannot *manage* or present *differently* (Youdell 2006). In the context of the project and its intents, this becomes highly problematic.

In practical terms, 12 trained professionals made up the team and worked in pairs in 5 schools to produce ethnographic accounts in Chile. These women and men belonged to different disciplines, including sociology, anthropology, education, occupational therapy, and psychology, and all had previous experience in doing school ethnographies. Pairs spent 8 months in each school producing field accounts through different types of documentation (field notes, field diaries, entry reports, etc.). To track the research processes, the full research team held 12 meetings between May and October 2013. In these meetings, these 12 professionals plus 7 senior researchers met and discussed notes produced in the school fields. In these meetings, the role of the senior researchers was to provoke deeper questioning on how to trouble school happenings in relation to the production of normalcy and difference. It is in this layer of the project that I locate myself and the insights I am sharing in this chapter. From my view as a senior researcher leading this group, the "becoming" of the ethnographer became both subjected to and the subject of research (Heckert 2010). This means that researchers as racialized, sexualized, gendered, classed, nationed, and aged entities became subjected to specific positions for me to understand what was presented as the *site* in their fieldnotes. In doing so, they uncritically reproduced the stability *of the field* in many different ways. As this became a multilayered, in-progress inquiry while the 12 researchers were *doing ethnographic work*, I came to create a second layer of analysis. Thus, the focus was on the ethnographers' possibilities to produce certain types of descriptions of schools and the possibilities of making visible the assumptions underlying them when writing and communicating their field notes.

Since the ethnographers worked for 8 months (3 days a week) in each school, they developed a long-term relationship with the school staff that allowed them to produce ethnographic texts through which intensities, regularities, and dissonances were presented. These texts, as cultural and social portraits of the observers, became data for me. I was interested in exploring how the fact of doing ethnography in five different sites can help me question stabilities in language that name and describe categories, and their relations in school sites. I read the ethnographers' accounts and was intrigued by the ways they normalize what they see and how these discourses were informed by specific assumptions of time and space as they produce knowledge about schools. My thinking was that paying attention to the ways researchers unconsciously use time and space in their ethnographic accounts allows me to see how they inscribe specific cultures, subjectivities, and relations as particular and unique, for instance, when they stabilize identities in their narrations as in, "I did not see any Peruvians in the schoolyard". Therefore, this is an invitation to focus on the turn to "data that escapes language or even representation" (Youdell 2010, p. 92). My questions were oriented to think about the ethnographer's possibility to produce ethnographic descriptions outside of her/his own sexualized, gendered, nationalistic, classed, and aged matrices of understanding and producing accounts and to explore ways to think about time and space differently to help expand this possibility. Therefore, my way of approaching these work meetings was through understanding ethnographic accounts *in the making* that later folded into possibilities to critically address knowledge and language used and produced by the researchers. I was constantly provoked by their descriptions and interpretations on how school organizes itself, where they see problems, what constitutes *the new* for them, what a politics of articulations rather than unities might do for them, and how thinking through nontraditional social and cultural frames could alter the force of *describing experiences in schools*. In other words, I intend to redirect attention to the ways lives are told and to rethink how such inquiry can be "attuned to the fluidity and incoherency of lived experience" (Browne and Nash 2010, p. 18), and to explore on the new political possibilities to think about who we are or may become.

The ways we organized the field research was inspired by the autonomy each pair of researchers had in terms of producing texts in each school. There was on average 60 field notes produced for each school. Although the research team was autonomous in producing their field notes, I asked that they include consideration of specific questions to be answered while in the field. The questions included: (a) How do you document *normalcy* in schools? How do you track dominant values in relation to gender, sexuality, class, nation, ability, and age in this particular school? (b) How are habits of gender represented at the school? Through which mechanisms, codes, signs, symbols, objects, protocols, and practices is it possible to narrate, describe, and observe these habits? What social feminine and masculine attributes are enacted in the school, in the neighborhood? How are women and men normalized in that particular school and neighborhood? (c) How is skin color organized at the school? What are the normative and valuable discourses associated to skin color at that school? How can I complicate the experience as an observer of skin color based on those categories and values that organize that experience for the ethnographer herself/himself?

I documented the group conversations around the problems and possibilities of responding to these questions in the production of ethnography in different school settings. This is the data that informs this chapter.

3.3   Something About Time and Space

When presenting critical theorizations of time and space as relevant in the production of ethnographic accounts, my argument is that both dimensions have been understood in separate and hierarchical modes (Massey 2005), which have developed the idea of space as a key element to enact the classroom, the school, the neighborhood, and the street and the idea of time as the succession of predictable pasts, presents, and futures within those spaces (schools' ideas of success and progress, evident developmental and emotional stages, predictable behaviors, unquestionable divisions of types of students, etc.). These ideas indicate the production of a motionless subject that belongs and corresponds uncritically to specific times and spaces. As Grosz (1995, p. 92) indicates,

> the subject's relation to space and time is not passive: space is not simply an empty receptacle independent of its contents; rather, the ways in which space is perceived and represented depends on the kinds of objects positioned "within" it and, more particularly, the kinds of relation the subject has to those objects.

To think and narrate time as a linear passing of units requires imagining and confining identities as being someone we already know, which in this chapter, is read as a source for the perpetuation of problematic stable cultural, social, and biological descriptions (the young, the poor, the vulnerable, etc.) to explain institutional spaces. Maintaining descriptions of schools based on regularities and stable practices and divisions suggest that dominant notions of time and space may operate silently on our backs when producing specific imaginations of relations, subjectivities, and correspondences between categories and lived experiences. What I am interested in is the question of, if notions of time and space are transformed, in what ways might our descriptions and imaginations of schools and who inhabit them shift? How do familiar notions time and space, as configurations of power (Ahmed 2011; Freeman 2010; Grosz 1995, 2005; Massey 2005; McCallum and Tuhkanen 2011; Thrift 2008), restrict our possibility to escape the humanistic version of the subject, progress, and development? If I choose to use time as resonating more with the idea of indeterminacy of the future, surprise, unpredictability, or newness (Grosz 1999, p. 4), in what ways does my own understanding of the past and present dialogue with the practices and subjectivities produced in ethnographic texts in the *now*? In what ways can we question the cause–effect relation that constantly acts behind our backs when observing? My argument is that when time and space are used in their dominant conceptualizations they allow the uncritical repetition of binaries, and as a consequence, school practices are presented as motionless cultural constructs. This is political.

3.4 About Ethnography

As I move through my questionings of what it is that structures my own stories of intelligibilities in schools, I pay critical attention to the versions of the *real* of ethnography represented by ethnographers. This requires me to understand that the ethnographers' own narratives are "effect[s] of the discourses of the real" (Britzman 2000, p. 28). This is particularly relevant when *the problem* that the ethnography narrates is hard to locate in one practice, one relation, one subjectivity, or one field. Tracking the production of the articulation between discourses of normalcy and difference in schools requires attention to the fluidity of concepts, how they are lived, and how they become real. The project I am referring to in this chapter did not focus on how *marginalized* identities have been repressed by some condition, person, or social structure (Samuels 2014). Instead, we directed the gaze toward the exploration of the dynamics that make it possible to speak of unquestioned normalcies in schools, and as a consequence, to think of *differences* as possible to be constituted, tracked, and monitored; in sum, as problems to be solved. This focus is a critical perspective on ethnography that casts a light on the possibility to document and reveal what is taken for granted by the researchers.

In order to utilize ethnography as a tool to explore the production of normalcy and difference in schools, a few questions guide my analysis: is—and, if so, how—is "the subject the effect of a certain type of question?" (Colebrook 1999, p. 122); what questions might we use to complicate ethnographic accounts in educational contexts? In what ways do normative understandings of time and space reproduce narratives of stable units in school settings (*the feminine girl, the disadvantaged student*, etc.)? Moving away from the humanistic notion of the subject as autonomous toward the idea that the subject is produced through constant movement and re-creation, as *unreal* (Britzman 2000; Pillow 2003), implies interrogating the uses of normative time and space in ethnographic research. Exploring some of the tensions of ethnographic research and writing when studying identity categories and institutional practices, requires attention to the ethnographer's ways of fashioning narratives, their uses of units and discontinuities, their insistence on maintaining subjects' common positionalities, the ways ethnographic texts embody specific notions of an essential self, and a view that these are critical dimensions for questioning *the real* of the stories we tell in ethnographic studies.

I consider the recognition of the postmodern turn within anthropology and sociology that states that ethnography is an

> intellectual approach rather than a method; a theory of research process, which is defined by its relationship to certain theoretical positions. One of the strengths of ethnography is the way that it seeks to link structure and practice, micro- and macro-analysis, historical, economic, political, and cultural factors. (Rooke 2010, p. 27)

Therefore, I focus on the power of ethnography to enact and produce particular cultural subjects (I refer to both the researcher and the researched). Thinking about ethnographies in schools differently requires the statement of a difference between those normative and declarative ways to do ethnographic work and those more deconstructive research practices. While a more reflexive ethnography "seeks to impart knowledge to a reader whose position is stabilized by invisible claims to a shared discourse" (Pillow 2003, p. 78); the deconstructive ethnography "disrupts the identity of the reader with a unified subject of enunciation by discouraging identification" (Pillow 2003, p. 78). Questions related to what it is that structures meanings, practices, and bodies in schools become crucial while in a more humanistic notion of ethnography the assumption is that the researcher holds the position of the detached, rational, and objective observer, and her accounts are understood as *real* possibilities to understand the Other. This might be called "the straight version of ethnography" (Britzman 2000, p. 230). I lean more on the deconstructive ethnography because it is concerned about how certain practices and bodies become intelligible while others become discounted. This is central to the ways ethnographic accounts are produced. In this orientation, "representation is always in crisis, knowledge is constitutive of power, and agency is the constitutive effect and not the originator of situated practices and histories" (Britzman 2000, p. 231).

I use these elements to trouble the narratives produced by ethnographers. I follow Britzman's (2000, p. 229) question related to the possibility of the existence of "an educational ethnography that exceeds the constraints of humanism. What if the ethnographer began not just to question the discourse of others but to engage the relation between the discourses that render ethnography intelligible?" Along with this idea, working in five different school sites, at the *same time*, provided the possibility to question the taken-for-granted stability of the narratives created by the researchers while in the field. I understand that "to fashion narration with the imperatives of poststructuralism means that the researcher must become overconcerned with experience as a discourse and with competing discourses of experience that traverse and structure any narrative" (Britzman 2000, p. 232). Experience, as a discourse, is relevant because it brings to the fore the problem of how the invention of the subject is "viewed as synonymous with 'experience' in education" (Britzman 2000, p. 232). Therefore, what researchers are describing as the *experience* of school subjects and their own experience as researching needs to be understood as the description of those discourses available to produce those particular descriptions. This has specific consequences on the ways we assign meaning to what we describe.

Having access to ethnographic texts from five different school sites helped me unpack notions of stability of meaning and the cultural and social matrices from where researchers produce ethnographic texts. This allowed me to critically raise questions about "what it is that structures meanings, practices, and bodies, about why certain practices become intelligible, valued, or deemed as traditions while other practices become discounted, impossible, or unimaginable" (Britzman 2000, p. 231). The apparent stability of the language used by researchers producing ethnographic accounts led me to attend to the ways the normalization of bodies is an essential and constitutive part of the possibilities to narrate schools. This language was most times expressed through unities (the "vulnerable male student," the "old female teacher," the "Peruvian female student," the "disabled young male student," etc.) rather than compositions; and anchorages (e.g., the strict relation between types of families and types of abilities students exhibit) rather than sporadic or simultaneous articulations, and most of the time they expressed in their field notes a rooted relationship between territory and the subject and static notions of time and space rather than a complex and shifting relation to them (e.g., Peruvians come from Peru). These three characteristics of their narratives are the ways I can tell they produce ethnographic texts under dominant notions of time and space: unities, anchorages, and correspondences. Thus, to shift the question from who is the student and who is the teacher to how is the subject—as a political and cultural form—institutionalized within and among schools, requires unsettling dominant notions of time and space. To work with five schools simultaneously allowed me to pay attention more attentively to the productive assemblage in the production of the articulations between normalcy and difference in such a way that the five schools were part of the racializing, gendering, aging, ableist, sexualizing assemblages where these categories were not constructed as "biological or cultural classifications but as a set of socio-political processes that discipline humanity into full humans, not-quite-humans, and nonhumans" (Weheliye 2014, p. 4).

While insisting on the political importance of questioning the possibilities of narrating school, most of the time I realized that ethnographic methods do not permit overlapping forms of attachment to cultural orders while questioning the same cultural orders through the observations. An effort to maintain unique and particular ways to politicize what the researchers observed was constant. As I tried to uncover the politics beneath the researchers' observations, I noticed that gendered, sexed, nationalistic, and aged descriptors did not seem to be understood as word choices to help them describe school contexts. They often referred to the workings of their prejudices while observing, instead paying closer attention to the politics of knowing.

Consider, for instance, the neutrality of gender when producing ethnographic accounts. It is common in Spanish to use male pronouns to describe activities that also can include girls, but does not recognize them explicitly. They are unnecessary to name. This simple fact produced several conversations on the authority of language and representation when producing ethnographic accounts where girls were part of the school landscape to be described. In Spanish language recognizing the existence of girls would mean explicitly saying "boys *and* girls" (niños y niñas), a convention that is usually considered unnecessary to specify. It produces the invisibility of girls or in other words, it invalidates the presence of girls from what is normal to say/write about schools and the operations of power to produce gender. This simple fact becomes a process of genderization in schools. This represents one way that the possibility of language has to offer produces only certain realities. In this case, unequal realities.

In our discussions throughout the project, I permanently insisted on the usage of male and female pronouns to describe and write ethnographic accounts. Otherwise, my sense of the *real* would have been completely *unreal*. This is critical when questioning the stability of language in creating ethnographic accounts of schools and points to a more general statement about gender and schools: the neutrality of gender in schools in Chile needs to be problematized. Even in official documents, it is expressed that to "save [physical] space," since naming girls and boys requires more words, the national curriculum explicitly indicates that official documents will use the masculine pronoun when naming girls as well. This is problematic as it assumes that masculine reference includes feminine, and this demands "muted sexuality" (Jackman 2010, p. 113). Therefore, it is necessary to continue to narrate stories of schools that make visible specific discourses about gender and sexuality in order to fully understand who are the ones who occupy particular spaces in schools. At this point, questioning ethnography requires naming and critically reflecting on the performances of the gendered, sexualized, classed, raced, and generational selves during the research process (Rooke 2010, p. 35). As we move into these considerations, we begin to see that it is not that ethnographers do research on *sites*; rather, ethnographers, because of who they are and what they imagine is the *site*, make possible and *real* gendered, sexualized, nationalistic, and aged narratives that latter become *the site*.

My concerns relating to the ways time and space act upon researchers' representations of bodies, relations, and practices deal with how "ethnography assures us that there is both a 'there' and 'beings who are there'" (Britzman 2000, p. 229). This reaffirms relations between time, space, and identity and in many different ways reinforces the problematic correspondence and fitting between lived experiences and imagined categories.

3.5   Scenes of the Uses of Space and Time

There is an interesting equation between time, space, and representation. Time and space, as critical dimensions to imagine and represent the world, are integral to producing children, youth, and teachers as social categories in school contexts. As Tsolidis (2008, p. 273) noted, "space and time conspires to make one school 'real' and the other 'unreal.'" Time and space are simultaneously created through action. Schools provide good examples of how to organize identities spatially and temporally either by mandating or allowing their presence in certain locations. Massey (2005, p. 127) reminds us that these "spatial organizations [are] deeply bound up with the social production of identities." There is much to explore about how space and its particular understandings affect the ways we narrate school. For instance, one of the ethnographic scenes in one of the girls-only schools addresses the spatial organization of the open areas and patios of the school. In this school, there is a special section of the playground with a locked fence, as one of the interviewees noted. This particular section of the patio is separated and one can hardly see it from the main patio. In different ways, it is constituted as an isolated section of the patio. This space is known as a hidden section where lesbian students go. As mentioned by one of the staff in charge of supervision of school breaks "it is necessary to lock this section of the patio otherwise it gets full of lesbians." This space is locked because there are "certain girls" who like to go to this section of the school. In this passage, space is used to *other* female students. The moral-inflected identities assigned to girls who "like" to go to this specific section of the patio are part of a discourse of "amoral" or "lost girls" for the rest of the school agents. The ways female students are *othered* through space deserve attention. There is a generalized idea that all sexual exploration needs to happen outside school, and indeed should not happen in school. The imagination is that spaces contain specific sexualities. Ethnographers recognize the sexuality of the place and then they can describe the effects of these distinct places occupied by these sexual differences (e.g., elementary schools vs. high school sites). It is only then that we can describe how they come to be in contact. Here, "differences are the consequences of internal characteristics" (Massey 2005, p. 68) of places. To identify bodies, they need to be *in* a place *in* time otherwise they become unreadable. I think it is important to question how space and its dominant notions narrow acceptable social identities that feed school ethnography and encourage the formation of marginal groups. Equating certain spaces with certain identities is a way to assign moral values to specific bodies and practices. These prescriptions reinforce particular cultural imaginings of sexualized youth identities.

The ways ethnographic accounts stabilize language assure strict narratives of gendered, sexed, classed, raced, and generational bodies that permit us to authoritatively describe *identities* in schools as stable, and in a clear relation, school as a particular space. This presumption that spaces are autonomous has enabled power to act (Massey 2005, p. 67), feed the imaginary strict narratives of identities that frame the "grid of qualification" (Manning 2009, p. xxi) that allows us to speak the school. For instance, the assumption that bodies perform in specific ways, for example, *the female vulnerable student, the male student at risk*, is a way to produce marginal and normal spaces and identities through a non-relational process. These *authenticities* and the ways they are constantly produced, discursively and materially as discrete identities, produced in neutral time and space, need to be questioned.

Descriptions of different spaces such as home, the neighborhood, the street, and school are presented as if they were individual units, completely differentiated one from another, and constituted primarily through their distinction of one from another, separation, and isolation from each other. Therefore, we anticipate that these places are different, that they belong and submit themselves to different purposes and goals, and that therefore *contain* different people, with different dispositions, attributes, and values. This way of organizing space and purposes informs common ideas. It is especially interesting to see how the narration of sexuality brings the language of inside and outside in relation to space in ethnographic accounts. For example, the popular idea that sexuality is a problem to be addressed and solved at home, rather than at school, which is a place to study and not explore ideas about sexualities. When issues of sexuality are presented, teachers argue that parents are responsible for talking about sexuality with their children.

These ways to represent difference in the ethnographic work suggest that differences are *real* and autonomous from what the ethnographers themselves imagine as the *real identity* of the place. Such ways to relay the truth of spaces and identities suggest that they are accessible products, and not produced from interaction "nor [within] the sphere of multiplicity nor as essentially open and ongoing" (Massey 2005, p. 71). On the contrary, to describe schools as a political space that produce identities requires acknowledgment of the "existence of trajectories, which have at least some degree of autonomy from each other (which are not simply alignable into one linear story)" (Massey 2005, p. 71). The spatial

> is the realm of the configuration of potentially dissonant (or concordant) narratives. Places, rather than locations of coherence, become the foci of the meeting and the nonmeeting of the previously unrelated and thus integral to the generation of novelty. The spatial in its role of bringing distinct temporalities into new configurations sets off the new social processes. (Massey 2005, p. 71)

This is relevant to the ways we construct narratives of the school site since it emphasizes the political nature of ethnographic work. How can we un-draw the distinct correspondence between identities and spaces and what for? In what ways may it help us see something unexpected?

Time is presented in the ways ethnographers narrate schools as the unfolding of some internalized story containing already established and recognizable identities and practices in schools. In many ways, the researchers' descriptions are reproducing the self-produced stories of the participating schools. Schools are constantly imagined and described by policies as "behind" or "advanced." This is what ethnographies in schools most of the time proliferate. As Massey (2005, p. 71) states, "… while representing time might take the life out of time, equating representation with space takes the life out of space." This has significant effects on the ways in which schools are presented and the ways in which categories and relations in ethnographic accounts proliferate.

For instance, in an interview with one of the oldest female participating teachers, she kept referring to her experience as a teacher as framed, as the fond remembrance of better times. She often recalled, "past times were better," indicating that school situations today are much more complicated than before. She used the past as a container of better social and cultural practices that made teaching a more enjoyable experience. She explicitly referred to the ideas of families and "normal" students:

"[today] parents do not worry about their children's performances in schools. Mothers should stay at home to take care of their children." Later, she complains about the inclusion of special education needs students in regular schools, noting that, she "was trained to teach normal kids." The idea that the past was composed of parents dedicated to supporting their kids in schools and the absence of children with special needs in schools is critically important. Schools from the past are constructed around dominant notions of specific social roles (women at home educating children) and the functioning of social institutions to produce specific identities. These notions of the past as containing specific social orders are ways to sustain explanations about students' performances, cultural practices, and particular meanings of school success. The notion that *today's schools* are composed of students with *social problems* who were not part of old ideas of the school is a relevant part of this narrative.

3.6 Final Thoughts

Sites, as usually imagined, are thought as spaces ready to be entered by the researcher to describe what is contained within them. In doing this, the complex relationship between space and subjectivities; and time and subjectivities in ethnographic accounts foreshadow the reinstallation of common sense and taken-for-granted notions of experience, power, and knowledge, "not only through interpretation and analysis but, significantly through the repertoire of methods available to the researcher" (Tsolidis 2008, p. 272). This is particularly relevant when describing school sites where we intend to understand the production and circulation of discourses of normalcy and difference. For instance, working with young people, women, and immigrants in school contexts implies the description of specific power dynamics that construct them and work against them in explicit ways. To get to know people and tell their stories is not enough for this purpose. Thus, we need to explore whose particular power relations and dominant values are produced in school ethnographies. To consider school as space that is "[…] not neutral, nor container, but instead prescribed by and in turn producing of, a range of unequal power relations that respond to social and material conditions nuanced through time" (Tsolidis 2008, p. 273) is imperative to politically transform the possibilities to become something we do not know yet.

Reflecting on the ethnographic process, I wonder about the ways we could produce descriptions of schools that promote fluidity and the possibility of the yet to come or appear. Imaginations of schools, students, learning processes, teachers, etc., are most frequently based on biological realities, age-based categories, and psychological processes that redirect our attention to causal and linear explanations. If we would rather emphasize the observation of those systems of reasoning, or discourses that circulate across schools to create the concepts of school, learning, development, child, youth, and teacher, we may turn to a different type of question and narration of what is the experience of normalcy and difference in schools. As Wise and Fine (2000, cited in Tsolidis 2008, p. 272) stated, "… as researchers, we need to account for the perspective implicit in our gaze and its potential to colonise those we describe."

As I move through my own questionings of the meanings of doing ethnographic work in schools, I think about how to account for the politics behind the idea that, "concepts must be experienced. They are lived" (Manning 2009, p. x). How do I observe to tell the lived concept? What are the kinds of questions I have to ask to imagine a different possibility to *tell* schools? The challenge would be how to experience schools, not as images of people contained by specific times and spaces, but as proliferations of particular relations that move across times and spaces. As Manning (2009, p. 5) states, "concepts are events in the making. An event in the making is a thought on the cusp of articulation—a prearticulated thought in motion."

My attention is posed on how the narration of more diffuse relations, subjectivities, and practices may affect the meanings of *experiences in schools*. What if I move from the understanding of school as a preexisting place that I *enter* to capture something that involves constant movement? Manning (2009) proposes that it is my movement that creates the space I will come to understand as the school. This will imply that "without that particular moving body, that particular environment does not exist" (Manning 2009, p. 15). If I define school as a site produced by moving things—meaning

> things that are in motion and that there are defined by their capacity to affect and be affected—they have to be mapped through different, coexisting forms of composition, habituation, and event. They can be "seen," obtusely, in circuits and failed relays, in jumpy moves and the layered textures of a scene. (Stewart 2007, p. 4)

As I move in my own way of framing these *possibilities*, I question my efforts to *know* how a school is presented by the collection of what a school means made by researchers and what would it mean to say something about schools by "performing some of the intensity and texture that makes them habitable and animate" (Stewart 2007, p. 4).

Through this process of ethnographic research, I have been oriented to question the politics of narrating the subject from the dominant languages of the static positions provided to subjects and times and spaces to be occupied. Knowledge ethnographers use to describe schools is an extension of the language of the sexed, gendered, nationalistic, and aged bodies we all know. As space takes the shape of a container where identities belong and where differences are conceptualized as temporal sequences (Massey 2005), ethnographic accounts resemble these prescriptions. As Massey (2005, p. 71) explains:

> The real import of spatiality, the possibility of multiple narratives, [is] lost. The regulation of the world into a single trajectory, *via* the temporal convening of space, was, and still often is, a way of refusing to address the essential multiplicity of the spatial. It is the imposition of a single universal.

As we move to other possibilities to produce ethnographic knowledge (data generation and analysis) about normalcy and difference, rather than seeking for closure, clarity, or definition, we should think of schools as institutions as an unfinished *now*.

References

Ahmed, S. (2011). Happy futures, perhaps. In E. L. McCallus & M. Tuhkanen (Eds.), *Queer times, queer becomings* (pp. 159–182). Albany: State University of New York Press.

Ahmed, S. (2012). *On being included. Racism and diversity in institutional life.* Durham & London: Duke University Press.

Baez, B. (2004). The study of diversity. "The knowledge of difference" and the limits of science." *The Journal of Higher Education, 75*(3), 285–306.

Barad, K. (2003). Posthumanist performativity: Toward and understanding of how matter comes to matter. *Signs: Journal of Women in Culture and Society, 28*(3), 801–831.

Béhague, D. (2015). Shaping the modern child: Genealogies and ethnographies of developmental science. *Social Science and Medicine, 143,* 249–254.

Britzman, D. (2000). "Question of belief:" Writing poststructural ethnography. In E. St. Pierre & W. Pillow (Eds.), *Working the ruins: Feminist poststructural theory and methods in education* (pp. 27–40). New York: Routledge.

Browne, K., & Nash, C. (2010). Queer methods and methodologies. An introduction. In K. Browne & C. Nash (Eds.), *Queer methods and methodologies. Intersecting queer theories and social science research* (pp. 1–23). England: Ashgate.

Campbell, E., & Lassiter, L. E. (2015). *Doing ethnography today. Theories, methods, exercises.* Oxford: Wiley Blackwell.

Chambers, I. (1994). *Migrancy, culture, identity.* New York: Routledge.

Colebrook, C. (1999). A grammar of becoming: Strategy, subjectivism, and style. In E. Grosz (Ed.), *Becomings. Explorations in time, memory, and futures* (pp. 117–140). Ithaca and London: Cornell University Press.

Davis, L. (2013). *The end of normal. Identity in a biocultural era.* Ann Arbor: The University of Michigan Press.

Department of Immigration and Migration of the Ministry of Interior and Public Security. (2016). Retrieved from http://www.extranjeria.gob.

Freeman, E. (2010). *Time binds. Queer temporalities, queer histories.* Durham & London: Duke University Press.

Gillborn, D. (2008). Coincidence or conspiracy? Whiteness, policy and the persistence of the black/white achievement gap. *Educational Review, 60*(3), 229–248.

Gillborn, D. (2010a). Reform, racism and the centrality of whiteness: Assessment, ability and the "new eugenics". *Irish Educational Studies, 29*(3), 231–252.

Gillborn, D. (2010b). The colour of numbers: Surveys, statistics and deficit thinking about race and class. *Journal of Education Policy, 25*(2), 253–276.

Gillborn, D. (2016). Softly, softly: Genetics, intelligence and the hidden racism of the new geneism. *Journal of Education Policy, 31*(4), 365–388. https://doi.org/10.1080/02680939.2016.1139189.

Grosz, E. (1995). *Space, time, and perversion.* New York: Routledge.

Grosz, E. (1999). *Becomings. Exploration in time, memory, and futures.* New York: Cornell University Press.

Grosz, E. (2005). *Time travels. Feminism, nature, power.* Durham & London: Duke University Press.

Haraway, D. (1992). The promises of monsters: A regenerative politics for inappropriate/d others. In L. Grossberg, C. Nelson, & P. Treichler (Eds.), *Cultural studies* (pp. 295–337). New York: Routledge.

Harwood, V., & Allan, J. (2014). *Psychopathology at school. Theorizing mental disorders in education.* London & New York: Routledge.

Harwood, V., & McMahon, S. (2014). Medicalization in schools. In L. Florian (Ed.), *The sage handbook of special education* (pp. 915–930). Los Angeles: Sage.

Heckert, J. (2010). Intimacy with strangers/intimacy with self: Queer experiences of social research. In K. Browne & C. Nash (Eds.), *Queer methods and methodologies. Intersecting queer theories and social science research* (pp. 41–54). England: Ashgate.

Jackman, M. C. (2010). The trouble with fieldwork: Queering methodologies. In K. Browne & C. Nash (Eds.), *Queer methods and methodologies. Intersecting queer theories and social science research* (pp. 113–128). England: Ashgate.

Kafer, A. (2013). *Feminist, queer crip*. Bloomington and Indianapolis: Indiana University Press.

Karping, I., & O'Connell, K. (2015). Stigmatising the "normal": The legal regulation of behaviour as disability. *UNSW Law Journal, 38*(4), 1461–1483.

Katz, M. (2013). The biological inferiority of the undeserving poor. *Social Work & Society International Online Journal, 11*(1). Retrieved from http://www.socwork.net/sws/article/view/359/709.

Korthagen, F., & Valsalos, A. (2010). Going to the core: Deepening reflection by connecting the person to the profession. In N. Lyons (Ed.), *Handbook of reflection and reflective inquiry: Mapping a way of knowing for professional inquiry* (pp. 531–554). New York: Springer.

Kumashiro, K. (2002). *Troubling education. Queer activism and anti-oppressive education*. New York: Routledge Falmer.

Kumashiro, K. (2008). *The seduction of common sense. How the right has framed the debate on America's schools*. New York and London: Teacher College Press.

Lather, P. (2013). Methodology-21: What do we do in the afterward? *International Journal of Qualitative Studies in Education, 26*(6), 634–645.

Lather, P., & St. Pierre, E. (2013). Introduction. Post qualitative research. *International Journal of Qualitative Studies in Education, 26*(6), 629–633.

Manning, E. (2009). *Relationscapes: Movement, art, philosophy (technologies of lived abstraction)*. Massachusetts: The MIT Press.

Massey, D. (2005). *For space*. London: Sage Publications.

Matus, C., & Haye, A. (2015). Normalidad y diferencia en la escuela: diseño de un proyecto de investigación social desde el dilema político-epistemológico. *Estudios Pedagógicos, 41*, 135–146.

Matus, C., & Infante, M. (2011). Undoing diversity: Knowledge and neoliberal discourses in colleges of education. *Discourse: Studies in the Cultural Politics of Education, 32*(3), 293–307.

Matus, C., & McCarthy, C. (2003). The triumph of multiplicity and the carnival of difference: Curriculum dilemmas in the age of postcolonialism and globalization. In W. Pinar (Ed.), *International handbook of curriculum research* (pp. 73–82). New Jersey: Lawrence Erlbaum Associates.

Matus, C., & Rojas, C. (2015). La normalidad y la diferencia en nuestras escuelas a propósito de la Ley de Inclusión Escolar. *Revista Docencia, 56*, 47–56.

McCallum, E. L., & Tuhkanen, M. (2011). Becoming unbecoming. Untimely mediations. In E. L. McCallum & M. Tuhkanen (Eds.), *Queer times, queer becomings* (pp. 1–21). Albany: State University of New York Press.

O'Connell, K. (2015). Bad boys' brains: Law, neuroscience and the gender of "aggressive" behavior. In S. Schmitz & G. Hoppner (Eds.), *Gendered neurocultures: Feminist and queer perspectives on current brain discourses*. Retrieved from https://ssrn.com/abstract=2581322.

O'Connell, K. (2016). Unequal brains: Disability discrimination laws and children with challenging behaviour. *Medical Law Review, 24*(1), 76–98.

Pillow, W. (2003). Confession, catharsis, or cure? Rethinking the uses of reflexivity as methodological power in qualitative research. *International Journal of Qualitative Studies, 16*(2), 175–196.

Pillow, W. (2015). Reflexivity as interpretation and genealogy in research. *Cultural Studies—Critical Methodologies, 15*(6), 419–434. https://doi.org/10.1177/1532708615615605.

Rooke, A. (2010). Queer in the field: On emotions, temporality and performativity in ethnography. In K. Browne & C. Nash (Eds.), *Queer methods and methodologies. Intersecting queer theories and social science research* (pp. 25–39). England: Ashgate.

Samuels, E. (2014). *Fantasies of identification: Disability, gender, race*. New York and London: New York University Press.

Schneider, J. (2002). Reflexive/diffractive ethnography. *Cultural Studies—Critical Methodologies, 2*(4), 460–482.

Skliar, C. (2007). *La educación (que es) del otro. Argumentos y desierto de argumentos pedagógicos*. Buenos Aires: Noveduc.

Stewart, K. (1996). *A space on the side of the road. Cultural poetics in an "other" America.* Princeton: Princeton University Press.

Stewart, K. (2007). *Ordinary affects.* Durham: Duke University Press.

St. Pierre, E. (1997). Nomadic inquiry in the smooth spaces of the field: A preface. *International Journal of Qualitative Studies in Education, 10*(3), 365–383.

St. Pierre, E. (2000). Poststructural feminism in education: An overview. *International Journal of Qualitative Studies in Education, 13*(5), 477–515.

Thrift, N. (2008). Non-representational theory. Space|politics|affect. London & New York: Routledge.

Tsolidis, G. (2008). The (im)possibility of poststructuralist ethnography—Researching identities in borrowed spaces. *Ethnography and Education, 3*(3), 271–281.

Weems, L. (2006). Unsettling politics, locating ethics. representation of reciprocity in postpositivist inquiry. *Qualitative Inquiry, 12*(5), 994–1011.

Weems, L. (2010). From "home" to "camp:" Theorizing the space of safety. *Studies in Philosophy and Education, 29,* 557–568.

Weheliye, A. (2014). *Habeas viscus. Racializing assemblages, biopolitics, and black feminist theories of the human.* Durham & London: Duke University Press.

Yoshino, K. (2007). *Covering the hidden assault on our civil rights.* New York: Random House Trade Paperbacks.

Youdell, D. (2006). *Impossible bodies, impossible selves: Exclusions and student subjectivities.* The Netherlands: Springer.

Youdell, D. (2010). Queer outings?: Uncomfortable stories about the subjects of post-structural school ethnography. *Qualitative Studies in Education, 23*(1), 87–100.

Youdell, D. (2011). *School trouble. Identity, power and politics in education.* London and New York: Routledge.

Chapter 4
Discomfort—Affects, Actors, and Objects in Ethnographic Intervention

Carolina Rojas Lasch

Abstract This chapter discusses the development of a productive circuit of observation and transformation of discursive practices regarding normalcy and difference in educational institutions. In addition, a conceptual and methodological analysis of the complex relationships between ethnography and intervention are presented. In working with educational institutions, both processes were nominally raised and sequentially planned as different processes. However, the boundaries between the ethnography and the intervention proved to be difficult to establish. This may be due to the fact that the study of the production of normalcy and difference is based on a political and transformational positioning that makes determining the limits of each impossible. Ethnography is a mode of intervention, and this intervention is nurtured, facilitated, and acquires meaning through ethnographic observation. In this chapter, I focus specifically on interventions associated with a professional development process for practicing teachers, but also on a more general understanding of the process of creating public policy that considers difference. The chapter discusses the instruments used for documenting the ethnographies and intervention such that they may be used or replicated in future research studies.

4.1 Introduction

In this chapter, I reflect on the relationship between ethnography and intervention when we take positioning ourselves from post-structural and queer approaches seriously. The ideas that I will expound on below are based on the work we developed during 2 years with teachers and other school agents to study the normal and transform the means of production of the different. Our purposes were to understand

I would like to thank Anita Sanyal for her help in the interpretation and editing of this chapter in English from the original in Spanish.

C. Rojas Lasch (✉)
Facultad de Ciencias Sociales, Departamento de Trabajo Social, Universidad Alberto Hurtado, Santiago, Chile
e-mail: carojas@uahurtado.cl

and transform the mediating processes and mechanisms by which the learning and teaching of normality discourses takes place in schools, and how associated with these discourses, different or diverse subjectivities and identities are produced and reproduced.

My interest in analytically exploring such limits, contours, and intersections of ethnography and intervention starts from a need to face emotions that circulated at different levels throughout the development of this project. By this, I refer to persistent nonconformity. In other words, these reflections are consequences of an act of confrontation between the emotional standpoint and the action performed. Although this feeling was never ignored by myself or by the team, I managed to see its predominance, value, and meaning in and for the work very late in the research process. Moreover, I would like to propose that this nonconformity, as a state, was consubstantial to the commitment we wanted to have concerning the theoretical approaches we adopted and above all, with the purposes of research and transformation that we had set for ourselves.

I have organized this chapter into four parts. First, I describe the sensation of nonconformity lived and problematized in its nature, by deploying it in light of the theoretical approaches that we set ourselves to work with. Second, I present and reflect upon the enacted practice within the project. Third, I reflect upon the theoretical methodological principles that were problematized in our work. Last, through what I have called an ethnographic intervention, I present a reflection about the ways in which a queer focus makes it possible to view ethnography and intervention as inherently connected.

4.2   Discomfort

During the second semester of 2012, a couple of university academics with whom I had been working on interdisciplinary topics invited me to participate in a project for which they had just obtained funding. The project was challenging because of the subject it addressed: the production of difference in the daily dynamics of schools. It was conceived as a process of construction, that is: construction of a research agenda, construction of a network of academics and institutions, construction of theoretical approaches to address diversity, and construction of a working model. In a broader sense, it was a project that, having very clear definitions regarding its purposes and theoretical approaches, challenged the rules and traditional orders of academic work in which the sequence of the definition of hypothesis, methods, and results is imposed as a logic of action. In this case, the project allowed room for creation.

Like every act of creation, the work was intense in energy and hours of dedication, and above all, intense in terms of the emotions that circulated around this process. It is with this in mind that I would like to pause. My purpose is not to describe the intimacy of a team of people, nor the psychological processes of its members, but to reflect theoretically and methodologically on the project's limits through the study of a specific feeling, which is discomfort. I focus, in particular, on two of the central praxes of the project: ethnography and intervention.

The confrontation of discomfort appeared little by little and due to different questions, but through the reactions we received, it came into focus. Reactions were organized into two large groups. First were those that alluded to the position from which we approached the study of difference and diversity, which included comments such as "it is too theoretical," "the language they use is not understandable," "everything proposed is abstract," "such a critical position does not offer anything concrete for schools to work with diversity." The second group of comments had to do with the practical work we were developing. Comments such as: "They do not know how they want to work," "they make things up along the way," "they do not fit a method," "what they do is not ethnography, because they never wrote it up," "ethnographic fieldwork is not done directly by the researchers, but rather by delegating it to young researchers," "it is a mode of neoliberal ethnography."

The expression of these types of comments occurred directly and indirectly in private spaces, behind closed doors, but also in instances of public academic events. However, the most interesting thing is that we made these same sorts of comments in a reflexive way, back and forth among ourselves, that is, between project research and personal capacity. They were reflections and states of discomfort that accompanied us on distinct levels, and never completely vanished.

At a distance, these commentaries provoke confusion and disagreements among colleagues, some of which are shown in this chapter as symbolic expressions of uncomfortable ways of creating knowledge, which reiterate a focus on methodological theory and demonstrate new ways of social transformation. It should be understood that discomfort does not refer to difficulties in the field, for example, within schools, their agents, or the context or object of investigation; rather, discomfort is consubstantial to a singular mode of production and transformation of knowledge, and is a means to learning.

Discomfort is sustained in the proposals made by affect theories by perceiving emotions in this way (Ahmed 2004a, b; Gorton 2007; Gregg and Seigworth 2010; Massumi 2002). Understanding emotion as a discursive practice makes it possible to investigate its effects. Following Ahmed (2004a), I am not interested in what emotions are; instead, I am more interested in what they do. More specifically, I view emotions as social and cultural practices. "Emotions are not *in* either the individual or the social, but produce the very surfaces and boundaries that allow the individual and the social to be delineated as if they were objects" (p. 10). In this sense, exploring discomfort will allow me to better understand the limits and scope of two of the central devices of our work: ethnography and intervention.

I identify two analytical approaches to understand discomfort. On the one hand, discomfort is associated with a resentful restlessness, something that bothers, and therefore, should somehow be overcome. In this sense, it is a feeling that can be useful to introduce something that happens in a way that is not anticipated. Thus, it becomes possible to see a moral dimension since the sensation indirectly reveals a normative and culturally accepted way of being and/or doing that could be altered. On the other hand, discomfort carries an intentionality of disagreement. It reveals an act of rebellion. In other words, the sensation is inundated with a feeling of willingness to remain a part of it, opposing the idea of letting it go. This manifests the notion that on a deeper level there is an aspiration to transform. This second understanding of discomfort opens up a highly political dimension. In the context of our work, the lived and resentful nonconformity transits within these two registers. As I argue, to remain in discomfort is consequential to the theoretical-methodological project of transformation that we assume.

Emotions understood as cultural and social practices allow for a view of their moral and political dimensions. Discomfort, then, corresponds to a moral and political feeling that is activated purposefully, by the intentional exercise of destabilization of the evident. In our project, this had implications in terms of our relationship with mainstream "management of diversity", particularly considering our conceptual approaches and positioning within the academic space. In light of this, our work was oriented to provoke changes in the ways of producing the problem and the identification of the subjects, areas, and forms of intervention. As I discuss later in this chapter, the project was based on the idea that our work was organized at different levels with the aim of creating processes of epistemological vigilance, which allowed us to superimpose moments of observation as well as install a permanent training process. We deterritorialized the production of difference as something inherent to schools and subjects in them, becoming aware of our own roles in reproducing that difference. In this way, we became part of the subject of study. At the end of the chapter, I expound on what I have coined *observational disposition* and *comprehensive involvement*.

4.3 The Project

The general purpose of the project was to set up a program to generate intervention strategies (design, implementation, evaluation, and potential impact on public policies) by means of an investigation of multiple cases (schools) and scales (levels of observation). The focus of intervention and research was the alteration of forms of knowledge within the social and cultural organization of difference, particularly in relation to ethnicity, gender, class, abilities, and their educational implications, both for learning and for community life.

The central premise that guided the development of the project is that human differences are constructed through situated social practices, which are organized in terms of a broader cultural discourse based on common sense, which predefines normality. An interdisciplinary approach and practice were central to promoting reflexive and critical debate on the possibilities of systems of production, of reasoning about difference, diversity, change, subjectivities, while at the same time, producing knowledge from the local configuration.

The project was executed in five educational establishments in Santiago de Chile, within which we worked with teachers and other agents involved in the schools. The first year was the development of the ethnographic investigation. In the second year, the intervention was implemented, for which the limits, as I show, became vague and pervious.

For the project, we gathered a team of 25 researchers who worked at different levels and with different degrees of participation. They all came from the fields of education and social sciences (sociologists, psychologists, social workers, philosophers), with experience in research on diversity issues but from different theoretical and methodological traditions. The project was implemented on three scales. A team of five researchers formed the lead research team, the group responsible for the development of the ethnography and the intervention. A team of ten ethnographers carried out fieldwork during the first year. The second year, a team of five monitors had the main task of executing and sustaining the intervention processes in the educational establishments. Additionally, a team of senior researchers carried out independent work according to their individual interests using material produced through the ethnography and intervention.

The ethnographic work involved the immersion of a couple of ethnographers in each of the establishments during an average of 7 months. The fieldwork was planned in four phases (Matus et al. 2019): (1) the Entry Phase into the field, which aimed at characterizing each establishment by paying special attention to the dynamics around which daily life is organized; (2) the Consolidation Phase, which focused on producing specific and detailed information regarding how markers of difference in each establishment operate (gender habits, skin color, vulnerability); (3) the Problematization Phase, which consisted of deeper work, focusing on unpacking the operation of the specific markers of difference we had detected in the earlier phase as important in each school (in some cases, this was gender, in others, vulnerability, sexuality, or ability). We produced ethnographic records that documented the meanings, practices, and assumptions shared by the members of each school regarding what is considered normal in pursuance of the following question: How do ideas, imaginaries, and discourses of normality—from which difference is significantly problematized in each school—work? The closing phase aimed at fine-tuning our documentation of daily practices, conducting interviews with relevant stakeholders and, in the case of some schools, ethnographic observations in classrooms.

During this process, we produced three types of ethnographic records: field diaries, process reports, and a final report in which the material collected during ethnographic work was organized in a standard format. Based on this information, we elaborated a Cultural Profile for each school. The profiles revealed two things. First, the marker of difference is situated according to its cultural context and social characteristics. The second considers aspects that, in relation to the particularity of their normative/institutional projects, caused difficulty for the "management of diversity". This document and its elaboration had great significance within the project; it was the only report we used to communicate something understood as results to the schools and funding agency. Moreover, these profiles were what made us public (in the sense of being directed to public readers). The ethnographic work, therefore, had strong political significance. The development of the Cultural Profiles, as well as their place and meaning in our work, was accompanied by important degrees of discomfort, manifested as intense and emotionally charged discussions among the members of the team.

During the second year, we developed an intervention process with teachers from each school. The intervention work involved the presence of a monitor (other than the ethnographer) at each establishment, who carried out two threads of in situ work (Matus et al. 2019) over eight months: accompaniment of teachers in the schools and a series of six training workshops. The former was oriented toward the development of a periodic interaction process between a monitor and individual teachers that were based on observation and self-observation, and focused on the problematization of the teachers' own pedagogical practices. The workshops were focused on developing two types of learning. The first was teachers gaining familiarity with concepts that help problematize the traditional idea of diversity based on fixed categories associated with specific forms of organization and power relations (gender, social class, race, etc.). The second dealt with teachers' understandings of their own biographies and experiences in which they learned ways of ordering within the categories, inciting a re-positioning of identity. The workshops were designed and conducted by the lead research team. The workshops occurred at 3-week intervals. In each, a specific theme was presented. In the interim between workshops, the monitor then worked with the teachers individually in the accompaniment process on the specific theme that was addressed in the workshop. The intervention work ended with the preparation of proposals for specific action to be taken in each school, which were presented to authorities and then set to be implemented.

4.4 A Way/Mode of Making Permanent Construction

I now reflect on how discomfort permeated the project's implementation while simultaneously configuring the means for research and intervention. To do this, I delve further into the three theoretical principles that justified and challenged us to think of new ways of doing research.

4.4.1 Instability of the Subject as a Principle

Following Youdell (2010), we started from the premise that the diverse or different subject in the school does not exist but rather is in constant production. The production of the diverse subject is due to the institutional actions of the school. However, it is also due to the ways we conducted ethnographic observations, and identified and objectified problems in the intervention. This involved destabilizing the meanings of discourses of identification, and instead, assuming that identities are in motion and therefore appealing to continuous dispersal. Our task then constituted resistance to "going to study" or "going to work with" the subjects identified as different, as if they were stable identities and subjectivities (women, migrants, homosexuals, etc.). In Butler's (1997) words, "resisting these processes through practices that unsettle the meanings of these discourses and deploy other discourses that have been subjugated or disallowed" (cited in Youdell 2010, p. 88). We tried to configure a mode of research and intervention in movement, oriented, as Youdell proposes (2010), to the development of a policy of practice.

In particular, addressing queer perspectives meant challenging traditional orders and rules of doing research, challenging the linear and sequential models and methods of knowledge within social sciences, problematizing the paradigms of representation and interpretation from which ethnography and intervention are developed. A methodical principle of our work was to avoid fixing the idea of others as an object, which allowed us to consider its circumstantiality. This is how the following uncomfortable and destabilizing question became central: What do we investigate if research consists precisely in constructing what has already been investigated? In contrast to the hegemonic tendency that prompts research to define and delimit a priori an object to be observed, we acknowledged that it was precisely in the act of observation and recording that the question about the normal and the different is constructed. And, in a similar way, the scope and content of the intervention with teachers was dependent on the processes that occurred in/during their daily practice. In other words, we assumed that the development of the queer focus to ethnography and intervention meant finding stability in sustained instability.

In practice, the main guideline for the team of ethnographers was to observe the daily dynamics of the normal in the school. Their immediate reaction was to ask: "But, how is normality observed?" Since the very purpose of our research was to observe how the normal occurs, this question was central and remained open. Such situations mobilized discomfort in the team. At times they insistently asked, "We do not know what else and where [to look at]… how do we look at new things?" In practical terms, this situation was further reinforced by the desire and/or need on the part of the ethnographers for the research team to orient their work and provide more standards and guidelines on what to observe and record, which we saw as typical of the way teamwork often develops.

This situation was not exempt from tensions and was felt at the level of ethnographers' subjectivity in interactions among ethnographers and between the ethnographers and the lead research team. In fact, during the biweekly meetings held throughout the course of study, where we shared field notes and collectively discussed the ways we were documenting, the objects we were describing, and the ways we were narrating the field, comments often arose, such as: "how do we continue if it is easier to recognize the abnormality over the normality within schools?" Appeals also appeared, such as: "the items of this project are being made up as we go along… the steps to follow have not been clear from the beginning. We cannot know where we are going and what they want [referring to the research team]." In these instances, much of the meeting time was devoted to calming the anguish of the ethnographers associated with the difficulty of producing what could be seen as normal in the school.

This is how we methodically translated the idea of destabilizing the subjects of research and intervention for the study on difference and normality. It operated as a construction exercise to be done in the process. We assumed that the questions surrounding research production and field of intervention would emerge in the very moment of praxis, that is, within circumstances of subjective production of the object of research. In other words, the study of the normal, and therein the different, only exists in the impossibility of a definition and, therefore, is in permanent discomfort.

4.4.2 Conscientious and Introspective Work Concerning the Use of Common Sense

While sustaining instability was a fundamental principle, we oriented toward a horizon of political and transformational research and intervention in a few ways. We wanted to develop the capacity for observing the ways common sense sustains research decisions and pedagogical practices (as an expression of hegemonic social and cultural orders); to problematize hierarchies that such decisions and practices produce, sustain, and construct as the normal and the different within school research; and to identify of how this permeates the objects of research and student learning. A premise was that neither ethnography nor pedagogical work are impartial or neutral in terms of their capacity to produce and reproduce what common sense indicates is normal. On the contrary, both are highly political and common sense operates through the invisible reinforcing, creating, circulating, and permanently distributing rules and order. Given this, a key dimension of our work around the study of the normal was to develop an introspective practice (Kumashiro 2003) aimed at transforming the personal experience of the subjects (ethnographers, researchers, and teachers) and politicizing the practice of knowledge and pedagogy.

Since our focus of interest was to affect the discourses we—researchers, ethnographers, and teachers—circulated as well as our own personal subjectivities, the project's goal was to altogether alter our ways of knowing, rather than change already established ways of conducting in-school research and pedagogical practice (as techniques or strategies for action). The idea of converting knowledge into our main focus is based on the premise that discriminatory practices are due to the perpetuation of naturalized systems of reasoning about identities, communities, and relationships, or, according to Kumashiro (2000), common sense. More specifically, we assume its correspondence to a way of social and cultural learning (Britzman 1992) that can also be unlearned (Matus and Haye 2015). This last idea is central as it opened a realm of transformative possibilities for challenging barriers and limits often encountered by critical perspectives. That is to say, to act toward an educational practice that is inclusive and more just was made possible only by assuming that normative, oppressive discourses can be observed in our practices and be altered or modified as a consequence of understanding them as learning.

Appropriating this principle implied the construction of a work dynamic (instances, exercises, dispositions, etc.) that was deconstructive. Specifically, this meant objectifying the categories we used in narrating our field observations and to make visible the categories we were using to construct visions of school life. We did this, for example, through exercises in the analysis of field notes made by ethnographers. In several work sessions, we used these types of exercises to help ethnographers describe how they observed color, gender, and vulnerability within schools. For this, we asked that their observations be shared with the whole team. The purpose was not the construction of a real record, nor one adjusted to the reality of the schools, but rather to disarm the record, to show limits in terms of the implicit discourse that was carried in the normal.

In the intervention, we did similar work through the mechanisms of the workshops and interactions between monitors and teachers. First, we addressed the content we would present: such as categories and labels of diversity, the problem of difference, the normal as a way of learning, denaturalizing the content of teaching, the performative work of school, and the design of responsive proposals for action. During the weeks between workshops, monitors' work with teachers involved working together on the tasks of observing practices, and developing a capacity to put into question all that was naturalized within the pedagogical practices of the participating teachers. This was only possible when the monitors avoided establishing themselves in a hierarchical position where they would be seen as truth carriers, and instead privileged the surfacing of doubt, error, and questioning (Matus et al. 2019).

4.4.3 From Self-observation to Reflexive Discomfort

The interest in placing the investigator at the center of attention within the investigative practice—in this case, this includes the researcher, the monitor and/or the teacher—is not new. Decades ago, Bourdieu (2003, 2004) wrote of the value and relevance of self-observation within the process of anti-objectivist knowledge. These works opened a significant vein within critical sociology. And, over the last decades in anthropology and in general, the idea of self-observation has become more complex in discussions specifically related to ethnography, and propose to resituate the ethnographer's experience, including tensions and impossibilities, within the practice of knowledge. Doing this includes paying attention to tensions in the field, the difficulties, the failures, and the impossibilities. In this effort, some analyses have delved into how emotions contribute to the understanding of the object of study, for example, the discomfort experienced in ethnographic fieldwork (Fassin and Bensa 2008). In general, these reflections have raised criticisms about the rules of ethnographic asepsis, which for decades has influenced the documentation of the field and writing, and has contributed to making the inherent and fundamental dimensions of fieldwork invisible. Thus, the illusion of a deproblematized ethnographic knowledge proceeds to break down. According to Fassin and Bensa (2008), this stance permits the revision of the conditions through which knowledge is verified, the analysis of the human relations that anchor such practices, a problematization of the results, and an understanding of their social effects. The authors refer to such theoretical uncertainties and empirical difficulties as an ethnographic concern, and should also be seen as a condition of intelligibility.

The interest in bringing the researcher into the research practice has also been strongly encouraged by feminist and postcolonial theoretical currents. These perspectives have allowed for the problematization of the implication of a gendered learner in investigative practice. As Gregorio (2014) suggests, what gives meaning to a decolonizing and feminist anthropological practice is our disposition to estrangement, not the journey and the "other" in itself (p. 302). In this sense, in addition to attending to the ethical and political effects of the knowledge process, these perspectives have challenged the ethnographic work to propose different means of investigation.

While in general terms it has been believed that through reflexivity the limits of the ethnographer's bias in the research process can be safeguarded and to some extent overcome, feminist and queer approaches have problematized the very idea of reflexivity. As Pillow (2003) argues, reflexivity has been advocated and recognized for decades as an inherent part of ethnographic work. However, she writes that this has led to a declarative, sometimes narcissistic or banal practice that needs to be revised. In this regard, Pillow warns that reflexivity, understood as a focal point for the researcher, has been extended as a way to legitimize and overcome the limits posed by the idea of representation inherent in ethnography. In light of this, Pillow proposes to go a step further and understand reflexivity as "reflexivities of discomfort," a critical practice that helps raise awareness of who and what reflexivity serves. Pillow also addresses how reflexivity is precisely convened to solve a deeper problem and appeals for an uncomfortable reflexivity that exposes disorder and uncertainty, which allows for deconstructive questions and doubts to be cast. Youdell (2010) continues this line of argument by proposing that assuming a queer approach to ethnographic work—whether as practice, subjectivity, or positioning—generates tensions that are productive in their un-resolvability. This can be usefully augmented by additional analyses, for instance, of the strange in the search of uncomfortable reflexivity.

In the framework of this work, we assume this principle of uncomfortable reflexivity precisely for its productive dimension. In relation to what was discussed earlier in the chapter, our ways of approaching diversity are left visible. This has produced disorganization, as well as presented questions about the limits in the way in which the subject has been approached within the local academic community.

In Chile, the dominant models in the study of difference in the area of education have been imbued with a strong biomedical discourse (which is most visibly deployed in the study of special education and disability) and have problematized diversity based on the objectification of the biological, social, and cultural differences of particular subjects. The "problem of diversity" has been understood as the differences that students endure that make it difficult for them to have a successful school experience. This has led to an assembly of discourses and practices that have guided the development of highly compensatory policies (Infante Jaras et al. 2011; Infante and Matus 2009; Matus and Infante 2011). In this context, our work came to create a shift in the way of understanding difference, by first reorienting our gaze toward the ways in which power relations are organized with regard to gender, social classes, race, and ability, among others. Doing this permitted us to see how otherness is configured and how subjectivities are produced. Second, we focused on developing critical observations of the processes and mechanisms through which the schools and research deal with how such issues are learned, produced, and reinforced by the existence of differentiated subjectivities. Our attention was on the subject that does the naming of the other/otherness (the teacher, ethnographer, or monitor), as opposed to what/who is being named (different identity groups, different characteristics or attributes, or the schools or the teachers). Our focus more specifically was then the unseen performative and oppressive work that is carried out in the school experience and in research and interventions associated with diversity and inclusion. Our work created an uncomfortable limit for more traditional academic and political communities, and we understood that our interest was in comprehending the actions that produce exclusion in the education system.

To study the normal from this research focus and practice is itself an act of nonconformity since it implies problematizing, in moral terms, the ways of assessing and evaluating the place assigned to difference in educational spaces, and in political terms, to transform ways of knowing and naming. We configured a mode of carrying out the ethnographic work and the intervention that prevented recognizing a clear distinction of the limits of both praxes. Above all, however, the movement permitted by the intersection of the two formed ways of altering the systems of reasoning about difference.

In the next section, I delve into the precise intermingling between ethnography and intervention. In doing so, I pay attention to the scope and focus of strategic mechanisms that mobilized the articulation.

4.5 Ethnographic Intervention

Academic literature that has focused on the relationship between ethnography and intervention has done so to reflect on the ethical and political limits and difficulties of ethnographic work. As an example, ethnographers sometimes face situations in which they feel compelled to intervene because of personal involvement with the participants (Dennis 2009; Puttick 2017). Additionally, when the ethnographer themself is affected, questioned, and/or changed during fieldwork demonstrates that the field itself is not constituted before the work of the observer (Lanas 2016). However, the link between ethnography and intervention has been scarcely developed in regard to its simultaneity and consubstantiality. It is this that is relevant to more closely consider in the context of this project. I propose a reflection on ethnography as a practice of transformation and intervention to destabilize the way of learning.

From an analysis of the critical debates that have been independently developed around ethnography and intervention, it becomes possible to identify shared practices that are ontologically defined, understood, and constituted in the establishment of power relationships. For example, Fabian (1990), referring to the idea of time, suggests that ethnography has formed its foundations in a denial of simultaneity. This means that there is a temporal distance between the subjects that study and those that are studied, that is to say between a *we* and the *other*. Here, the former are conceived in the present, which situates the researched in the past. Hastrup (2004) has also problematized the notion of otherness and the construction of ethnographic objects, reflecting on the idea of evidence in anthropological fieldwork. In this regard, he affirms that the nature of knowledge generated through ethnography cannot be sustained by evidence as something that is observed from the outside. Instead, we are an active part of the reality under study, and the object of that knowledge is ontologically emergent.

> The anthropologist must engage the world under study, but must also at the same time realize that the anthropological object is emergent. Because knowledge is gradually incorporated, the object has no fixed ontological status, be it as a culture, a society or a community. It emerges in consequence of a particular intervention and analytical scope. Conversely, the anthropological subject does not stand outside of the situation under study, and at both levels we can see how the particular relation to the object of necessity bends back into the object itself. (Hastrup 2004, p. 468)

From the perspective of the field of intervention, Simmel (1998) reveals that the act of assisting reinforces the precariousness of the assisted by positioning them as the lower on a social scale. And, from an interactionist perspective, Goffman (1968) problematizes the reparative character of intervention, which is based on the assumption of a defective subject; the monitor, is the provider of technical experience. An extensive debate about power relations in interventions also comes from Foucauldian[1] approaches. These analyses have shown that every act of intervention implies being invested in an authority to the extent that they embody processes of domination and control. That is, the establishment and stabilization of power relations are inherent to the very nature of intervention.

As these critics suggest, it is possible to see that ethnography and intervention share a common nature. This has to do with the appearance that they can only be constituted in praxis through a didactic interaction, which requires a designation and naming of subjects. Such a relationship is an ontologically hierarchical measurement, as ethnographers and monitors are the ones who define others, the studied, and intervened upon.

This commonality prompts me to think about the scope and limits of the way in which we conducted this study on differences and normality. Is it possible to conduct ethnography without producing otherness? Is it possible to intervene without producing the intervened-upon subject? Is it possible for researchers to merge into the observed and be themselves transformed? I believe it is all possible, but only by breaking with the comfort of certain orthodoxies and deploying two strategic processes: observational disposition and comprehensive involvement.

---

[1]In regard to these approaches, the debate reported in *Revista Espirit* (April–May 1972) in which M. Foucault and J. Donzelot (among others) participate should be consulted. In addition, the following report that was published 26 years later in the same magazine (March–April 1998), in which R. Castel, M. Autés, and J. Donzelot, among others participated can also be consulted.

4.5.1 Observational Disposition

It is possible to identify that observational disposition coming from ethnographic work becomes a fundamental practice for problematizing normality. By this, I mean the capacity to pause and observe daily life in schools and document it. Later, this can be reflexively revisited as texts that permit the observation of the concepts, which can help detach us from the need to name or label. This was what we did with the team of ethnographers. We used this experience to inform what we then did with monitors and, in turn, with teachers. The underlying idea is that it is not possible to think about transformation in ways of knowing unless we start with objectifying our own possibilities and limits of observation and naming. In this sense, observational disposition becomes a way of opening up reflection. Meanwhile, the process distances itself from an exercise directed at showing or reporting what is seen in order to make a suggestion for change.

Observational disposition is certainly an uncomfortable strategy for asking about how difference is produced (both in research and in pedagogical action). The capacity to ask oneself about the limits of our own means of identifying is, therefore, the central element in the deconstruction of what appears to us as normal. In this sense, ethnography and intervention were fused into the mode of work that structured the project.

In our experience, this implied eliminating two products in terms of which the ethnography and an intervention are usually evaluated: ethnographic writing and the transformation of a reality. Conventionally, ethnographic work is assumed as a methodical whole, contemplating scope and outcome through writing, that is, the initial time of observation and documentation, which later leads to the production of an ethnographic text. From this premise, the consecration of ethnographic production is the production of a narrative. However, as I have alluded, it was our decision not to write an ethnography. This is justified in that our purpose was not to report what was seen, but to produce a transformation, to modify a way of working in schools. In this regard, several authors have already advanced a critical reflection on ethnographic writing and have warned of their representational risk. For example, Johannes Fabian, who writes shortly after boom of the debate about *Writing Culture*, problematizes the work of anthropology as a practice of representation. This suggests that writing about the other is an act of subjugation and discipline. Meanwhile, examining alternative genres of writing such as dialogue and poetry does not really solve the problem. Fabian (1990) highlights the dialogical nature of fieldwork:

> To preserve the dialogue with our interlocutors, to assure the other's presence against the distancing devices of anthropological discourse, is to continue conversing with the other on all levels of writing, not just to reproduce dialogue. Preserving the dialogue with interlocutors ensures the other's presence against the distancing devices of anthropological discourse. Also, to continue talking with the Other at all levels of writing, not only to reproduce the dialogue. (p. 766)

As discussed earlier, the production of the Cultural Profiles at the end of the first year was central. The meaning of these texts in no case attempted to describe the visible, but rather to open a conversation with schools. This can only be understood in a broader temporality that contemplated and established a commitment for the second year of work in the schools, as a process of intervention.

The Cultural Profiles were a small document of no more than five pages that we delivered to the teachers. They contained a brief description of normative dynamics at work in the schools. The daily life of schools was organized with respect to what school agents identified as "problems of diversity". The identified themes were: gender, sexuality, vulnerability, and nationality. Associated with this, the text alluded to forms and management mechanisms and/or the formal and informal administration of difference observed in the establishments. Finally, we suggested questions or topics that could be worked on the following year.

These documents were delivered to the schools, but their main dissemination was an extended workshop with all the teachers. In this workshop, the contents of the Cultural Profiles were presented and were accompanied by ethnographic citations. We carefully considered these instances since we feared that we would show critical elements not apparently visible to schools. However, the dynamics achieved were highly productive in the sense that, in the words of the teachers, they "felt recognized" in the end, despite resistance or justification some demonstrated upon seeing our findings. This exercise was key to legitimizing the observation work to generate context for teacher training in the second year, but above all, to open a discussion.

In other words, these documents founded and sustained in ethnographic accounts, helped cultivate a willingness to be observed. They were a reference of what they were learning to do for the second year, during workshops and accompaniment.

Similar to the sequential forms in more conventional ethnography, intervention is defined as a logical process associated with phases within a planning process: diagnosis, strategy formulation, implementation, and evaluation of the same. However, in our case, this formula for action was disarmed and re-configured as a rhizome-shaped process. The intervention was planned for the second year and limited to the training of teachers. It began as a way building from the ethnographers' and our work as researchers from the moment in which we asked ourselves the question about the normal approach.

The overlapping modality of ethnography and intervention implies waiving the possibility of measuring the performance by evaluating the transformation of reality resulting from the intervention. By this, I refer to the possibility that at the end of our two years of work in the schools, we could demonstrate that the schools are less exclusionary, less discriminatory, and therefore, fairer and more just. This situation was uncomfortable and complex in terms of justifying what was done to funding institutions and our colleagues. However, our ways of transforming the ways of knowing acquired value and lost the sense of failure, which resituated observational disposition as a central element in our work. Our transformative purpose was refigured on two different levels. On the one hand, there was a verification of a change in language in the ways in which ethnographers, monitors, schools, and teachers refer to diversity issues; and, on the other hand, participants developed the capacity to ask themselves about their ethnographic or pedagogical practices.

4.5.2 Comprehensive Involvement

The second strategic process that allowed us to reflect on the consubstantiality of ethnography and intervention is the action of comprehensive involvement. Both ethnography and intervention share a particular modality of commitment to their objects and subjects. Moreover, it is possible to say that these require and sustain the establishment of a connection and are legitimized by a close presence in the spaces of daily life to be studied or transformed. In this sense, it is important to reflect on the limits and scope of how this occurred within the framework of our own work. However, the involvement and distancing of intervention are somewhat different from that of ethnography. While in the former, involvement finds its limitation in its extreme dependence on the intervened-upon subject, in conventional ethnography, distancing is ultimately required to be able to objectify what is being studied. As such, involvement finds its limitations within the achievement of research purposes. In our case, comprehensive involvement was essential to the development of a politics of knowledge production for school dynamics and the transformation of ethnographic and pedagogical practices.

In a different register from that of dependence and distance, the articulated practice of ethnography and intervention are required to configure relationships of commitment and trust. In more general terms, this involved mobilizing and making explicit our politics and moral codes. This was not done in an abstract sense, but instead, it was associated with constructing, explicitly explaining, and sharing the goals of transformation, thus defining a normative framework of relationship to ensure the desire and the willingness to let oneself be transformed. With regard to schools, for example, the invitation made was to establish a collaboration in these terms. Of the fifteen schools that we invited, only five wanted to become involved. Within this framework, the promise of intervention and support for the development of transformative actions validated and legitimized the ethnographic work, which in turn, mitigated fear of the extra-critical practice that usually accompanies research processes. Knowing that we could contribute with ideas that would benefit the institutions and/or teachers through intervention allowed us to be more legitimate as researchers.

One of the important devices in the construction of this comprehensive involvement was the elaboration of Collaboration Agreements. This instrument, which had no legal value, made it possible to develop a 2-year work plan. At the same time, it was a promise of commitment to what occurs in the future in the schools.

Throughout the two years, we had a constant presence in the establishments, first through the ethnographers and then through monitors and senior researchers. Undoubtedly, this favored the construction of interpersonal bonds between agents and provided a context of security and confidence to install and sustain a state of discomfort and critical observation of the oppressive processes of schooling. The nature of the relationship we established compels and affects. It gave us access to situations that we would not otherwise have had easy access to (for example, situations of sexual abuse within the establishments) and made us face situations that we might have avoided or felt helpless in, in the context of research alone (Marchand and Rollin 2015).

This articulation between ethnographic work and intervention led to the implementation of a permanent mode of restitution and not *ex post*. Undoubtedly, this was key. We made the phenomena we were studying intelligible and we provided comprehensive support to help teachers understand (Marchand and Rollin 2015). In regard to the extent that we were challenged to keep reporting our observations and make accusations about the oppressive practices of the schools, we were also building our own discourse, positioning, object of investigation, and focus of intervention.

4.6   Final Reflections

The development of ethnographic work and intervention on the production of differences from a queer approach allows for the political value of discomfort to be revealed. More than a feeling experienced or observed from a reflexive position, I have understood this as a state of epistemic and methodological vigilance, being inevitably higher in the production of effects. Discomfort is not the consequence of a material and objective process associated with a particular research project; it is a necessary force that allows and produces problematized forms of addressing diversity. In other words, affect circulating within academic work makes it possible to challenge the limitations of intelligibility, as well as the orders and rules of action. In other words, discomfort has the effect of situated production by questioning the normal. Through this process, social and cultural deconstruction become possible. It is then and only then that an opportunity is opened to alter the potential that the normal has to identify and establish different groups and subjects.

Throughout this chapter, the analysis of discomfort has allowed me to describe, show, and reflect on the interference in the school dynamics in five schools, with the purpose of deploying inclusive and anti-oppressive practices. This project is based on the development of a praxis that I have called ethnographic intervention. Its main particularity is that it conceives the ethnographic and interventional work in their consubstantiality. They are processes that nourish and merge with each other from two elements that share common ground; on the one hand, the development of an ethnographic disposition, and on the other, the deployment of personal involvement. As shown in this chapter, our work was oriented to deploy these dispositions both with researchers and teachers, to investigate and to change the pedagogical practices.

To extend the impact of the work presented here, it is important to form a dialogue and offer it as material to answer contingent questions in the field of contemporary anthropology: To whom is it directed? How does it work? How can fieldwork be communicated? As described by Marcus (2012), due to the *Writing Culture* of the 80s, a reflexive display within anthropological work opened the question about what is exchanged in fieldwork: how and to whom is it communicated? This question has returned, been updated, and become more complex over the years. "These same criticisms appear in the today's same impulses to find ways, means, and modalities that mix the ethnographic discourse within the anthropological reinventions of the fieldwork as a research process" (Marcus 2012, p. 63). New, strongly interdisciplinary approaches challenge as they deploy more flexible, creative, and original forms of action based on fieldwork. New technologies help to think of new ways to show and make publishable ethnographic production.

In some ways, our project gives depth to this reflection. It shows how the production of ethnographic material unfolds in temporal terms during the construction process itself. This is true for researchers, ethnographers, and teachers. It is in this exercise that it becomes possible to problematize the idea of normality. At the same time, through this process of communication and making fieldwork public, the ways of knowing of such agents are intervened. It is then that a new way of thinking about the value of public and political senses of ethnographic and interventional tasks can be realized.

To conclude, it seems important to invoke an open discussion by Didier Fassin. In his text "Why Ethnography Matters: On Anthropology and Its Publics" (2013), he makes the distinction between what would be a normative and analytical approach to studying the public and political sense of ethnographic work by citing authors such as Shaper Hughes from anthropology and Michael Burawoy from sociology. Such works aim to reach audiences that are not only academic, but also those with a militant vocation since it is oriented to open space for subjects to speak. Fassin's (2013) analytical proposal is for the sciences to go beyond the moment of making academic production public and urges the extension of investigation of forms of production as they are received. This means that part of what we study ought to include reactions, criticisms, and implications for the people or institutions of whom we speak. I argue that it is provocative to add a third approximation to understanding the public and political aspects of ethnographic work. As exemplified in this chapter, ethnographic production, *itself*, is viewed as a way to problematize the everyday in investigative and pedagogical practices and to promote the transformation of the researchers and the researched. The emphases that our project placed on resistances and sustained discomforts permitted a general movement toward the uncomfortable destabilization of processes, subjects, and identities. And, by doing this, we enact Fassin's idea to promote the politicization of everyday life through ethnographic work.

References

Ahmed, S. (2004a). *The cultural politics of emotion*. New York: Routledge.
Ahmed, S. (2004b). Affective economies. *Social Text, 22*(2), 117–139.
Bourdieu, P. (2003). L'objectivation participante. *Actes de la Recherche en Sciences Sociales, 150,* 43–58.
Bourdieu, P. (2004). *Esquisse pour une auto-analyse*. Paris: Éditions Raison d'agir.
Britzman, D. (1992). The terrible problem of knowing thyself: Toward a poststructural account of teacher identity. *Journal of Curriculum Theorizing, 9*(3), 23–46.
Dennis, B. (2009). What does it mean when an ethnographer intervenes? *Ethnography and Education, 4*(2), 131–146.

Fabian, J. (1990). Presence and representation: The other and anthropological writing. *Critical Inquiry, 16*(4), 753–772. Retrieved from http://www.jstor.org/stable/1343766.

Fassin, D. (2013). Why ethnography matters: On anthropology and its publics. *Cultural Anthropology, 28*(4), 621–646. https://doi.org/10.1111/cuan.1203.

Fassin, D., & Bensa, A. (Eds.). (2008). *Les politiques de l'enquête. Épreuves ethnographiques*. Paris: La Découverte.

Goffman, E. (1968). *Asylums: Essays on the social situation of mental patients and other inmates*. Harmondsworth: Penguin Books.

Gorton, K. (2007). Theorizing emotion and affect: Feminist engagements. *Feminist Theory, 8*(3), 333–348. https://doi.org/10.1177/1464700107082369.

Gregg, M., & Seigworth, G. J. (2010). *The affect theory reader*. Durham: Duke University Press.

Gregorio, C. (2014). Traspasando las fronteras dentro -fuera: reflexiones desde una etnografía feminista. *Revista de Antropología Iberoamericana, 9*(3), 297–322.

Hastrup, K. (2004). Getting it right: Knowledge and evidence in anthropology. *Anthropological Theory, 4*(4), 455–472.

Infante, M. D., & Matus, C. (2009). Policies and practices of diversity: Reimagining possibilities for new discourses. *Disability & Society, 24*(4), 437–445.

Infante Jaras, M., Matus Cánovas, C., & Vizcarra Rebolledo, R. (2011). Razonando sobre la idea de diferencia en las políticas educativas chilenas. *Universum (Talca), 26*(2), 143–163.

Kumashiro, K. (2000). Toward a theory of anti-oppressive education. *Review of Educational Research, 70*(1), 25–53.

Kumashiro, K. K. (2003). Queer ideals in education. *Journal of Homosexuality, 45*(2–4), 365–367.

Lanas, M. (2016). Emerging emotions in post-structural participant ethnography in education. In M. Zembylas & P. A. Schutz (Eds.), *Methodological advances in research on emotion and education* (pp. 111–124). Switzerland: Springer.

Marchand, A., & Rollin, Z. (2015). Ce que l'intervention fait à la recherche dans un contexte de maladie grave. *Santé Publique, 27,* 331–338.

Marcus, G. E. (2012). The legacies of writing culture and the near future of the ethnographic form: A sketch. *Cultural Anthropology, 27*(3), 427–445.

Massumi, B. (2002). *Parables for the virtual: Movement, affect, sensation*. Durham: Duke University Press.

Matus, C., & Haye, A. (2015). Normalidad y diferencia en la escuela: Diseño de un proyecto de investigación social desde el dilema político-epistemológico. *Estudios pedagógicos (Valdivia), 41*(especial), 135–146.

Matus, C., & Infante, M. (2011). Undoing diversity: Knowledge and neoliberal discourses in colleges of education. *Discourse: Studies in the Cultural Politics of Education, 32*(3), 293–307.

Matus, C., Rojas-Lasch, C., Guerrero-Morales, P., Herraz-Mardones, P., & Sanyal-Tudela, A. (2019). Diferencia y normalidad: producción etnográfica e intervención en escuelas. *Magis, Revista Internacional De Investigación En Educación, 11*(23), 23–38.

Pillow, W. S. (2003). Confession, catharsis or cure? Rethinking the uses of reflexivity as methodological power in qualitative research. *International Journal of Qualitative Studies in Education, 16*(2), 175–196.

Puttick, S. (2017). Performativity, guilty knowledge, and ethnographic intervention. *Ethnography and Education, 12*(1), 49–63.

Simmel, G. (1998). *Les pauvres*. Paris: PUF.

Youdell, D. (2010). Queer outings? Uncomfortable stories about the subjects of post-structural school ethnography. *Qualitative Studies in Education, 23*(1), 87–100.

Chapter 5
The Production of the Problem of Difference in Neoliberal Educational Policies

Marcela Apablaza

Abstract Within the framework of an educational system based on administrative and financial neoliberal principles, this chapter responds to questions related to how educational policies produce and circulate discourses of *difference* and how such discourses play out in schools. The aim is to problematize Chilean educational policies of inclusion focusing specifically on mechanisms of production, operation, and articulation, as well as the ways educational actors circulate discourses of difference. To do this, I analyze three components: (1) policy documents, (2) the administering body, and (3) the school by unpacking discourses related to the policy of school community life and the inclusion of students with special needs. These discourses are tied to government rationality that develops the problem as a depoliticized matter of identity, linked to the deficit or lack of particular student subjectivities and therein, points to the objectification and management of, and intervention on social and cultural differences in a neoliberalized educational system.

5.1 What Is Problematic in Policies of Inclusion?

[In education] We will ensure that excellence goes hand in hand with inclusion, which does not mean discriminating, but rather awarding fair merit in all socioeconomic classes of our society. (Proposals from Sebastián Piñera's administration, Chilean President, 2018–2021).

Policies of inclusion are an essential part of the discussion of how countries approach issues of social differences in the educational field. For at least two decades, discourses of inclusion have occupied various fields of the political arena, their main principles being equality, justice, and law. Their importance continues to grow (Rizvi and Lingard 2013). Encouraged by international organizations, such as UNESCO, the World Bank, and the OECD (Infante et al. 2011; Matus and Infante 2011), countries have developed inclusive policies in order to meet the social demands of certain groups categorized in a position of *inequality*, *difference* and/or *exclusion* regarding their possibilities of social, political, and/or economic participation.

M. Apablaza (✉)
Facultad de Medicina, Universidad Austral de Chile, Valdivia, Chile
e-mail: marcela.apablaza@uach.cl

© Springer Nature Singapore Pte Ltd. 2019
C. Matus (ed.), *Ethnography and Education Policy*, Education Policy
& Social Inequality 3, https://doi.org/10.1007/978-981-13-8445-5_5

The manner in which the policies produce and elaborate discourses of difference is an issue of concern that requires problematization, above all, in societies that call themselves democratic and that function under neoliberal rationality.[1] The politics of inclusion utilize a certain logic that implies identifying a group of individuals, making use of specific strategies of demarcation, under specific identity criteria. In conjunction, these policies develop, manage, and administer the possibilities that influence social participation of such individuals.

The thesis I develop in this chapter demonstrates a problematic characteristic that comes along with the question about issues of difference yet to be solved or addressed by policy, which has been developed into identity markers (Bacchi 1999).

Such depoliticization operates through the obscuring of essentialist and naturalized discourses with respect to the subjects that policies claim to represent. In this way, the maintenance of a fictitious state of equality is perpetuated through the promotion of inclusive policies, and an externalizing marginality. In everyday life, this produces subjectivities that finally end up occupying categories as *different, others*, or *diverse*. This is in contrast to a social group that maintains and reaffirms, in turn, a position of privilege, under categories of *normal, heterosexual*, or *white*, framed in discourses of normality (Matus and Rojas 2015).

As long as these ways of understanding *difference* in educational policy persist, as a neutral and objectifiable category based on identity markers, without examining the mechanisms and conditions that produce such differences, the discourses of difference will continue to function individually, fixed and determinate in an apparent rejection of the normality discourses. This maintains the status quo on the social inequality that the policy intends to counter and in turn, will continue to reaffirm and ensure the privilege of those who reap the benefits of the *normal* category.

This way of problematizing inclusion policies allows us to examine the operational mechanisms of the policy and their effects on the processes of subjectivation of the individuals that the policy aims to represent. It also makes new practices visible, which the school, as an institution and its agents, has constructed within the new inclusive policies.

In this analytical exercise, I analyze policy as discourse.[2] That is, I assume social configuration not only as the result of, but also as a generator of discursive networks

---

[1] I use the notion of neoliberalism proposed by theorists like Brown (2015), Laval and Dardot (2013), who under the inspiration of Michel Foucault, consider rationality as a particular form of reason that configures all aspects of human existence in economic terms. Therefore, its scope would be given by the management of conduct and the production of subjectivities, under the principle of maximum freedom, and above all under the central premise of the "economization" of the different dimensions of life, whose impact does not only respond to the monetization of everyday behaviors and activities, but also refers to the commercialization and managerialization of noneconomic valuation schemes, such as education, health, and justice, among others. In Brown's (2015) words: "as an order of normative reason that, when it becomes ascendant, takes shape as a governing rationality extending a specific formulation of economic values, practices, and metrics to every dimension of human life" (p. 30).

[2] By discourse, I refer to the basic unit of social configuration, which is independent of the substratum that supports it (linguistic or extralinguistic), allows us to understand social organization (Scott 1992). There are three central components that are densely articulated: discourse-power-knowledge.

made up of institutions, actors, strategies, economic measures, theories, architectures, laws, and a heterogeneity of practices and objects linked together. I would like to emphasize that understanding policies as discourse alludes not only to the text or the document (Ball 1993), but also to the rationalities behind practices and strategies whose purpose is to guide the conduct of individuals (Pillow 2007).

Foucault (2006) calls this new rationality about politics *governmentality*. It is a set of tactics, strategies, and normative frameworks that achieve their fundamental purpose with the maximum possible freedom: to drive the behavior of the subjects towards specific ends. In this sense, policies are assumed as the government's mentality, whose actions and effects go beyond the limits defined by the policy document itself.

Regarding this point, Allan (2003) emphasizes that the policy works as a limitation of the possibilities of behavior on the part of the subjects/agents that it tries to represent. In this process, the discourses in circulation (texts or practices) produce certain effects on the way in which subjects are named, and the way in which their agents relate to each other. Consequently, discourses shape the ways in which the social field is organized (Allan 2003; Ball 1993; Laclau and Mouffe 2011).

Considering this argument, I seek to question the ways of thinking about differences—articulated within discourses of normality and especially within neoliberal rationality—in educational policies, specifically in the Chilean legislative framework linked to inclusion.[3] In particular, I am interested in making visible the ways in which neoliberal rationality produces, governs, and manages discourses of difference in an educational context, such as in Chile. In this process, I illuminate the discourses that policies consider as well as those that are left aside, and the government logics and technologies it puts into play.

This allows us to uproot what has been installed and fixed—partially—as a *given* and *natural* social phenomenon that works as a requirement for the conditions of historical production of existing differences in schools. This allows us to re-create other forms of production, which should always remain open to change in constant aperture and sufficiently mobile as to not create and solidify a new order that superimposes the same rationality that is intended to be questioned.

In the following sections, I present some reflections about the discourse produced in an apparatus made up of three components: the policy document, the administrative organization, and scenes from ethnographic material of a school in southern Chile, which for reasons of confidentiality, I name under the pseudonym *Sur Austral*.[4] In this attempt, I use the analytical logic provided by studies of governmentality

---

In Foucault's words: "the practices that systematically form the objects of which they speak" (Foucault 2011b, p. 68).

[3] When I discuss the legislative framework of inclusion or Chilean diversity policies, I refer to policy as a document. I include in that category the set of laws, policies, and orientations in relation to the issues of diversity and inclusion. In the Chilean case, they have been developed from identitary marks (social class, disability, gender, ethnicity, among others).

[4] Sur Austral is an elementary school located in a peripheral sector of a southern Chilean city. The student body is made up of students of low socioeconomic status, classified according to public policy as an at-risk population due to the School Vulnerability Index (90%). One of its

and Political Discourse Analysis (PDA), as well as the understanding that there is a political–economic framework from which inclusion policies arise, in an attempt to articulate hegemonically the way in which these policies operate within the educational field, where different practices, strategies, and forms of resistance converge.

Initially, I delve into the articulation of the neoliberal educational system with Chilean inclusion policies. Later, I further examine the specific problem the policy has produced within inclusion and difference issues, specifically, under the use of identity markers as a key mechanism of installation. Subsequently, I analyze the politics of school climate and its articulation with the marginal difference. In this exercise, I examine strategies that a school uses to *intervene* on its students in order to reorient their behavior and above all to fulfill the government's purposes that go beyond the school space: security.

5.2 Rights, Differences, and Education as a Consumer Good

We require, without a doubt, in this modern society, a greater interconnection between the education and the business worlds, because education serves a double purpose: the presence of culture is a consumer good, to be able to take better advantage of the instruments and opportunities for the personal fulfillment of the people. But also, education has an investment component. (Declaration from President Sebastián Piñera during his first period of administration, July 19, 2011).

In order to analyze Chilean inclusion policies, we are forced to consider the basic principles that underpin our current educational system, particularly, the neoliberal rationality that puts a strain on and disputes the principles of justice and law, a characteristic of contemporary democratic societies and for which countries elaborate and raise policies around matters of inclusion and difference.

The declaration made by Sebastián Piñera, a Chilean businessman and current President in his second term (2018–2022), about education as a consumer good was not politically strategic. However, it is a true reflection of our current educational system and the market logic that governs it: *globalization, free market, examination, standardization,* and *accountability* (Bellei 2015; Carrasco 2013a).

Specifically in the field of education, the concept of *market logic* refers to those policies that, inspired by neoliberal models, have intensified their financing and administration processes based on the operation of market forces. These policies configure the educational field and its institutionality under in a spirit of *manageral-*

---

particularities is the large decrease in enrollment within the last 10 years, dropping from 1,000 students to now 300 students. This led the school to open its doors to all policies that would allow it to survive financially. That is why Sur Austral relies economically on two critical programs: the School Integration Program (SIP) and the Preferential School Subsidy Law (SEP Law). Likewise, it also has a multidisciplinary professional team dedicated to the SIP and school climate. This is composed of: three psychologists, one social worker, one occupational therapist, one speech therapist, and five special education teachers.

ization (Fardella et al. 2012; Sisto and Zelaya 2013) and competition dynamics (Bellei 2015). Certainly, such rationality has profoundly modified the entire framework. Its main effects are: reduction of the state apparatus, privatization of educational services, stimulation of schools by competition under a business and self-management perspective, and transformation of families from social actors to consumers (Ball and Youdell 2008; Power and Frandji 2010).

In the Chilean case, the internalization of the market logic materialized initially during the military dictatorship, causing serious consequences for the educational system. First, the decentralization of the state administration of schools, whose delegation fell to the municipal governments (denominated municipalization of education), which later expanded to the private sphere, was established through shared financing. Second, the introduction of the financing system based on the *voucher* (subsidy to the demand) was implemented, which granted the system the *quasi-market* condition. Third, the introduction of a series of control and administration mechanisms were put into place, typical of the business world, called *managerial-ization*, whose materialization can be seen in accountability policies, performance measurement systems, and the elaboration of rankings (Bellei 2015; Carrasco et al. 2015).

Furthermore, two other key components link our educational market system. First, freedom of education safeguards the autonomy of the school regarding their educational projects (that has a negative effect on the implementation of the discourse of inclusion). Second, school choice ensures that these agents behave like true consumers, stimulating said behavior by using school performance information as a mechanism measurement of public scrutiny, whose essential goal is to stimulate competition between schools (Carrasco 2013b; Carrasco et al. 2015; Seppänen et al. 2015).

Regarding the interrelation between neoliberal rationality and the management of differences, I believe it is relevant to make some distinctions, particularly surrounding the economic rationality that underpins inclusion policies and the way in which said rationality operates in different dimensions.

On the one hand, funding policies related to Special Education Needs (SEN) are established through an additional differential system of subsidies, according to a specific criterion that ultimately depends on a diagnosis. Based on compliance with certain requirements and conditions based on an individual diagnosis (under biomedical criteria), an additional subsidy is delivered. In this way, differentiated resources are assigned to schools, according to the *complexity* of students' diagnoses, or in a more official language, according to the type of Special Educational Need (SEN) (transitory or permanent) that the student has. For example, a student with a diagnosis of Specific Language Disorder, which falls into the transitory category of special educational need, is granted a smaller subsidy, with respect to a student with intellectual, visual, or auditory disability, who enters the permanent category of SEN.

On the other hand, the same policy regulates its financing through the quota system. Decree 170 regulates the operation of the School Integration Programs (SIP) (MINEDUC 2009) and establishes a maximum of seven student placements for SEN per class. In specific, SIP allows for five students with transitory SEN and two with permanent SEN, under the logic of establishing a minimum baseline necessary to finance the support of specialists; and generalizing its scope under the inclusive approach, its action would be generalized to the entire class. However, this condition has allowed schools to use it as a form of selection and exclusion, whose aims is not only related to SEN students' concentration, but also as a way to safeguard their results and position in the ranking.

These effects portray the productive dimension of neoliberalism and its positive articulation regarding differences. That is, these effects demonstrate the way in which the neoliberal principles that underpin educational policies are reaffirmed by discourses of difference in schools. Beyond reviewing the evident economic calculation that differentiates the greater or lesser cost of students according to individual criteria (students with SEN and students without SEN), we see that a school works under a set of rules from the educational system centered on neoliberal principles, such as competition for funding, the freedom of families to choose the school, and at the same time the freedom of the school to choose whether it will have SIP or not. This ends up developing new forms of student selection, based on the calculation and management of differences. These practices of calculation and management can be understood as forms of resistance that the educational agents develop for the school's subsistence.

On the one hand, those schools that maintain greater prestige, determined by their place in the school rankings choose not to have SIP, thus ensuring an enrollment composition that allows maintaining their good results on standardized tests. This situation encourages families to *freely* choose other educational establishments that offer SIP; this decision is mainly based on whether or not their child will have the specialists who will support them in their educational process. In this way, the school does not discriminate, nor does it directly exclude a child with SEN, but rather the family in their right to choose the educational establishment for their child, chooses another school.

On the contrary, those schools that do not have a good reputation choose to include SIP in their educational projects in order to survive. The increase of students with SEN means that they will also be able to increase their enrollment, capturing those families that seek schools with SIP and along with it, receive additional subsidy. Regarding the result of standardized tests, these schools prepare what can be defined as a practice of resistance, because as the regulations permit, schools make use of the option to exclude the results of the permanent SEN students' exams in the reporting of scores. This means that they may exclude permanent SEN students' scores, safeguarding the ranking results as much as possible. Such practices can explain to a certain extent the increase in SEN diagnoses in schools, specifically intellectual disability.[5]

---

[5]In 2005, the number of students belonging to SIP amounts to 41,023 (Tenorio 2011). In 2011, with the implementation of Decree 170, those numbers increased to 130,139 students; in 2013, they increased to 221,416 students (Fundación Chile 2013). In 2014, there were 251,092 students who belonged to SIP (MINEDUC 2015) and in 2016, that number increased to 319,217 students (MINE-DUC 2017), of which 17.6% corresponded to students diagnosed with an intellectual disability;

A similar exercise can be applied in social class-oriented policies, specifically towards students considered to be of a low socioeconomic level, catalogued under the label "priority student" or "vulnerable". The Law of Educational Preferential Subsidy (known as the SEP Law) (MINEDUC 2008) establishes a financing system, based on an additional increase in the general subsidy, to "correct" the effects of "social inequality". This is under the assumption that the schools with the highest concentration of *vulnerable* students require more funding because it is more expensive to educate students in this context (Falabella 2014).

In this way, the debate reopens to reflect on how economic rationality is installing new logic and new effects on the configuration of certain school cultures. This happens because the distinction of *vulnerable* or *priority* students complies with the market logic that accompanies our educational system, focused on results (ranking), more than a matter of social or legal justice. Specifically with this policy, the neoliberal rationality broadens its scope, by means of the incorporation of new technologies linked to psychosocial intervention and school climate. As we will see later, the main goal of these technologies is public safety rather than educational or pedagogical improvement.

Next, I go more in-depth on how the neoliberal rationality works in a constant and subtle way in inclusion policies through the deployment of identity makers. Within this, cultural politics become a focus of attention, masking the discourses of normality and the conditions for the production of social inequality.

5.3 Identity Markers as a Neoliberal Strategy

In the educational field, a political–legislative framework that rests on technical rationality has been developed. This framework aims to solve or mitigate social inequality and its effects of discrimination and exclusion (Bacchi 2009). Based in social sciences, this rationalist focus brought about another manner of understanding social problems by decentering the political attention in favor of a neutral, technical-instrumental understanding of the phenomenon (Allan 2003; Baez 2004; Rizvi and Lingard 2013). This new form of knowledge sought to objectively delimit the problem in order to more effectively address and resolve it in the future.

Under this objectivist logic, a set of educational policies is generated in Chile that is based on an affirmative action approach. Their purpose and intention are to move towards more egalitarian or *inclusive* societies by developing programs and technical guidance that delimit the target populations based on rigorous and standardized measures. The results, in turn, determine proposals of concrete actions.

Examples of this are policies linked to *vulnerability* such as the SEP Law (MINE-DUC 2008), policies linked to SEP students through SIP (MINEDUC 2013), as well as gender and migration policies for students through distinct technical orientations

---

a percentage that almost triples the prevalence of intellectual disability according to international literature (Fuenzalida 2014).

and education plans (MINEDUC 2015, 2017). Thus, difference is marked and protected by identitary and legal structures and becomes a key strategy for the production of discourses of diversity in Chilean schools.

The Chilean case has been the subject of analysis based on its neoliberal political reforms (Bellei 2015). This interest makes sense as neoliberal rationality has permeated not only economic spaces, but also social politics. Brown (2015) stresses that rather than understanding neoliberalism as an ideology or a set of policies based on the market or with the purpose of maximizing capital, we can instead conceive neoliberalism "as a normative order, which in its broad and subtle scope, becomes a rationality of government that, when extended, takes specific forms of market values, practices and metrics for each dimension of human life" (p. 30).

If we analyze the differences in the educational context, as an area of neoliberal economization, we can trace the way in which inclusion policies have internalized new facets of knowledge. In turn, this generates effects such as the transformation of educational practices, new forms of management and new educational agents as subjects. All of these fall under a normative rationality based on premises that are not only related to monetary aspects, but also are overlain by social demands, the law, participation, recognition of merit, security, and even recognition of identity.

While the *affirmative action* approach has contributed to generating new forms of social participation of identity groups that such policies claim to represent, it is necessary to ask how the operation of educational policy produces and reproduces discourses of difference and how such discourses are triggered in schools. In light of privilege, placing emphasis on identity or justice for certain Othered groups is problematic in several ways. I intend to unravel this perspective in the following paragraphs.

Predominantly, this rationality as sustained by identity politics addresses the issues of difference from the language of *tolerance*. As a result, this rationality results in three possible origins in regard to the issue of difference: the individual identity based on where one comes from; a conflict whose roots are inherent in natural, cultural, racial or ethnic differences; or in the interrelationship of the two (Brown 2008). Placing emphasis on the inequality or injustice of certain social groups reconstructs the problem as an individual and private issue, rather than questioning the historical, contingent, and political conditions, and therefore, power relationships. Therefore, certain individuals are constructed as *different* or *other*, and subsequently, as objects of inclusion or tolerance.

This rationality, as Brown (2008) points out, corresponds to the tactic of depoliticization of the phenomenon. This government strategy aims to legitimize the neoliberal discourses in technocratic policies, based on a logic of instrumental rationality that is stripped of acts of power and where the discourses of justice, equality, and tolerance are reviewed as a *moral* domain, rather than a political one.

Secondly, the depoliticization of these difference-linked discourses provokes a positive and productive articulation of the neoliberal venture in various ways. In one sense, the apparent separation between economic rationality and cultural policies has facilitated the consolidation of neoliberalism under the principles of freedom, individualism, and consumerism. Here, the proliferation of identity groups as separated from an economic issue, have allowed the diminishing role of the State to be obscured and economic policies to be promoted as transcendental principles, even in the case of demands for civil-identity rights (Duggan 2004). An example of this is the inclusion policy linked to SEN or gender policies from a corporate focus.

Notwithstanding, these same principles—that individualism under a lens of civic morality of *tolerance* and market shapes social life and the subject based on business or consumption logic—are situated in a dissociated plane that prioritizes essentialist logic of representation or totalization policies about the construction of certain cultural groups. Some examples include: associating a migrant a priori with delinquency or learning difficulties; or linking indigenous people in Chile to violent extremist groups (as in the case of the Mapuche people); or the relationship between social classes of affluent/poor associated with honesty/delinquency. Such examples fail to consider multiple intersectionalities of people's history and contingency is bulky.

This reduction rescinds the participation of the economy, market relations, the implication of the State or the historical element of production that conditions the conflicts or inequities associated with these groups. Returning to the example of the intercultural policy, one element that affects the problematic relationship between the State and the Mapuche people that is ignored in this reduction is the economic interest of forestry companies towards the disputed lands. Instead, the focus of the conflict is set in the victimization of the *peasants* (by businessmen) in the allegedly extremist conflict where the Mapuche people tend to be held wholly responsible, justifying the State's response of criminalization and military intervention, redirecting the focus away from the economic, social, and political inequality faced by this population.

As Brown says (2015), "it eliminates colonialism, capital, caste or class stratification and external political domination from accounts of political conflict or instability. In their stead, 'culture' is summoned to explain the motives and aspirations leading to certain conflicts" (p. 20).

Additionally, within this process, discourses about identity politics within the educational field have been disguised within concepts such as *diversity* as a mode of neutralizing the languages linked to *difference* (Ahmed 2007; Baez 2004; Infante et al. 2011). Hence, to discuss the subjects who take the role of *The Different* or *The Other*, inevitably refers to a rhetorically unattractive idea: a subaltern or subjugated position in relation to a privileged position. However, the language of diversity gives greater relevance to the rescue of particularities, but from a universal perspective. It utilizes a depoliticized and neutral language, eclipsing the existing power relations that participate in these discursive constructions.

Expressions such as "we are all different, so we must accept and respect such differences" illustrate how cultural differences are approached in public policy today, based on the language of tolerance, and how the differences are neutralized and set to replace the individual. As noted earlier, in this configuration of discourse, power relations are hidden behind the constitutive and biological idea of being different and in turn, conditions the production of differences such that they operate as fixated and immutable (Brown 2008; Infante et al. 2011).

According to Infante et al. (2011, p. 150), this "system of reasoning *difference*" has penetrated and given shape to the central axis of inclusion discourse within the

Chilean political framework, where discussions put into circulation a mechanism of operation and regulation, intimately bound to neoliberalism. Thus, thinking about social and cultural differences in this way allows certain power regimes to perpetuate, which contributes to the generation of subjects with specific attributes that reinforce the market system, that is, disciplined, efficient, and productive subjects.

5.4 Policy of School Community Life and the Marker of Vulnerability: How to Effectively Govern the Marginal Difference?

One of the ways in which neoliberalism operates in the production of *difference* can be seen in the coordination of the National Policy of School Community Life[6] (MINEDUC 2011b). This policy arises in response to the growing rates of school violence and the orientations of international organizations, which Chile regarded with marked interest (MINEDUC 2011b). In this way, it converts into a key strategy for eradicating violence within schools.

This policy was created with individual rights in mind, as a move to make the school responsible for maintaining healthy interactions within it. Framed from a legal perspective, with school climate as a control mechanism, this policy functions by determining duties and rights of varied agents who inhabit the school (MINEDUC 2011a, b).

In this sense, the art of government focuses on its performative nature. It develops a normative context that promotes specific *allowed actions*. Nevertheless, the subjects are the ones who transform their practices towards specific governmental ends, taking precautions against regulating the behavior of others as well as oneself, maintaining the maximum freedom possible (Laval and Dardot 2013; Lemke 2011).

Under this analytical framework, the mentality of the neoliberal State creates a control apparatus by using the Policy for Healthy School Environments. According to the Chilean Law of School Violence (MINEDUC 2011a) and its respective decrees and technical guidelines, this mechanism delimits the actions that educational agents must carry out. Above all, it supervises and scrutinizes their compliance through a specific institution, the School Superintendence.

The school's governance mentality materializes in a reproductive sense and with appropriations, through different governmental technologies. Here, we highlight the *Strategic Plan of School Climate*, where schools commit to generate specific actions for the prevention and promotion of a *healthy* school climate. This plan is comprised

---

[6]The Policy of School Community Life, framed within the Chilean Law of School Violence, corresponds to a set of regulations and technical guidelines that regulate the school climate within Chilean schools. Its assumption is to guarantee the basic conditions necessary for the achievement of quality learning (MINEDUC 2011a, b) from the regulation of sanctions in case of violent acts, to matters of prevention of school bullying, and other transversal issues such as citizen formation, sexual, and environmental education (MINEDUC 2011a, b).

of: a *code of conduct* that standardizes the forms of behavior and the system of sanctions of the different educational agents, principally of students and their families; the *General Inspection Team*, school personnel in charge of student surveillance and the application of sanctions in the event of an act of violence; the *psychosocial team*, professionals in the psychological and social work areas are in charge of coordinating diagnostic and intervention actions; and finally, the technologies of the self, materialized in *extracurricular workshops* and *activities*, whose intervention strategies use recreational resources and community spaces as effective forms of subjectivation.

In this respect, I would like to delve into two technologies of the self, which, due to their subtle, less regular, and innovative characteristics, transform them into two of the most sophisticated technologies. First, I refer to the extracurricular recreational activities that the Sur Austral School developed as part of its school climate policy. Second, I address the extracurricular workshops that Sur Austral makes available to its students. I consider both subjectification technologies, as Foucault (2008) emphasizes, techniques that activate operations around the subjects' bodies, their souls, their thoughts, and therefore their behaviors, in such a way that it transforms them according to a particular objective, in this case, the formation of neoliberal citizens, which at the same time carries a second objective: the prevention and sanitization of *vulnerability*.

The scenes of ethnographic material that I present below are useful to visualize the purpose of these technologies that function as social security systems, beyond the educational-pedagogical space. We can see the regularity and discontinuity with which they work, the way they are installed, and the place they occupy in daily life in scholarly and extracurricular life, and with families and the community.

5.4.1 Scene No. 1: The Police's Visit to the School

All school activities are suspended so that students, families, and all personnel of Sur Austral School can attend the artistic show organized by the local police at the school.

The performance begins with a show of canine–police training, where an actor pretends to be a criminal who steals from a person and the police officer walks around with his police dog. The master of ceremony (a police officer) asks the children to describe the offender so that the policeman and his dog can catch him.

I am struck by the way in which certain traits and characteristics of *the delinquents* are presented. In this case, the extra was characterized as an unkempt man, with ragged clothes, long hair, a wool cap, and designer shoes. The master of ceremony reminds the children that they should always pay attention to people with these characteristics, because they can be suspicious and that they should notify the police immediately.

Later, they present a folkloric ballet number and end with a popular music band.

The day before, one of the police officers responsible for the show told me that these types of activities are carried out as a way to engage with the community and to gain more information about the area since there is a lot of micro-drug trafficking. (Field Notes No. 18, November 13, 2014)

In this scene, the type of technology of the self responds to a sophisticated exercise of power, where subtlety is the key means of production. Its political purpose is masked in its recreational nature, exposing it as a depoliticized and disinterested situation, or rather oriented toward the improvement of the school climate. But as we know, the same decision that tries to strip this practice of its political goals is in itself a political action (Baez 2014).

Finally, the moral imperatives that sustain these government technologies reinforce, with little questioning, the conditions that make it possible for the emergence of problematic elements within the school climate. In this way, the school and policies converge to ensure the problem, and at the same time, seek to counter it. In this sense, the interest in individuality and relationality is lost, and the population, biopolitics, and the security systems that are deployed are at play. Here, what counts is the dissemination of said rationality, a logic that naturalizes the disciplinary apparatus of school climate and emphasizes individual responsibility, rather than promoting a rationality of agency and transformation amongst subjects that are socially located within a setting of marginality.

Next, I refer to another technology of the self that the school, and particularly the school climate policy as an apparatus, has put into operation. I refer to extracurricular workshops, activities that are traditionally used in all educational establishments. In the case of Sur Austral, extracurricular activities contribute in an arranged way, with the control apparatus created by the school climate policy. Specifically, I analyze the mural workshop, for its potentiality and subtlety, qualities that make up a key field of subjectivation for the students.

5.4.2 Scene No. 2: Mural Workshop

This workshop is an initiative implemented by the school's psychosocial team and is conducted by an art teacher. Its purpose is to strengthen the *proper school climate* and is aimed at students from fifth to eighth grade. At the time of the ethnography, nine students (six female and three male) participated. Specifically, the students design their own murals while the monitor guides their technique. In its second year of operation, the school requested that the topics of school climate are explicitly addressed in the mural. In the first year of operation, the content of the murals had been freely chosen, without emphasizing any particular topic. In response, the teacher leading the workshop tells me that in the murals, it was a challenge to connect to sociopolitical commentary and resistance with the institutionalized accepted approach reflecting a proper school climate. (Field Notes No. 13, October 10, 2014)

By contrasting the first- and second-year murals, whose emphasis is on "good school climate," it is easy to distinguish the ways in which policies operate and function. Here, we have a mural focused on generating processes of awareness and agency, represented in the phrase "Free Rivers, Living Communities" (see Photograph 5.1). This promotes the language of liberation and the agency to resist that the community (in this case, educational) can exercise in a broader social, political, and economic context. It also reflects part of the local community's history where Sur Austral is located.

Photography 5.1 Mural Workshop Year 1

In contrast, we observe the other murals and their approach oriented towards "healthy school climate" (see Photographs 5.2, 5.3 and 5.4). These discourses focus on healthy and unhealthy behavior as well as the *victim* and *aggressor* relationship. In this way, the language of agency, resistance, and political space is transformed, in a seemingly neutral, moral, and hygienic discursive field. Within this new logic, pastoral and political power can be traced, as its premises are based on moral principles, on good and evil. Civic formation in its own right makes use of the intervention and direction of certain moral canons, which, in their interaction with neoliberal democratic principles, conform to a circuit of rationality that combines the ways in which processes of subjectivation are configured (Lemke 2011).

As in the previous scene, participatory methodology where the students have *authorship* over the murals (downplaying the teacher's leadership, who in turn serves the government goals as demanded by the school) consolidates the overlap between disciplinary power and especially self-governance as a key technology of the self. Such self-governance is key in the internalization and appropriation of depoliticized discourses of *a healthy school environment*, discourses that operate and circulate as productions of truth (Foucault 2008, 2011a; Lemke 2011).

The innovative nature of the mural workshop appears *alternative*, veering from the traditional, and could constitute a different political space of greater resistance. However, we still see in the images the same discourses that the school addresses in its policies, which is based upon the central focus of improving the school climate. Statements linked to *health*, such as "healthy coexistence" and "play healthy", contrast with the *unhealthy* and *vulnerable*, which reveals a hygienist treatment of these

Photography 5.2 Mural Workshop Year 2 (with emphasis on "good school climate")

Photography 5.3 Year 2 "Play Healthy"

Photography 5.4   Year 2 "Protect the Defenseless"

issues centered on the frame of normality-abnormality and closely linked to moral parameters of the idea of a *good citizen*.

Finally, through a repeated technique of micro-practices that circulate in the daily routine of an extracurricular workshop, the political mechanism points to the administration of the educational community through subtle tactics, daily practices, and the domain of spaces that were previously occupied exclusively by the community, which the State's mentality could not permeate. Unlike the rationality of the welfare states (whose strategies of government are focused on large state apparatuses), the logic of neoliberal government (based on autonomy and freedom) and government tactics are overturned to such spaces that were previously out of reach, resorting to community intervention as a subtle way to achieve their goals. Therefore, it is logical to resort to popular techniques such as murals or the artistic show to capture the community's attention. Using more traditional techniques, the community would not be challenged to adhere with the new governmentality (Foucault 2006, 2009; Youdell 2011).

Nevertheless, what the State and Sur Austral School did not consider is that such discourses of the *good citizen* do not coincide with the governmental project that the students and their community adhere to. The confrontation of both projects persistently threatens the school's institutional identity, at such a level that it is somewhat antagonized by the community itself. Therefore, the school no longer has the power that it had a few years ago. This is proven daily by the transgression of minimum standards imposed by the school (punctuality, uniform, guardian's attendance to meetings, compliance with the school's order, confrontation of guardians and students with the members of the school, such as teachers, administrators, managers, and the like).

In this context, these technologies function biopolitically. Under the use of knowledge categories about certain delimited individuals in a specific social group (e.g., *at-risk population*, *vulnerable students*, among others), biopolitics responds to the calculation established by said knowledge, in order to intervene in time to contain the (already calculated) effects of what may happen, in the case that there is no such government intervention (Baez 2014). In this manner, we can distinguish the government's aim to contribute to the multiplicity of *scholarly* activities, which the school and the state government deploy.

Under this framework, we see the way in which the school climate policy is situated as a central problem in the school. Specifically how it is configured from a focused on deficit, hand in hand with school violence and social class articulation, particularly among the poorest groups. This constitutes and reaffirms a problematic idea of school coexistence coupled with school violence, vulnerability, poverty, and marginality.

This policy is a clear example of how neoliberalism operates in the different dimensions of human existence. Its interest in citizen education and, above all, in citizen security, configures a security control apparatus, articulating a heterogeneous network composed of a governmental institutionality (Ministry of Education and School Superintendence) and a local school institutionality.

Beyond the subject itself and the configuration of certain subjectivities (*to be different*), the school as a cultural device, with a new rationality of government based on school climate discourses, configures a new school institutionality. In such relations the principles of normality/abnormality are present and the ideal of the *good citizen* prevails. This system of particular knowledge states that through strategies and tactics deployed in a subtle and repetitive way, the school produces new subjectivities. Not only subjectivities of students, but also subjectivities of teachers, directors, administrators, families, and the school itself.

5.5   From the Tolerated Difference to the Marginal Difference: Effects of Neoliberal Inclusion Policies

By analyzing the production of *differences* in their correspondence with neoliberal rationality, we are led to understand how differences articulated to identity markers make up a chromatic multiplicity, which, under the rules of the educational market, elaborate two types of *difference*. First is the *tolerated difference* associated with SEN capacity whose acceptance entails an economic income necessary for the school's subsistence, even though it involves challenges for the institution. Second is the *marginal difference*, whose production would be marked by the correlation among poverty, vulnerability, and violence, which emerges from more radical and less desirable *difference*.

Considering the other difference, located in *otherness* itself, *difference* is the most acute and problematic marginality for the school, the state apparatus, and for society itself that has been individualized as an effect of an advanced liberal society, but at the same time, should not be tolerated. I refer to the difference that highlights the phenomenon of vulnerability, which is then transformed into school violence, in total deviation of the civilizing-citizen mission, which has currently been entrusted to schools.

Under this scenario, the school assumes a role as the guarantor of social order to reduce the maximum damage that the abject *difference* can cause in the near future—either as a dropout from the school system, a lawbreaker, a consumer of illicit substances, a practitioner of non-heteronormative sexual activity, and the like.

In such a way, the school generates strategies, mechanisms and tactics to fulfill this purpose, developing and installing an entire disciplinary-control apparatus, as in the case of Sur Austral School. A complex surveillance system, internalization of police discourses, penitentiary and judicial discourses, protocols for the management of acts of violence, security technologies based on prevention of certain behaviors, government technologies materialized in a set of extracurricular activities and psychosocial interventions, all contribute to transforming the school's *ethos*. In other words, even though the school preserves its civilizing goals, it converts its exclusively pedagogical and formative mission into a security apparatus.

This interaction cannot be seen as disconnected, or even as a casual articulation, but instead, as a part of government logic which aims to safeguard democratic principles, freedom, and social equality, minimizing the effects of said principles within neoliberal State rationality. In summary, a new school emerges focused on risk prevention, with citizen education as the government's mission, not for the purposes of the agents, rather for purposes of containment and security of the population.

On the contrary, a different phenomenon occurs in inclusion discourses connected with SEN. As discussed earlier, SEN have become the desirable *difference* and at the same time necessary *differences* for the school system's survival. However, this does not mean that they are at the center, but rather that policies of inclusive education (the SIPs) operate under the logic of the reproduction and affirmation of cultural differences. This is not in a sense of identity vindication, but in a sense of *managerialization*; that is, where they are arranged and put to work from an economic-administrative perspective to safeguard the solvency of the institution and at the same time, its integrity in producing the end results that it must in order to continue functioning.

Although, this way of managing differences does not antagonize, nor subalternize the students that are included in the SEN category, it still produces the difference from a marginal space. Even though these differences linked to SEN are more valued and accepted than the differences that derive from the problems of school climate, in this case, the problematic elements lie in the delimitation of the diagnosis and the uses that are assigned to the category of the *different*, given that they underlie the purposes of government that the school develops to respond to the State's mentality.

Finally, the perspective of law built on an assumed notion of childhood is diluted as a result of the intensification of technologies of control that the governmental apparatus operates with.

Consequently, as long as the market and *accountability* rationale that dominate our educational system are not modified, possibilities for transformation are scarce despite major reforms. Together with systems of control and sanctions in which schools are included, the maintenance of a *voucher* based financing system (according to standard-based results or through additional subsidy in the case of affirmative policies), ensures a highly neoliberalized educational system. This will continue to governmentalize schools and push them to generate self-governance forms, which allow them to survive market demands.

The current functionality of educational policies surrounding social and cultural differences, framed in a neoliberal normative context, will hardly disrupt the current hegemonic order. This is because the government goals are oriented, on the one hand, to the management of difference based on an economic calculation, for which schools obtain greater resources; on the other hand, they point to national security in terms of preventing effects of marginal difference.

Despite the inauspicious scenario, one of the possibilities exposed in this chapter is the attention to the positions from which it is possible to work and destabilize certain forms, which until today are stable and fixed. For example, to consider the practices the school develops before the fiscalization or rendering of accounts, which make them visible. Problematizing and including such practices as part of the current debate is a space that may open paths to mobilize new discursive networks within the context of school policy.

In conclusion, with this research I seek to re-politicize the language of *inclusion*, but above all to question the connection between *normality* and *difference* and how such languages create a productive dialogue within neoliberal rationality and globalization.

References

Ahmed, S. (2007). The language of diversity. *Ethnic and Racial Studies, 30*(2), 235–256. https://doi.org/10.1080/01419870601143927.

Allan, E. (2003). Constructing women's status: Policy discourses of university women's commission reports. *Harvard Educational Review, 73*(1), 44–72.

Bacchi, C. (1999). *Women, Policy and Politics: The construction of policy problems*. Great Britain: Sage.

Bacchi, C. (2009). *Analysing policy: What's the problem represented to be?* Frenchs Forest: Pearson Higher Education AU.

Baez, B. (2004). The study of diversity—The "knowledge of difference" and the limits of science. *Journal of Higher Education, 75*(3), 285–306. https://doi.org/10.1080/00221546.2004.11772257.

Baez, B. (2014). *Technologies of government: Politics and power in the "information age"*. Charlotte: Information Age Publishing.

Ball, S. (1993). What is policy? Texts, trajectories and toolboxes. *The Australian Journal of Education Studies, 13*(2), 10–17.

Ball, S., & Youdell, D. (2008). *Hidden privatisation in public education*. Brussels: Education International Brussels.

Bellei, C. (2015). *El gran experimento. Mercado y privatización de la educación chilena*. Santiago: LOM.

Brown, W. (2008). *Regulating aversion: Tolerance in the age of identity and empire*. New Jersey: Princeton University Press.

Brown, W. (2015). *Undoing the demos: Neoliberalism's stealth revolution*. Cambridge: Zone Books Near Futures.

Carrasco, A. (2013a). Performative mechanisms of educational institutions in Chile: Steps towards a new cultural subject. *Revista Observatorio Cultural, 15*, 7.

Carrasco, A. (2013b). Politics based in privatization, standardization, examination, and educational accountability: The anglophone experience. *Pensamiento Educativo, 50*(2), 163–172.

Carrasco, A., Seppänen, P., Rinne, R., & Falabella, A. (2015). Educational accountability in Chile and Finland. In P. Seppänen, A. Carrasco, M. Kalalahti, R. Rinne, & H. Simola (Eds.), *Contrasting dynamics in education politics of extremes* (Vol. 37, pp. 53–80). Rotterdam: Sense Publishers.

Cooperativa, Radio (Producer). (2011, July 19). Presidente Piñera: la educación es un bien de consumo. Retrieved from http://www.cooperativa.cl/noticias/pais/educacion/proyectos/presidente-pinera-la-educacion-es-un-bien-de-consumo/2011-07-19/134829.html.

Duggan, L. (2004). *The twilight of equality: Neoliberalism, cultural politics, and the attack on democracy*. Boston: Beacon Press.

Falabella, A. (2014). The performing school: The effects of market & accountability policies. *Education Policy Analysis Archives, 22*(70). Retrieved from http://www.redalyc.org/html/2750/275031898024/.

Fardella, C., Sisto, V., Morales, K., Rivera, G., & Soto, R. (2012). Rendición de cuentas y trabajo público. La Ética en Tensión.

Foucault, M. (2006). *Seguridad, territorio, población*. Buenos Aires: Fondo de la Cultura Económica.

Foucault, M. (2008). *Tecnologías del yo*. Buenos Aires: Paidós/I.C.E.-U.A.B.

Foucault, M. (2009). *Nacimiento de la biopolítica: Curso del collège de France (1978–1979)* (Vol. 283). Madrid: Ediciones Akal.

Foucault, M. (2011a). *El gobierno de sí y de los otros*. Buenos Aires: Fondo de Cultura Económica.

Foucault, M. (2011b). *La arqueología del saber* (A. Garzón, Trans. 2ª ed.). México: Siglo XXI.

Fuenzalida, R. (2014). *Los estilos educativos y su relación con la psicopatología en niños y adolescentes con discapacidad intelectual: un estudio comparativo entre Chile y España*. (Doctoral), Universidad Autónoma de Barcelona, Barcelona.

Henry, M., Lingard, B., Rizvi, F., & Taylor, S. (2001). *The OECD, globalisation and education policy*. Oxford: Pergamon Press.

Infante, M., Matus, C., & Vizcarra, R. (2011). Reasoning about the idea of difference in Chilean educational policies. *Universum (Talca), 26*(2), 143–163.

Laclau, E., & Mouffe, C. (2011). *Hegemonía y estrategia socialista: Hacia una radicalización de la democracia*. Buenos Aires: Fondo de la Cultura Económica.

Laval, C., & Dardot, P. (2013). *La nueva razón del mundo*. Barcelona: GEDISA.

Lemke, T. (2011). *Foucault, governmentality and critique*. Colorado: Paradigm Publishers.

Matus, C., & Infante, M. (2011). Undoing diversity: Knowledge and neoliberal discourses in colleges of education. *Discourse-Studies in the Cultural Politics of Education, 32*(3), 293–307. https://doi.org/10.1080/01596306.2011.573248.

Matus, C., & Rojas, C. (2015). Normalidad y diferencia en nuestras escuelas: a propósito de la Ley de Inclusión Escolar. *Docencia, 56*, 47–56.

MINEDUC. (2008). Ley Subvención Escolar Preferencial (Ley SEP), Congreso Nacional, 20.248 Stat.

MINEDUC. (2009). Set standards to determine students with special education needs who will be beneficiaries of special education grants. Decree 170 C.F.R.

MINEDUC. (2011a). School Violence Law, 20.536 C.F.R.

MINEDUC. (2011b). *Política Nacional de Convivencia Escolar*. Santiago: Ministerio de Educación. Retrieved from http://www.convivenciaescolar.cl.

MINEDUC. (2013). *Orientaciones Técnicas Para los Programas de Integración Escolar (PIE)*. Santiago-Chile: MINEDUC.

MINEDUC. (2015). *Educación para la igualdad de género. Plan 2015–2018*. Santiago: MINEDUC.

MINEDUC. (2017). *Orientaciones técnicas para la inclusión educativa de estudiantes extranjeros*. Santiago: MINEDU. Retrieved from https://migrantes.mineduc.cl/wp-content/uploads/sites/88/2017/12/Orientaciones-estudiantes-extranjeros-21-12-17.pdf.

OCDE. (2018). *Chile, primer país sudamericano miembro de la OCDE*. Retrieved from http://www.oecd.org/chile/chileprimerpaissudamericanomiembrodelaocde.htm.

Pillow, W. (2007). 'Bodies are dangerous:' Using feminist genealogy as policy studies methodology. *Journal of Education Policy, 18*(2), 145–159.

Piñera, S. (2017). *Programa de educación: mejoremos la sala de clase*. Retrieved from http://educacion.sebastianpinera.cl/.

Power, S., & Frandji, D. (2010). Education markets, the new politics of recognition and the increasing fatalism towards inequality. *Journal of Education Policy, 25*(3), 385–396.

Rizvi, F., & Lingard, B. (2013). *Políticas educativas en un mundo globalizado*. Madrid: Ediciones Morata.

Romero, M. (2017). Piñera presenta sus propuestas en educación con énfasis en mejorar la calidad. *Emol*. Retrieved from http://www.emol.com/noticias/Nacional/2017/10/12/878944/Las-propuestas-de-Pinera-que-apuntan-a-mejorar-la-calidad-en-la-educacion.html.

Scott, J. (1992). Experiencia (M. Silva, Trans.). In J. Butler & J. Scott (Eds.), *Feminists Theorize the Political* (pp. 773–797). New York: Routledge Inc.

Seppänen, P., Carrasco, A., Kalalahti, M., Rinne, R., & Simola, H. (Eds.). (2015). *Contrasting dynamics in education politics of extremes* (Vol. 37). Rotterdam: Sense Publishers.

Sisto, V., & Zelaya, V. (2013). La etnografía de dispositivos como herramienta de análisis y el estudio del managerialismo como práctica local. *Universitas Psychologica, 12*(4), 1345–1354.

Tenorio, S. (2011). Formación inicial docente y necesidades educativas especiales. *Estudios pedagógicos, 37*(2), 249–265. https://dx.doi.org/10.4067/S0718-07052011000200015.

Youdell, D. (2011). *School trouble. Identity, power and politics in education*. New York: Routledge.

Chapter 6
Normalcy and Deviance: The Production of Schools and Their Subjects

Anita Sanyal Tudela

Abstract This chapter aims at describing the ways everyday discourses of the school produce normal and deviant subjectivities, and how these contribute to the continued production of the school itself. I draw from the ethnographic studies to make descriptions of an all-girls school and a mostly boys school, and pay special attention to the ways gender and sexuality discourses predominate definitions of who students are in each and stabilize subjectivities that continue to work to produce institutional identity of the school. This chapter responds to two principal questions: How is the normal produced within specific school contexts, and how does it frame the production of identities of students and teachers? How does the specific structure of normalcy contribute to the construction of the individual school? In the analysis that follows, I emphasize the ways in which normal and its deviants are ordered. I argue that these orders serve a productive function in that they permit the sustenance of the school and its mission. The identities ascribed to types of students, especially in terms of gender and sexuality help a constant mechanism of production of the school through locally and institutionally meaningful processes.

6.1 Institutions and Intelligibility

Understanding school practices through the lens of discourse permits the ability to see the ways school subjects are produced through everyday normalized mechanisms for naming and managing students. Such practices become normalized through their tacit repetition in everyday forms through language and actions that are readily accepted as natural and *the way things go*. In the case of schools, children are normalized and constrained so as to produce students, a category that is widely generalizable to some level. Students are produced in opposition to teachers and constitute normalized categories of age, race, and ability, and are overlain by other features such as innocence and vulnerability (Baker 1998; Bloch et al. 2003). The simultaneous pro-

A. Sanyal Tudela (✉)
University of Maryland, College Park, MD, USA
e-mail: asanyal@umd.edu

© Springer Nature Singapore Pte Ltd. 2019
C. Matus (ed.), *Ethnography and Education Policy*, Education Policy
& Social Inequality 3, https://doi.org/10.1007/978-981-13-8445-5_6

duction of teachers and other professionals in school settings is set up in opposition to students, and serves to reemphasize series of constraints designed for individual self-regulation and social control.

> The productive elements of power move from focusing on the controlling actors to the systems of ideas that normalize and construct the rules through which intent and purpose of the world are organized. The effects of power are to be found in the production of desire and in dispositions and sensitivities of individuals. (Popkewitz and Brennan 1998, p. 19)

Institutions serve as a site for the production of subjectivities that make up a governable citizenry. As Fassin et al. (2015) explain, institutions

> … are thus the site where the state is produced. This production does not occur in a vacuum: it operates in an ideological environment and under regulatory constraints. Nor does it exist in abstraction: it proceeds from the individual and collective actions of the agents. (p. 6)

The normative discourses that structure values and subjectivities translate into tacit, unquestioned ideas about what is acceptable, good, or proper, and what is unacceptable or bad. The circulation of value judgments that determine the production of subjects come to define a common sense and shared understanding of a social scenario (Fassin et al. 2015). Within institutions, regularly shared normalized discourses reiterate taken for granted ideas about who school actors are and the identity performances that matter. These discourses work to constrain the possibilities for who can exist, and what actions can be taken, as well as set limits for where these possibilities end, therefore recognizing the limit of what it means to participate legitimately in the institution (Phillips et al. 2004). Fairclough lays out the mechanism through which institutions produce and constrain identities:

> Each institution has its own differentiated settings and scenes, its case of participants and its own norms for their combination… It is, I suggest, necessary to see the institution as simultaneously facilitating and constraining the social action of its members: it provides them with a frame for action, without which they could not act, but it thereby constrains them to act within that frame. (as cited in Phillips et al. 2004, p. 638)

While we can rely to some extent on generalized notions of children and students, we can also see the limits of generalizability when we think about schools as institutions that, for themselves, must continually be reconstituted (Phillips et al. 2004). In this sense, we can view the institution as having a locally defined identity that relies on persistent processes of social construction in order to maintain its existence. In this sense, while there are some more universal notions of students and teachers shared across institutions, discourses within institutions constitute specific versions of such actors and their roles, which are enmeshed in the "'reasoning' inscribed [in] technologies [of] how the teacher supervises … as well as a way in which teachers and children become self-governing actors in the spaces of schooling" (Popkewitz and Brennan 1998, p. 9).

Butler's (1990) notion of intelligibility helps us to focus the lens on the ways institutions construct themselves as individually recognizable, how they come to have locally specific and meaningful identities, and how they can be distinguished from one another. While Butler's use of the idea is attentive to subjectivation and the making of individual subjects, in this chapter I find it useful to underscore this notion as contributing to the maintenance of institutions—in this case, schools. Ultimately, schools use subjectivation (Butler 1997; Davies 2006) processes to make their students; however, we see these subjectivities as contributing to a broader collective institutional identity that is at once generalizable (schools have similar characteristics, e.g., the school building, dominant organizations of schooling and classes, etc.) and unique (each school has its own identity, ways of naming, and constructions of school actors). As we explore institutional discourses to understand the production of school subjectivities further, we can also see the ways students and teachers are constrained into sets of attributes that are valued and devalued.

The way in which the production of the normal student is upheld at schools can be seen by looking at the specific school profiles and other ethnographic accounts. We can see the ways in which processes of gendering, classing, sexing and sexualizing, attributing ability or any other natural innate characteristics, and extending such attributions to families have contributed to producing normal and accepted subjectivities, as well as, deviant, problematic or unacceptable ones. In addition, the ways that such processes operate to stabilize hierarchies within the school become visible. These processes of subjectivation help the school continually maintain and reinforce its intelligible identity, and they are also the effects of power (Foucault 1982). In the sections that follow, I present two school profiles, each followed by an analysis of the specific ways particular versions of school subjectivities are produced. Gender prevails as an essential framework for understanding the stabilizing mechanisms in the productions of subjects. I focus on the ways the normal school student is produced, the conditions for this production, and the role of the teacher in this production. In the discussion that follows, I use the idea of *moral economies* (Fassin et al. 2015) to develop a larger frame by which the processes of subjectivation can be understood in the contexts of specific school sites. I argue that students, teachers, and schools are produced through articulations that rely on specific processes of subjectivation that operate to confirm already accepted morally defined forms.

6.2 Institutionalizing Gender: Quillaye School

Quillaye School is an all-girls school serving kindergarten to twelfth-grade students. The school's mission is to educate girls to fit a particular and well-defined profile of the ideal girl student. The school participates in the series of national programs dedicated to supporting special needs and vulnerable students, including the School Integration Project (*Proyecto Integración Escolar* or PIE) and the Preferential School Subsidy Program (*Subvención Escolar Preferencial* or Red SIP). Quillaye School's participation in the PIE and SEP helps it define its overall goals for the formation of students in the school.

Dominant discourses in the school revolve around notions of academic excellence and are enacted in the expectation for students to achieve high scores on standardized exams and college entrance. In practice, there are celebrations for high performance and disappointment for not achieving high enough scores. Test preparation and extra support for lower performing students is a normal practice and talk about the importance of the results of such tests is widespread among the school staff and well known among students.

Another logic that contributes to the specific normalization of children in this school relates to the learning and reinforcement of virtues and specific ideals related to gender, and their behavior as *señoritas*. The expectations for upholding these school values include any situation in which they are in uniform or representing the school and extends to situations off school grounds. This version of femininity is dictated by expectations of specific behaviors and physical appearance.

Teachers maintain positions of authority and have the capacities to sanction and evaluate the behavior, dress, disposition, and academic performance of students. Teachers see themselves as supervisors and managers of innate behaviors that contradict the ideal. Students who interfere or resist the values of the ideal imagined student pose problems for the school that have to be dealt with or are otherwise relegated to private intervention and removed from public view. Teachers view their roles as helping to contribute to the prevention of resistant behaviors during the early formative years, by focusing on intervention before the students can demonstrate more resistant behaviors, such as: noncompliance with the performance and dispositions surrounding academic excellence, resistance of the physical expression of the *señorita*, or *proper young lady* (e.g., short or boy-cut hair, heavy makeup, other expressions of individuality in terms of dress and physical appearance), and engaging in same-sex relationships or sexual behavior.

The *problem* of lesbianism is recognized by the outside community, as well as within the school. However, the silencing and hiding of deviant behaviors from the public view is an active strategy for maintaining the school identity—that Quillaye School remains an institution dedicated to the formation of *good girls* or *señoritas* that embody virtue and proper values, strive for academic excellence, and exercise discipline and self-control.

Even though formal selection for the school is prohibited, another strategy for maintaining the school's vision is a series of informal selection mechanisms. There is a lengthy and arduous admission procedure that involves the collection of large amounts of paperwork, parent interviews with the director, and large periods of wait time for confirmation of enrolment. After eighth grade, students have to reenter an admissions cycle before starting high school. Community members and parents reported that such processes provide significant challenges for enrolling a child. These mechanisms contribute to the school's maintenance of a high academic standard and ensure the fulfillment of the institutional mission.

6.2.1 *Producing Normal*

The production of the Quillaye School student and their limits and counterparts works through the continued disciplining of student identities primarily along lines of age and gender. The normal student is reified in constant comparison to the imaginary ideal student the school wants to form. The ideal student is one who fulfills the expectations for a set of traditional characteristics of women, who at once demonstrate academic excellence and embody aspects of traditionally valued forms of femininity, as written in the institutional mission of the school, "The improvement of the person consists of the development of her own faculties through the exercise of virtue, with the goal of seeking good, truth, justice, and beauty." In the words of teachers, the ideal student is one who is,

> ... attentive, that they know how to listen [...] they practice their reasoning in class, and, despite being little, understand the line of discussion in class and continue to respond to questions that come up. I try to maintain an active class with these girls. I try to call on them to respond or I get close to them. And one girl, who had finished, brought me her notebook and I gave her a smiley face, congratulations – I keep encouraging her so that she keeps acting like a good student (elementary).

> A student who pays attention to the norms, who studies, who is disciplined (elementary).

> We hope for a girl who is disciplined, who lives up to standards in class. This is to say that she works hard and is respectful, and who has opinions and creates beautiful things, but up to a certain standard, so she can do more things (secondary).

While the ideal student is who the school aspires to educate, it remains an imaginary figure to which the normal student is constantly compared. In the normal student arises an image of everything the ideal student is not. In other words, students are constructed according to what has to be controlled in them or otherwise managed or changed in order for them to appear more like the ideal. The following quotes refer to primary education students:

> Sure, they use makeup, they talk about boys [...] they talk about sex. I know they talk about these things and they worry about music like La Violeta, Justin Bieber. They go to concerts and dances.

> They are very consumerist. Everything, even their backpacks are $30.000 [equivalent of ~50 USD] and above, and they have the rollers. They have lunch boxes that match their backpacks. I am talking about the majority, not everyone, but the majority. Their pencil cases are high fashion, the latest arrivals. Whatever is in style is what the girls bring. Many walk with cell phones. It is surprising, from kindergarten until 12th grade, they have the latest fashions.

> The girls are more aggressive. These days we don't see girls that play with dolls. And, [the younger girls see] that the other girls are aggressive and copy whatever they see. [This happens above all] with the younger ones.

In general, students are described as *"agrandadas;"* they act older than they are and are concerned with superficial topics and value things that teachers feel are superfluous and unnecessary, or distracting from school goals, including academic engagement and proper girl behavior. There is an additional note in the last quote that implies that the normal child of today is not the same as the normal child of the past. Times have changed and children are different.

Students' school behavior goes against the accepted version of who students should be and encompasses a more insidious set of descriptors. Students "do not

follow rules. They come [to school] and do what they want. They want to be themselves…attended to. They are stubborn…You tell them something and they say 'yes,
yea Miss,' but they do whatever they want" and "lie to get out of something." Teachers
further describe violence and the tendency for students to bully each other:

> Among the students, in past year, you might hear: "You hit me, I am going to report you to
> my mother." Not now. Now, they say things like: "Be careful, because I can bring a gun,
> because my mom was a police and I know where she keeps her gun…" And, the moms come
> to the school and say: "How is it possible that you can have these types of girls?" and "this
> is what they learn at home."

The production of high school students is in many ways similar. Students are
described as "cry-babies, jealous, manipulative, unfair, complicated." One teacher
adds: "They are capable of disregarding agreements and commitments to save themselves." An administrator comments that high school students are very "revolution-
ized," "they argue back," "they argue about everything, even boyfriends."

In another interaction, teachers describe the tendency for high school students
to leave the patio or classroom a mess. One teacher even reflects on whether this
tendency is common to women, since, in her experience, boys are too active during
the break to eat, and therefore, leave no mess.

> The girls pay little attention to their surroundings. After break times, they leave the patio [a
> mess].

> It shocks me that they leave so much garbage in the classroom. When I arrive in the classroom,
> it is like … crazy. […] Could it be that women are naturally tchotchke collectors, that we
> like little figures or other little things? I don't think so because previously, this school was
> for *niñitas*[1] and it wasn't like that […] Boys aren't like that. They come to break time and
> they don't even take time to eat their lunch because they are busy playing soccer, [and] they
> don't generate that much garbage. I've thought about this before …

In the production of the normal student and her limits, the profile extends to
versions of the family to which the school behaviors and problems are attributed.
There are strong opinions about the liberties mothers, in particular, give to their girls
and how this is different from the past.

> I think they lack the modesty that the little girls from before had more of … I think we
> mothers were inculcated with [modesty] also.

> … they come from home … their mothers permit them to come with eye shadow, lipstick
> on, their hair down, [and] tight pants.

What is implicit in these quotes is the assumption that times were better in the
past—girls complied more with the expected norms, and that the liberties they are
allowed in terms of coming to school with sunglasses, lipstick, and their hair down,
in part, is what makes them deviate from the expected standards.

Assumptions around the affordances of having a nuclear family are evident and
the absence of the father is considered a negative factor to the girls' upbringing.

---

[1] *Niñitas* refers to the traditional notion of little girls comprised of innocence, goodness, and appropriate femininity.

"[Sometimes mothers are] young, single, they live with their step parents [...] Nowadays we are seeing some 60% of students live without their fathers, a large majority of them." Teachers note that "sometimes there is a male presence, but it is not the biological father."

Parental influence is noted as a cause of bullying and more extreme, violent behaviors in the school.

> Girls from first grade on get so attached for whatever reason. During break, they play, if someone [...] hits them a little bit harder, the other hits back even harder and it gets bigger and bigger. There are a lot of parents that say "if they hit you, hit back." So, the problem is that all the parents talk about bullying, and against violence, but [that means that] you can't go around saying "if they hit you, hit back." [...] So then, there are a lot of things [one could do] talk to the teacher, talk to the other girls, talk to parents [...] so then, there comes a moment that the mothers get tired of their girls always being victims. And, in order to not get bullied yourself, you bully others. In the end it is like a vicious cycle. If the mom says to hit, it will happen. If, in the house the mother validates [that behavior], it doesn't matter that she ends up in the principal's office because she has to defend herself.

One teacher describes the long-lasting effects the students suffer from parents as

> The girls shield themselves a lot in family problems.
>
> ... they use the excuse that "parents are separating" or that she "doesn't have a father." [...] but the girl is going to grow up to be 20 or 25 years old and [when something difficult confronts her in life] she is going to need to go to a psychologist. She can go to the guidance counselor. There are fathers and mothers that hide this and some moms even admit it. Later [the girls] shield themselves with family-related problems. It is like the girl is like that because her parents separated, so there isn't anything we can do.

6.2.2 Gender and Sexuality

We see the way gender plays out in the quotes cited earlier by noting the assumed characteristics of students (they use makeup, they are attentive to fashion, behave in specific ways, respond in specific ways, etc.) and the comparisons made about the nature of boys versus girls. We can see gender, and more explicitly, the heteronormative standards, more strongly as we tune into comments related to what it means to be a girl. The following excerpts are from an interaction between one of the ethnographers and a teacher:

> Girls are more detail-oriented. They are attentive to every detail, and if I am not mistaken – correct me if I am wrong, they are very complicated. They have problems with everything and are sensitive. If they have a conflict with a classmate, they make a huge fuss. Girls are also more caring, affectionate, always giving little gifts or getting close. Boys are more relaxed. They aren't sensitive like girls and if they have problems with their classmates, they immediately resolve them. [...] If a boy comes to class all sweaty, it doesn't matter because during break, boys play soccer, and it seems like they are not bothered by being sweaty. But, if a girl comes in all sweaty like that, or with her hair all messy, I send her straight to the bathroom to clean up and gather herself.

Teachers' personal stories also play explicit roles in how they interact with students and the focus of their surveillance. One teacher recounts her experience as a *tomboy* in a mixed school, "[I was] chubby, not-pretty. I really wasn't interested in fixing myself up. I wore clothes that were three sizes too big for me, and I played with boys *"como machito."*[2] As she explains, her education was "difficult" and "came at a big cost because I never could find a boyfriend and I had to change. I lost weight and tried to be more feminine." In her role in the school, when she notices a student who dresses masculine or has a masculine attitude, this teacher makes it a point to speak to her so that "[the student] doesn't make the same mistakes" and highlights the "benefits of being feminine." Femininity plays a part in the affective relationships she maintains with students since "as teachers we expect [close personal] relationships because [students] are girls."

The narrative of who girls are is set within a frame of standards that define the presumed nature of girlhood. Teachers note that students are

> very sexualized. They talk about intimate things about themselves, in a vulgar manner, talking about their genitals. They touch each other, and how they dress and make themselves up, uff. This is sexualized conduct that exists in women [...] women, the students are more emotional and [are susceptible to being swayed into homosexuality].

They also express worry about what is interpreted as an increasingly young age that students begin to engage in sexualized behavior:

> They date a lot, and from [a] much younger [age] have relationships that are more serious than one would think. The boyfriend is, for example, a studious boy, who keeps a schedule (not the other way around). But, he could also be a *flaite*,[3] the opposite of what one would want as a mother, not a prince. They have ear expanders (spacers for ear piercings), big, baggy pants, [and] tattoos.

Sexuality, more directly, comes into view as the topic of lesbianism and homosexuality is described as a problem. Community members and parents are aware that homosexual behavior is happening at the school and have expressed concern over the vulnerability of their daughters and the responsibility of the school. As an example, parents expressed concern about "the cases of lesbianism in the school." Parents' sentiment, expressed at a recent parent meeting, includes feeling that their younger children are witnessing homosexual behavior that makes them susceptible as well: "their girls see the older students kissing each other and come home and tell their parents all about it." They ask that the school control the potential for younger students to come into situations of witnessing such behavior, and therefore becoming persuaded toward homosexual tendencies. This causes a strain and discomfort for teachers who do not believe the topic is a school issue. The teachers readily accept that the younger students are "weaker and are more easily convinced." The younger students are at more risk and deserve stronger attention from the school than the older students in order to prevent homosexual behaviors. This idea is confirmed in

---

[2] She describes herself as acting like a boy and playing with the boys, a tomboy.

[3] *Flaite* is used to refer to students who represent a stylized rebellious youth. This is a negative term that describes someone who is usually brown skinned, low socioeconomic status, and/or uncultured.

the words of a school administrator, "I've realized that if you treat them well, they respond well. It isn't necessary to scold them…well, in primary education you can scold them, but in high school, you have to treat them well."

While some teachers are more open to homosexuality as a part of normal behavior and believe girls should have freedom in this respect, others are more hesitant and less sure or explicitly resistant about "how such themes are being addressed in school" or feel that they "don't have the tools to deal with sexuality at the school." The general positioning is that this topic should be within the purview of parents and not the school.

6.2.3 The Role of the Teacher

Teachers see helping push students toward the correct path for expression and development as part of their role:

> … they are not able to recognize [the correct path] … I tell them sometimes, that they should tell me the truth because if I know the truth straight from them I will defend them no matter what happens. Sometimes I have to defend the younger girls from the older ones. [The older ones] treat [the younger ones] like dolls, or they take their lunch or their money. I imagine that this has always happened, but this is why we need trust. I trust them as a teacher, because they have to have trust me in order to tell on someone. Like, for example, to tell the truth about what happens at home with their family, but when the time comes, they have to realize that it is their responsibility [to speak up]. […] At times, I have spent a very long time asking for the truth, because, [if I do not] the girls say "I told you. I told the teacher and she didn't do anything." So, in communicating problems, you have to have trust, until someone says, "it was me. I made a mistake."

However, she also acknowledges the limits of this position: that there are moments where one needs to make a stronger appeal to the authoritative voice because trust does not go far enough.

The same teacher says:

> … but there are others that you have to threaten with sending her to the principal so they tell the truth. What is worrying is that they are really little. […] When they get to 5th, then 8th grade, they [have much more experiences] so, if they are not able to make small mistakes earlier on or get into some mischief, then later what can you expect if they are not able to recognize, or more directly, they blame someone else. You end up saying to yourself, "Shoot. Who is telling the truth and who isn't?"

> … so there are other forms that girls can use to defend themselves: they can make good arguments, they can name someone else, whatever they can do, but it is pretty complicated when one tries to teach something at school and in class, and you see that they have learned the opposite. […] Sometimes, they believe their mothers much more than they believe [us teachers]. […] Sometimes, if the girl has permission to make a complaint, if someone hits her, or if someone spits at her, you sometimes find it exaggerated. They say they are going to tell the principal, but they don't even know [the other girl]. Sometimes [it is for such] common, everyday things, the level of tolerance is so low. [You can't be telling on someone for such small things, like someone hid a pencil or something like that.]

6.2.4   Synthesis

Part of what we can see in the ways the students are constructed in Quillaye School relates to the presumed nature of girls, some innate biological essential character-istics that are universal to all girls. Teachers' need to push and tame these essential characteristics plays out as surprise and frustration toward girls' behaviors and the persistent notion that the students are defined by the distance they represent from the ideal. This harkens back to Wagener's (1998) point relating to the pathologiza-tion and sexualization of womanhood—girls and women have a natural and innate tendency toward sex and sexualized behaviors that must be controlled. This logic creates a natural and persistent goal for the school to discipline these aspects away for fear that younger girls can succumb to influences and natural tendencies to which they are particularly vulnerable. In this way age also becomes a structural feature in defining the range of what is acceptable, as well as the forms of addressing issues.

6.3   Saving Students: Alerce School

Male students make up 71% of the student body at Alerce School, which provides first through eighth grade education. Like Quillaye School, Alerce participates in the PIE and SEP programs. The school defines itself as being an "open school." That is, it is open for all who are interested in attending, including rolling admissions throughout the year. The policy structures of PIE and SEP play a big role in facilitating the positioning as an open school and provide support (specialists, funding) for incoming students. Children participants in each of the programs are deemed *special* and designated a top priority so that their needs are met. Teachers and other school officials are explicit about this school being a place that accepts all children, and in particular, those who have not been successful in other school settings. Along with a disposition for the acceptance of all students, teachers express a deep commitment to affective and otherwise non-pedagogical support for students. This means teachers' roles are defined not solely by a responsibility to educate in the formal academic sense, but also, that the roles extend into the necessity for them to be caring and accepting of students who have problems. Taking on an affective and caring role for students in need, as well as paying attention to the types of "issues" or problems students face in their home lives, is a regular part of what teachers do. Members of the faculty share examples of students who need extra care and attention, including a place to rest and/or wash clothes, services that the school provides.

   While the school sustains itself on its identity as an *open door* school, the ongoing integration of new students and the weight of responding to the students' various needs create a tension that remains at the heart of the school. On one hand, the supports provided under the policy programs provide the school with funding and resources based on enrolment and the specific categorizations of students that arrive, which help the school stay afloat in the midst of low enrolment. On the other hand, these "special students" (the ones who are brought in under the policy frames) create challenges for teachers in getting through daily processes by causing "difficulties" or "complications" in daily school life. It is a dilemma that is at the heart of the school's survival and identity. In this sense the school lives in a constant state of emergency. There is some push back from teachers who feel that the school's limits are superseded for existing in this state (the constant addition of students throughout the year, more and more difficult situations, more challenges with student behavior), which provokes feelings of dissatisfaction and resistance.

Saving students from difficult situations, providing a safe place, and helping guide them toward paths of success is a big part of the discourse utilized by teachers about students. Alerce School students are described as coming from challenging homes and family situations, having a high amount of special education diagnoses, and different levels of *vulnerability*. In general, they are described as lacking in the basics for learning and lacking in the values for school success. While students are seen in many different ways as lacking, they are also described as "affectionate," "caring," and in need of maternal attention. This is the profile of the normal student at Alerce School. Difference/deviance is generated along two principal lines. The first are students who go against the general school spirit of inclusion and caring, and "abuse the weaker [students] and/or pose threats" and/or whose families are immersed in "drugs and cultures of delinquency." Students who are exposed to drugs/drug culture have problems with attendance and concentration in class, and are otherwise causes of problems in the classroom and school. Teachers feel these students are beyond "saving." Gender is also a theme through which normal and deviant school identities are reified. While previous descriptions refer mostly to boys, there are distinct lines of differentiation for the girls. The school culture is described to be predominantly masculine and girls are expected to fulfill traditionally gendered roles and responsibilities. For example, they are expected to maintain their appearance, keep their hair tied back, and act like *little ladies* (*señoritas*). There is little similar discourse for boys, who are understood to "need" more attention and maternal style caring, and for whom being *messy* or *disorganized* (*desordenados*) is part of being a boy.

6.3.1 Producing Normal

The normalization of students at Alerce School happens along multiple lines that create and sustain prototypical school subjects, while simultaneously constructing the Other and less acceptable variants. Teachers readily take on or resist the culture of the open school and the notion of extending their roles toward more caring and affective roles. Their overextension seems to be part of what is understood as simply what teachers in this school do.

One specific and notable way student identities are normalized is through a stable and constant discourse of deficit relating to students backgrounds, families, and home lives, which structures their potential for academic success. This deficit discourse is accompanied by a construction that relates to students' affective dispositions to produce a subject that experiences important deficiencies in his life, a situation which makes him vulnerable and in need of attention, affection, and otherwise crave for care. Consider, for example, this series of quotes from teachers in a focus group meeting:

> The [normal student] could be a boy student, since there are more boys in this school. It could be a boy with problems, parental absence, where parents do not take care of their needs [...] an unmotivated and very talkative boy student.

> I think that, due to what they lack, the students are affectionate. It is like one characteristic of all of them is that they are affectionate. [...] They like to hug, to touch. There are many boys like this. It is almost like they expect you to welcome [or embrace] them. This has to be precisely because of what they lack [in their home environment]. I feel like this has changed the relationships between teacher and student [...] in comparison with two years ago, the students are much closer to the teachers. There are disciplinary problems. I am making a comparison between what I saw and what I now see; I feel like, now [...] the students have a closer identification with their school.

> [The normal] kid is [...] I don't know if this is the right word, but, easily distracted [*disperso*], hyperactive, they want to always do things. [...] They want to learn, but don't know how, so they get close to you and they look for the affective aspects. They seek the shelter [and protection] that they don't have in their families.

> The normal student is the one who comes to school in search of something. He doesn't know what, but he is looking for something. He knows he has to come to school, and he is in search of something. Here is where we, as teachers, enter the game, because not everything is learning. Here is where we still haven't made the connection with what the Ministry of Education is asking of us. They are always asking for content, only content and very little person-to-person relationships. So, I think that, because of this also, from last year until now, the students are closer to us. It feels certain, because they are in search of that attachment. They don't have this; it disappeared when they were much younger. Now they don't really exist like a family. They search for the attachment, so here we are. And, now, how can we be prepared [enough] as teachers. We also have our difficulties and challenges, our own stories.

> I agree about that bit relating to wanting to always hug. He wants you to talk to him and he trusts us. I think they search for this because there isn't someone to listen [at home].

> So, I have worked in two other schools, but my previous school was one with much more need in economic terms. But this school has much more need in terms of affection, more social need [...]. It is really shocking to arrive to a school that is poorer in terms of social and affective factors. I don't know, but for example, all the kids have cell phones and tablets. Some even have computers. But, no one asks them how they are, or no one is in charge of them or responsible for the things they do. But, all this is also part of what it means to be a parent: to be responsible even of the negative things that the student does.

It is evident from the teachers' language that there is ready acknowledgment that certain parental "absences" or other family deficit conditions related to parents' commitments to support the school are characteristic of the normal child at Alerce School. These students suffer problems at school in that they are generally recognized as being "unmotivated," "talkative," or otherwise weak in terms of potential for school success. These challenges are constructed as the normal student at Alerce School since the school serves principally students who are not able to succeed in other schools and defines itself as being accepting to all those in need. Students with special education diagnoses or who are otherwise labeled as vulnerable confirm this norm. These students are those who are brought in under the policy frames of PIE and SEP and are those who define and sustain the school.

We can also see, in the second quote, that students' affective dispositions are added to the deficiencies that students have. An absent parent, usually the father, or an otherwise undesirable or lacking home life is cause for students to have dispositions of caring, loving, and needing affective attention from teachers. Finally, as we saw with Quillaye School, we can also note some references to a notion that these are different times compared to how things were in the past. Children were inherently different in the past and this fact relates to the construction of teachers' role as readily responsive to students' needs in this particular time and place.

While this is recognized as the normal student in the school, another set of quotes help identify the Other; the ones that continually push the limits of the school and who otherwise presses at the school's ability to *deal* or otherwise carry out daily classroom and school activities.

> There is a group of students that are getting very close to becoming delinquents because their families are involved with drugs, and in those cases for example, I have parents that ... the only thing they worry about is that their boys don't get into drugs or delinquency. But, they don't see education as a path because they are so absorbed with all of those sorts of problems. The only thing they want is to keep the kids in school, that they don't get thrown out [expelled] from school because of the risk of falling into drugs or delinquency.

> These factors influence the learning of the entire group [...] And, an additional factor we have is about discipline and self-control inside the classroom, which determine much of the learning, independent of special education needs and other things we encounter. This will determine how the work inside classrooms plays out, and obviously impacts learning. So, the boys with disciplinary problems – all the students that we are talking about in relation to drugs or delinquency – many times have concentration problems in class [...] [The students] with disabilities or special needs really need special support and time with someone who will support their learning. [The distractions] will affect them ...

> For example, we have a family in the school that we know is involved in criminal activities and the kids barely ever come to school. So, you see how they have these problems, [the kids] live in a world submerged in criminal type activities. [The family] feels like they have the right to not send the kids to school and to mandate that the school passes [to the next grade] the kid anyway through intimidation. They have done this.

> ... when I arrived here, or when I had a problem – I don't remember the exact situation – But, they told me: "No. You have to let those kids pass [to the next grade] because of their situation and parents' involvement in drugs." And, I felt intimidated because in the past someone from that family hit a teacher. [...] So, they talk to you like this so you feel intimidated and you let the kids pass. In reality, it is pretty shocking.

In these cases, families are beyond an acceptable limit of dysfunction that is the norm for this school and are considered causes of the most extreme cases that pose a problem for the school. Families are held responsible for providing children with specific values that favor or put students at a disadvantage in school settings: "It is probably that the families are not educating their children and passing on values." In this sense, students are positioned beyond a clear boundary between what or who is acceptable, able to be rescued, and in need, and those who cannot be helped, pose a problem for the school and teachers, and are seen as students who generally do not fit into the acknowledged range of the majority of the school's work. We can also see the ways teachers become pressured to let these students pass, therefore permitting the axis of difference and the ongoing existence of the problem.

6.3.2   The Role of the Teacher

While students are constructed in such a way that define the normal and deviant student, teachers and other school staff (e.g., the individuals that manage the policy enactment in schools) are simultaneously constructed as managers of these student identities. While teachers experience struggle and hardship around having to manage the needs of this population, they still count it as part of their role as teachers in Alarce School.

> I notice that the more times a student leaves the classroom, the less integrated he is. When a student is stuck to me, it means he isn't integrated and it is a challenge for me. Maybe another teacher could say something like, "awww, how cute to have them right next to you like little chicks," but to me that is not integration. This isn't normal in my view. This shouldn't make us happy. When a kid says, "ah!" (raising his hand to wave from far away), then I feel better about it because he has [made space for himself in the classroom]. I think that our students are so dependent on us and they are [always saying things like] "What about now, Miss? Is it ok, now?" They have fewer abilities to make decisions about themselves. They are easily influenced. We have had a lot of problems because of this sort of thing. I think the student population has been diverse, which is not worse or better than before, but it is different. And, the students these days they demand more tools that I truly don't think I have.

> It is complicated because they come pre-programmed from home to act in certain ways. And, here in the school, it is like they try to replicate it. I have experienced this many times. I point out to so many kids so they act like they should, and the girls too, like "Listen, you are a lady." [They answer] "Whatever profe" and I feel like [I want to tell them to] "talk properly!" Talking about more normal things ... I don't know, but it seems like we are in over our heads, but in the classroom, I think the students have to act with a certain standard of normalcy.

6.3.3   Synthesis

The Alerce School defines itself by being able to attend to the particular profile of children that are seen as normal. This normality is defined by situations of precarity, lack of resources and support, but also lack of important values for school. Through such notions of deficit, students are constituted as having particular characteristics. Families occupy an important role in the provision of acceptable values or standards, and are held responsible in the most extreme cases that define the Other, and this provides an ongoing constant challenge for school staff. The school and teachers occupy the role of addressing issues and providing support. Teachers are explicit about their role extending beyond instructional responsibilities, to encompass a more affective and nurturing set of dispositions toward students in need.

6.4 Moral Economies and the Production of School

In the earlier sections of this chapter, I described the ways the normal school student is produced in two schools in which the ethnographies were carried out. What comes to light through the quotes and analysis presented above are the locally meaningful ways that normativity operates and the specific combinations of student subjectivities that come through in the expectations and discourses of teachers. As we look across both the cases presented in this chapter, we see gender and being played out in specific and important ways. I interpret these as being related to larger structural discursive mechanisms that produce the students and the schools. While Alerce School is a school for boys and girls, the discourse of teachers strongly leans toward descriptions of masculinity and childhood—the normal child is explicitly recognized as male since there is an overwhelming majority of boys. Descriptions focus on a vulnerable subject that lacks appropriate caring and nurturing figures in their home experiences. Teachers take up an active maternal and caring role and use it as a structural force guiding their notion of professional responsibility. In comparison, while Quillaye is a girls-only school, the notion of a normal student is described within assumed and very specific versions of acceptable and unacceptable femininity. Age plays out in specific ways as well in this context. A period of rescuability seems to taper off as girls mature into high school and transform into threats or challenges to the innocence of others. In both cases, children—especially young ones—occupy the position of needing surveillance, guidance, and moral, intellectual, and economic rescue, and as such vulnerability is a marker of the very nature of the child (Baker 1998). Descriptions of students rely heavily on the vulnerability of students to negative ends that are principally dictated by outside school factors that are inherent to the child (family, community, cultural influences) or are otherwise seen as the essence of childhood, a period of open possibility for falling onto the wrong path.

We can use the work of Fassin et al. (2015) on moral economies to help us understand the role teachers take and the frame in which their professional actions and thinking are set. Teachers in both schools feel responsible for guiding students in the appropriate direction or toward an assumed horizon of possibilities for success, and see this role as a part of their professional responsibility. Fassin et al. (2015) explains:

> … the agents of these institutions also work in reference to a certain professional ethos, to the training they have received, to an idea they have of their actions, and to a routine they develop: the principles of justice or of order, the values of the common good and public service, the attention to social or psychological realities, or the ignorance of one or the other, all products of their professional habitus, influence the manner in which they will respond to state injunctions and behave towards their publics. (p. 6–7)

In each case described above, the professional roles of teachers are produced along with those of students and in response to the deficits and vulnerabilities described in earlier paragraphs. Teachers are actors who contribute to the production of students through deliberate processes of evaluation and judgment of what is acceptable and what is not. Through this frame, they themselves are continually produced. We can understand the production of teachers' professional role as a moral economy in that it necessitates the installation and deployment of particular values and affects that uphold the norm:

> Moral economies represent the production, circulation, and appropriation of the values and affects regarding a given social issue. Consequently, the characterize for a particular historical moment and a specific social world the manner in which this issue is constituted through judgments and sentiments that gradually come to define a sort of common sense and collective understanding of the problem. (Fassin et al. 2015, p. 9)

In Quillaye School, teachers make up a sort of moral police that is vigilant over the unwieldy nature of girl students, steering them away from threats. In Alerce School, values and affects are related to the dispositions of the children toward being cared for and the role of the teachers in this school in providing this care and other guidance toward the correct path. In both cases, sets of values about who students should be, and the roles of the school and teachers influence the thoughts and practices of all actors. Teachers come to understand such values and effects as common sense, unquestionable, and an integral part of their professional identities.

The school institutions in this story are continually constituted within the frames of the specific moral economies described above. The processes of subjectivation described in earlier sections are the ongoing mechanisms of production that maintain the legitimacy and intelligibility of the school as a whole. Subjectivities of students and teachers are ordered, and the definitions of acceptable and unacceptable for both come to the fore. It is through these processes that the norms and limits for who one can be in a particular institutional setting are defined, limited, and stabilized.

References

Baker, B. (1998). Childhood-as-rescue in the emergence and spread of the US public school. In T. S. Popkewitz & M. Brennan (Eds.), *Foucault's challenge, discourse, knowledge, and power in education* (pp. 117–143). New York: Teachers College Press.

Baker, B. (2002). The hunt for disability: The new eugenics and the normalization of school children. *Teachers College Record, 104*(4), 663–703.

Bloch, M. N., Holmlund, K., Moqvist, I., & Popkewitz, T. (Eds.). (2003). *Governing children, families and education: Restructuring the welfare state*. New York: Palgrave Macmillan.

Butler, J. (1990). *Gender trouble and the subversion of identity*. New York: Routledge.

Butler, J. (1997). *Excitable speech: A politics of the performative*. New York: Routledge.

Davies, B. (2006). Subjectification: The relevance of Butler's analysis for education. *British Journal of Sociology of Education, 27*(4), 425–438.

Fassin, D., Bouagga, Y., Coutant, I., Eideliman, J. S., Fernandez, F., Fischer, N., et al. (2015). *At the heart of the state: The moral world of institutions*. London: Pluto Press.

Foucault, M. (1982). The subject and power. *Critical Inquiry, 8*(4), 777–795.

Phillips, N., Lawrence, T. B., & Hardy, C. (2004). Discourse and institutions. *Academy of Management Review, 29*(4), 635–652.

Popkewitz, T. S., & Brennan, M. (1998). Restructuring of social and political theory in education: Foucault and a social epistemology of school practices. In T. S. Popkewitz & M. Brennan (Eds.), *Foucault's challenge, discourse, knowledge, and power in education* (pp. 3–35). New York: Teachers College Press.

Wagener, J. R. (1998). The construction of the body through sex education discourse practices. In T. S. Popkewitz & M. Brennan (Eds.), *Foucault's challenge, discourse, knowledge, and power in education* (pp. 144–169). New York: Teachers College Press.

Chapter 7
Diversity and the Failure of the Civilizing Project

Laura Luna Figueroa and Alfredo Gaete

Abstract In this chapter, we show how the diversification of the school population in two Chilean public schools has turned into a crucial means for survival and an awkward problem at the same time. Coigue School and Alerce School, despite many contradictions between their discourses and their practices, seem to have embraced diversity as a value by making it the core of their educational projects. The ethnographies carried out in these two schools illustrate the deep discomfort caused by the presence of children who are "different" because of their nationalities, their cognitive abilities, their conduct or other aspects. They also make evident that another, older agenda, which we call *the civilizing project*, still prevails in school daily practice and resists against discourses on diversity. We argue that attempts at student homogenization, inspired by the ancient values of nationalism and progress, have undermined the diversity project, but without making school members truly engage with the civilizing project either.

7.1 Introduction

In Chile, many school classrooms are now far more heterogeneous than ever before. After almost two centuries, during which most of the students had the same nationality and ethnicity, and more or less the same initial set of physical and cognitive abilities, it is now easy to find a wide variety of these and other aspects, especially in nonselective schools. One reason for this *diversity turn* is the recent awareness of the universal right to education and, consequently, the quick broadening of educational coverage in the country (Ministerio de Desarrollo Social 2016). But there is another reason. In Chile, it is relatively unproblematic for state-funded schools

L. Luna Figueroa (✉)
Center for Educational Justice (CJE), Centro de Estudios Interculturales e Indígenas (CIIR), Pontificia Universidad Católica de Chile, Villarrica, Chile
e-mail: lluna@uc.cl

A. Gaete
Pontificia Universidad Católica de Chile, Villarrica, Chile
e-mail: agaetes@uc.cl

© Springer Nature Singapore Pte Ltd. 2019
C. Matus (ed.), *Ethnography and Education Policy*, Education Policy
& Social Inequality 3, https://doi.org/10.1007/978-981-13-8445-5_7

to apply student selection mechanisms and to charge an additional fee to families.[1] As a consequence, many students whose families are not able to pay the additional fee, or who have been rejected by schools for academic, behavioral or religious reasons (Valenzuela et al. 2010), end up entering nonselective educational centers. The former is the situation for many immigrant families who arrived in Chile during the last two decades from other Latin American countries, whose economic possibilities are relatively restricted; the latter is the situation for many students who have been labeled as having *disorders*, *conduct problems*, *special needs*, and so on. More generally, because currently almost everybody goes to school and many (both public and private) educational centers are selective, those with no enrollment profile, especially those with no monetary cost for families, have significantly increased their levels of student diversity. Indeed, each year they have more students who are different from the *normal* students accepted in private schools not only from a socioeconomic perspective, but also because of their behavior, their cognitive abilities, their bodily aspect, and their ethnic and national origins, among other markers of difference.[2] Moreover, they also differ among themselves in all of these aspects.[3]

This, of course, has been noted by teachers, who feel that they have not been prepared for this heterogeneity during their initial training at university or other training centers in the country. As some of them put it, they were trained to teach what are assumed to be *normal* students, not to face diversity (Gaete et al. 2016). So they are somewhat uncomfortable in these heterogeneous contexts, mainly because they feel that they do not have the pedagogical tools required to do well in them. Some even believe that children with special needs[4] should not be attended by them (regular teachers) but by specialists in special schools (Vega 2009). The children in their classes are not who they would expect to be teaching; they are too different.

This diversity turn has been both acknowledged and reinforced by policy-makers in laws providing extra economic resources for schools that have been affected by it.

---

[1] The 2015 Inclusion Law was meant to stop this, by prohibiting both selection and family fees in state-funded schools.

[2] Perhaps the socioeconomic dimension is the only one in which a certain homogeneity can be found in some of these schools. If we consider any other aspect (nationality, cultural background, cognitive abilities, etc.), heterogeneity is the rule. This contrasts strongly with what happens in private schools attended by the highest socioeconomic classes, where these kinds of differences among students are far harder to obtain. As a former student of one of these schools put it when asked how he would describe his schoolmates at that time: "They were all the same as me—all of them" (Madrid 2016, p. 279). Public schools with no selection mechanisms and expensive, non-state-funded private schools seem to be two marked extremes in the homogeneity–heterogeneity continuum regarding student intake, even though in terms of their socioeconomic composition they are both relatively homogeneous.

[3] *Diversity* is not a clear notion or fact that everybody can easily agree on. What we refer to as diversity or heterogeneity, is the complex phenomenon associated with the dissimilarities between *normal* students and others, the dissimilarities among the latter, and the variety of dimensions or aspects that those dissimilarities can obtain.

[4] Special needs is a highly controversial concept in the literature on diversity and inclusion in education. We employ it throughout the text since it is a crucial category in educational policies and programs and therefore, it is largely employed in educational practices.

Thus, despite the difficulties teachers have teaching diverse students, many schools are openly welcoming to such students. Moreover, given the voucher system that was implemented in the country some decades ago (Paredes 2016), taking students who have not been (or would not be) accepted in other schools becomes very attractive for educational institutions struggling with financial sustainability since schools are funded according to the number of pupils they have. Moreover, the state offers extra money for children with special needs through the Program for Educational Integration, and for children categorized as a *priority* in the School Preferential Subvention Law.[5]

All of this has brought enormous challenges to daily school practices and, as we argue in this chapter, to the schooling project itself. We reflect upon certain difficulties, contradictions, and dilemmas that two Chilean public schools must face as a result of the proliferation of difference in their enrollment rates. Based on an ethnographic analysis of social practices in these institutions, we show how the problems they are experiencing with diverse students are tied to the idea of schooling as a civilizing project—an idea that emerged with the first educational establishments of the republic and which is still in place in Chilean schools, despite having lost much of its previous thrust and appeal. We describe how this project is displayed, experienced, and resisted in both schools, and also its progression against the pressure of another, more recently adopted project, which we refer to as the *diversity project*. By this we mean the institutional attempt, also present in the two schools, to turn the diversification of the school population into something desirable or positive. This attempt is usually conveyed by resorting to the conceptual framework of multiculturalism and inclusion. However, and this is part of what we argue too, these alleged multicultural and inclusive endeavors are weak or superficial and do not manage to replace the quite entrenched view—inherited from the civilizing project—that one of the main purposes of schooling is to homogenize people. Our main tenet is that both schools struggle to carry out these two incompatible projects—the diversity and the civilizing project—not only because they perceive at some level that it is logically impossible to succeed in doing so but also because the assimilationist view concealed under the (false) labels of *multiculturalism* and *inclusion* is quite hard to achieve in practice. School members experience this as a vacuum of meaning, in so far as they end up believing that neither of the two projects that are available to make sense of schooling can, in fact, be carried out.

The chapter is structured as follows. First, we present an overview of the general conceptual framework guiding our analysis. Then for each of the two schools, we offer a brief ethnographic description, focusing on the elements that are relevant for the purposes indicated above. Each description is followed by an account of how the diversity project is dealt with in every school and how it is experienced by the school members. Next, we elaborate on the conception of schooling as a civilizing project

---

[5]The label *priority* is used in Chilean law to identify children experiencing poverty. The School Preferential Subvention Law, enforced since 2008, provides extra funding for children whose socioeconomic conditions are deemed to be an impediment for their achievement (see Valenzuela et al. 2013).

and show how such a project is enacted in the two schools. Finally, we present our discussion of how this conception and implementation of schooling clash with the diversity project, and the way in which this is experienced in both schools.

7.2 School and the Production of the Person

Our analysis draws on anthropological approaches to the study of school practice. Ethnographic insights into school life have allowed schooling to be seen as more than a functional device operating either for the imposition of a political order (Meyer 1977; Ramirez and Boli 1987) or for the reproduction of the social structure (Bourdieu and Passeron 1977). A solid body of ethnographic analyses of daily school practice and subjectivities reveals the weight of human agency in the process of educating citizens. Students, teachers, and other school members do more than simply pass on and absorb messages: they can also ignore them, reinterpret them, and resist them (Apple and Weis 1983; Giroux 1983; Levinson et al. 1996). The process of socialization, which is supported and generated through schooling, is mediated by the person who has an active and creative role in both reproducing and resisting social order.

From this point of view, schools are "sites for the formation of subjectivities through the production and consumption of cultural forms" (Levinson et al. 1996, pp. 13–14). Without denying the (undeniable) reproductive role of the school, the focus is on the production of the person through social practices. Schools are "communities of practice" (Wenger 1998) in which a group of people regularly coexist and actively participate in a "joint enterprise", constructing a "shared repertoire" that is comprised of symbols, words, stories, ideas, routines, gestures, actions, and so on (p. 83). The production of the educated person occurs not solely as an effect of structural social conditions; it is a process that takes place within a specific community, by means of the unique ways through which people experience social conditions in intersubjective relations and build meaning together. Processes of sense-making, discourse production, negotiation, and resistance are crucial components of the complex phenomenon of citizen education at school. School practice is, in this sense, the embodiment of sociopolitical projects, which can be permanently re-signified in people's participation in specific communities of practice. From this perspective, researchers, especially from critical and resistance theory (see Evans 2006; Everhart 1983; Foley 1990; Levinson 1996; Luna 2015a, b; McLaren 1986; Willis 1977), reveal the tensions and fractures between those projects and the views and experiences of the participants in the community of practice of each school.

The basis of our analysis is the ethnographic material produced within the NDE project in six schools in Santiago, as explained in the introduction, but our attention is focused on two public schools, namely, Coigue and Alerce. We mostly rely on the description of daily school practices during nonclass instances, for example, hall situations, children's interactions at break time, and extracurricular events. Observations at class time are also taken into account, with a focus not on pedagogical relations but rather on social interactions between children and between children and adults. Particular attention is paid to instructions and normative practices that show a clear intention to rule children's behavior. Finally, we also consider information from both formal interviews and informal conversations with school teachers and authorities that make explicit the contradictions between the officially declared multicultural or inclusive project and school members' perceptions and experiences.

7.3   Coigue School and the Diversity Turn

Coigue School is a public school located to the northwest of the city center of Santiago de Chile. It has several features that are common to many other Chilean public schools: low academic achievement (measured by means of standardized tests), a high percentage of children categorized as *vulnerable*,[6] and high levels of discontent among staff. Teachers frequently complain about the lack of resources, the amount of administrative work, and the pressure to improve academic achievement in what they experience as bad working conditions.[7] Additionally, approximately one-third of its students have been classified as having special needs and are part of the Program for Educational Integration, which was created a year before the study was carried out. Moreover, there are a few students who receive permanent medical attention in a room especially designed for the purpose, called the *hospital room*.

In recent years, the school's enrollment has decreased abruptly, going from 1,000 students to 300. Due to the voucher scheme, under which, as previously mentioned, schools obtain state funding according to the number of pupils they have, the school has suffered dramatic economic consequences. The abolition of all selection mechanisms was the way the school coped with them, resulting in a diversification of the student population. Unlike in the recent past, when the school served mainly Chilean families in relatively good socioeconomic situations, nowadays the majority of students (60%) come from immigrant families (from Perú, Ecuador, Colombia, and Bolivia) with poor socioeconomic conditions or who are even experiencing poverty. As a cleaning assistant explained:

> The school used to have many more children [...] There used to be "good status people" here. Now things are different. Children are from the middle class like me [...] There have always been foreigners, but there were only a few. Then, when children started to leave the school, *peruanitos* [little Peruvians] came, because there is no discrimination here.

Despite the evident signs of discomfort that the presence of immigrants provokes among the staff, the school has made a significant attempt to turn this situation into its hallmark, especially in circumstances in which staff dissatisfaction has produced

---

[6]For a critical analysis of how the term *vulnerability* is employed in educational policies and practices, see Gaete and Gómez (2019).

[7]These seem to be some of the main reasons why Chilean teachers have especially high attrition rates (see Gaete et al. 2016).

a general detachment from the school project (we will return to this shortly). Furthermore, a diagnosis by the National Drug and Alcohol Prevention and Rehabilitation Program revealed a lack of sense of belonging and identification with the school among students. In this context, a multicultural image was shaped as the chance to give new inspiration and a reinvigorated identity to the school community. A new school hymn was composed, in which a direct reference is made to the different flags and colors that are now part of the school community—and different kinds of representation of the multicultural character of the school started to occupy both the calendar, with several extracurricular activities, and the facilities, with symbols and paintings alluding to different nationalities.

7.3.1 The Display and Experience of the Multicultural Project in Coigue School

Coigue School's concern with creating both a self-representation and a public image as a multicultural school is reflected in the big wall painting of the so-called *small yard*, where flags from Chile, Perú, Ecuador, Argentina, Panamá, Colombia, and Bolivia are painted around the term *Latin America*. The latter appears written in big letters in the middle of a natural landscape of sea, sky, hills, and animals, which seems to suggest the harmony of different nationalities living together. In addition to this wall, in the *big yard*, another representation exalting the cultural peculiarities from different Latin American countries was being painted during the fieldwork year: a figurative map of Latin America where different icons (typical dresses, musical instruments, important statues, etc.) allude to the identity of each region. In other parts of the school, the exhibition of several writings done by the children themselves reaffirms the message of *sameness in difference*, with sentences such as: "We are all equal.... Latin America always united."

The crucial event in which the school's multiculturalism is performed and enacted is the Family Latin American Festival. Every year, a group of students represents a Latin American country by performing a typical national dance during the Festival. The spirit of the event is transmitted in big writing on a blue background, which reads: "Latin America, only one people." The different countries are represented by their flags, the Chilean one obviously being larger than the others. The event starts with the singing of the Chilean national anthem—albeit sung without much vigor or enthusiasm by the assembly. As aforementioned, every year a group performs a characteristic dance: salsa from Cuba, cumbia from Colombia, tango from Argentina, and so on. Colorful dresses are worn by the girls who perform in the show. After the dances, the whole school community is invited to share typical food from each country.

Another way in which engagement with the multicultural project is shown is participation in the Intercultural Encounter, which takes place in Yungay Park, a well-known public space in the center of Santiago. Here, many schools of the neighborhood exhibit dance performances from different zones of Chile and other countries. Coigue School takes part with a dance from a Latin American country. However, there is no chance for a proper *encounter* here, for the groups and their audience leave after their own presentation. In this sense, the event seems to have a merely performative character.

Beyond these events, which are all part of the school calendar and impact the children's school participation insofar as they require the rehearsal of the shows, there are no institutional orientations, either pedagogical or social, or of any other kind, to approach the issues that the presence of children from different countries or cultures may raise. The challenge of taking into account the cultural or academic background of immigrant students for a more situated pedagogy appears only as an individual initiative, and it is neither encouraged nor supported by an institutional policy or plan. This was confirmed by a math teacher in an interview, who pointed to the lack of school programs on this matter. Having noticed that foreign children bring to school different ways of performing mathematical operations, as a personal approach to student heterogeneity, she had decided to study the methods they had been taught in order to provide these children with proper support.

A delicate situation is produced with content that may be particularly problematic to teach to students from other countries, especially when they cover military facts and international relations between Chile and other Latin American countries. The 1879 Iquique Naval Battle, which took place during the Pacific War (against Perú and Bolivia), is taught in a way that is not substantially different from how it would be taught in any other Chilean public school. In particular, the presence of both Peruvian and Bolivian students does not lead teachers to question the appropriateness of the academic content presented in most Chilean history textbooks, which is that Chilean people rightfully defend their country from the intrinsically unfair actions of Peruvians and Bolivians. The math teacher, for instance, acknowledged in an interview that Peruvian people have "their own truth" about history and that they must be listened to. However, her admittance of different perspectives on historical facts did not prompt her to challenge the idea that some perspectives count more than others: Peruvian and Bolivian people, she concluded, simply have to accept without protest the international agreements on the division of the territory, all made after Chile won the war.

Although the presence of immigrant children does not lead to questioning the way in which school members see historical facts, it does frequently appear as the referent, more or less implicitly, which informs the way in which current situations of school life are seen, valued, and experienced. Indeed, in many nonformal interactions, the students' condition of being foreigners is alluded to as an explanatory matter, as the object of a paradox and sarcasm, or as an explicit threat.

During informal conversations, teachers refer to the high presence of immigrant families as the cause of parents' poor participation in school events. Children's *at risk* condition (so diagnosed in the National Drug and Alcohol Prevention and Rehabilitation Program report mentioned above) is immediately associated with the Peruvian supposed cultural habit of drinking. Children's positive characteristics are also explained by virtue of their "culture": Venezuelans are good at music because it is in their blood, whereas Colombians are shrewd because they have been trained in Escobar's culture.

Irony and sarcasm seem to be useful tools to cope with disappointment when certain milestones in school life do not take place in the way they used to, or are expected to. This is true of the comment, "They are all Chilean!", followed by laughter from a teacher celebrating the prizes obtained by students—all immigrants—who participated in a soccer championship. Discomfort is also expressed with laughter by a teacher when asked about the dance that children were preparing for an event: "They are all Peruvian and foreigners!—he prompted—There is such a mixture of races! I don't know what will happen with this, we are all mixed." In both cases, the teachers' comments seem to reveal the disappointment created by the fact that the protagonists of important school achievements and events are not Chilean people. Performances that nurture school pride and image are led by immigrants, a fact that seems to diminish their value. The creator of the Latin American Festival, at the beginning of the event, exclaimed: "Nationalities do not matter, let's show we are all Chilean!", which also reveals the idea that the presence of different nationalities may discredit the school image, and therefore, since it cannot be concealed, at least efforts must be made to keep it low profile.

While teachers and adults were cautious about expressing their worries or distrust about the presence of immigrant students, some Chilean students explicitly manifested their aversion to them. On different occasions, insulting and racist comments toward immigrants could be heard. "Dirty indian!", a child shouted to a girl with Andean features, while one girl commented, "There are a lot of black people and they stink!". Furthermore, on the school's Dream Wall, where children are invited to report their dreams, one can read: "My dream is that Peruvians go home."

We believe that these assertions provide evidence that not only is multiculturalism in Coigue School not sufficiently engaging to inspire a new sense of identity, as it was meant to, but it is also explicitly resisted. Further on in this chapter, we describe how the civilizing project, based on ideals of cultural homogenization, acts daily in school practices, invalidating (implicitly) multicultural pretensions.

7.4   Alerce, the Open School

Alerce School is located in the center of Santiago, in an old neighborhood with a high percentage of immigrants. This is reflected in school enrollment, with approximately 50 of its 200 students being immigrants, mainly from Ecuador and Argentina. Most of the children come from families with low educational levels and high socioeconomic instability, indeed, 63 students are considered a *priority*. Moreover, 15 students have been categorized as having special needs: 11 have been diagnosed with a cognitive deficit, 2 with Asperger syndrome, and 2 with auditory disability. However, 47 children receive professional attention in the Program for Educational Integration, since they are deemed to have special needs, even if they have not been diagnosed with a specific condition. Furthermore, there are another 11 students who are not part of the Program for Educational Integration, even though some teachers believe they should be. Extra support is provided by specialists to children with academic and socio-emotional difficulties, with resources obtained through the School Preferential Subsidy Law (*Ley SEP*), which, as aforementioned, provides funding to schools with priority children. A further feature of the student population is its high level of rotation: children can leave, but they can also get into the school at almost any time of the year.

Because Alerce was one of the few schools in Chile that in 2002 began implementing the Program for Educational Integration, it is publicly acknowledged as an *inclusive school*. However, its inclusiveness is also related to the welcoming spirit of the school, whose children approached it "either because of adaptation difficulties or due to academic issues, which make them unwanted in other schools", as the principal explained. In 2008 she took on the leadership of the school and gave a new impulse and meaning to inclusion by implementing significant changes in order to improve the general quality of the educational provision: reorganization of the management team functions, teamwork and peer cooperation for the improvement of teaching practices, and different strategies for parental engagement, among other measures. These changes reactivated teachers' commitment and sense of responsibility toward children's learning and well-being. The new leadership encouraged staff into adopting the idea that every child can learn and that the school mission is to provide children with all they need to fully develop their potential. The idea that learning occurs through integral development has made teachers and staff place greater emphasis on students' socio-emotional dimensions, and particularly on the creation of affective bonds with them. Nevertheless, the principal's inclusive approach has not found general acceptance among teachers, who cope daily with the difficulties of providing adequate responses to a high and growing number of children's cognitive, academic, emotional, and material needs.

7.4.1 The Display and Experience of the Inclusive Project in Alerce School

Beyond the school entrance, banners depict the school's vision for visitors: "Educating the child, foreseeing the responsible youngster of tomorrow, educated in the value of justice, trusting his/her capacities to be positively integrated into society." The principal, in her first meeting with the ethnographers, presented the school as "different" based on the kind of students it takes, which are "special". "We are an open school, an inclusive school", which makes things more difficult, she added. What makes the school enrollment "different" or "special" is "the high number of vulnerable or special needs children", said the principal, using the categories one finds in the country's educational policies. She explained "vulnerability" in terms of a lack of affect, poverty, situations of abuse, and parental abandonment, which are deemed, among other factors, to be the main reasons for children's rebellious and aggressive behavior. Being conscious of children's backgrounds helps teachers to react in a welcoming and dialogical way to insurgent attitudes. For instance, Benjamín, a 10-year-old Year 1 student, is approached with conversations and hugs when he tries to escape from the classroom. The teacher explained this reaction by arguing that what children need most is affect. The school takes responsibility for the provision of basic emotional containment, as well as for the satisfaction of basic biological needs. Therefore, it has become part of the inclusive tenet to keep a mattress in the principal's office for a child who has sleeping problems at night because he shares a bed with his brother and father. It is also accepted that another child takes a shower when he is at school, since he comes to school dirty. Families are criticized harshly for their lack of commitment toward their children, which is proved—according to staff—by their poor participation in parents' meetings, lack of collaboration, and lack of care.[8] In order to overcome the difficulties of communication and relations with families, the school has established the *Papinota* (memo for parents) system, consisting of the use of text messages sent to parents' cell phones with reminders about meetings or comments on their children's performance.

Problems relating to children's abilities are addressed through the Program for Educational Integration, which is carried out by a team of specialists: a psychologist, a speech therapist, and two special needs teachers, who work with children in the classroom and in a special room where they take some children for specific activities. They usually intervene in complex situations where children have what is considered as *antisocial behavior* or present an emergent issue that forbids them from staying quietly in the classroom. For instance, children who are deemed to suffer from "decompensation", because they shout, or try to escape or beat somebody, are taken to the trampoline in order to restore their balance. Pushing balls, recently purchased by the school, is meant to have a similar function. Some of the children are also given medication to handle their behavior. However, despite this plurality of strategies designed to deal with children's particular conditions, no pedagogical changes or adaptations have been made to provide them with more flexible assessments or extra support.

In line with the findings of contemporary educational research in the country (see introduction), teachers' general opinion is that they do not have the competencies to attend to children's needs. They also believe that the support provided by the Program for Educational Integration is totally insufficient, as the number of children classified with special needs or ability issues exceeds the maximum accepted for public funding. One teacher noted that it is the very fact of having an integration program that has created the increase in the number of children with special needs, since it made the local authority send such children to the school. However, the definition of who needs support from the Program for Educational Integration is

---

[8]This negative discourse about the families is widely extended among schools in poverty contexts (Gaete and Gómez 2019). It usually shows a deficit ideology (Gorski 2016), as well as an uncritical way of thinking, by means of which teachers "succumb to, and reinforce, the negative images society tends to construct of families experiencing poverty" (Gaete and Gómez 2019).

so comprehensive that most of the children easily fit it. Indeed, in Year 1, 75% of children are considered part of the program, albeit most of them informally, since the attention provided by the program is not financially covered in most cases. However, as pointed out above, there are also children that, according to the teachers, should be part of the program but are not, either formally or informally. Therefore, there is a general feeling among teachers that the number of children with special needs goes beyond the school capacity to cope with the associated difficulties.

So, while the principal, in a meeting with the parents of children in the integration program, encouraged them by reminding them that Alerce School had given hope to their children and that, with their help, the children would learn, the teachers expressed skepticism, anguish, and fear. One teacher described the vertiginous increase in the number of special needs children as "a disaster". Despite the sort of ethical or moral commitment that many teachers manifest toward the students deemed *at risk*, they feel totally overwhelmed and, more or less explicitly, judge the school as irresponsible for accepting special needs students beyond the maximum established by public policy—even if they understand that it is due to the general decrease in student enrollment, which makes the application of filters or subtle forms of selection unviable. Fears about becoming a special school and ending up performing another professional role—psychologist or social worker—rather than that of educator, appeared in many conversations with teachers. One teacher, who had been working in the school for less than a year, commented that she was exhausted; she loved her job, but felt she was drowning. She described in quite clear terms the tension with the school authorities, mentioning that when the teachers complained about the problematic situations of some children who were particularly disruptive, the answer was that the "school door is wide open", which made her feel like she had her hands tied. "What should I do? I need a float! And I can't have it!"

On the other hand, teachers with a long history in the school made several nostalgic comments about Alerce School's past. Both students and parents used to "participate more" and "respect teachers more." One teacher sustained that the lack of a sense of authority is due to psychologists who have emphasized children's rights, causing them to fail in their duties. In the past, another teacher complained, children who passed from preschool to Year 1 used to come "clean, properly combed, and shy, but later on, when preschool was abolished in the school, we started receiving in Year 1 children who had not had any pre-school experience, who had not studied…uuuh. Now Year 1 children kick the teacher".

The idea of setting a limit was recurrent in the teachers' discourse. "One can be highly committed to helping children, but there's a limit you clash with", one teacher said. Complaints that the number of special needs children was above the legal "limits" were numerous. The need to evoke the idea of borders or limits in a context where teachers are explicit about being overwhelmed because of their daily experience of "difference" reveals the concern with reaching a point in which the school itself may lose those basic conditions that define it as such. The daily manifestations of what seems to be the ungovernability of diversity make real, in teachers' eyes, the threat of becoming something other than a school. Daily practices of providing satisfactory basic needs (such as affect, sleep, toilet), or of coping with antisocial behavior, create the idea that the work carried out in school looks more like the task of a social worker than educational labor.

In Alerce School, inclusion is perceived as a challenge that goes beyond staff capacities, since the circumstances—for example, the number of children with special needs—make it too hard to achieve. However, it should be noted that in this school, being inclusive does not seem to be simply rhetorical; nor does it mean accepting everybody. It also implies changes in staff attitudes (more focused on affect and basic needs) and expectations (lower in terms of achievement).[9] Moreover, several strategies are being implemented and incorporated into the school's daily life in order to attend to children's needs. In the next sections, we analyze how several of these strategies (e.g., the pushing ball or trampoline), despite being designed as an inclusive or welcoming answer to diversity, are expressions of clear intent of normalization within the framework of the civilizing project.

7.5   Schooling as Civilizing

Regardless of the discourses and practices introduced in the school functioning as a result of the adoption of a multicultural or inclusive scheme, school life in both centers is regulated by a set of norms, rules, routines, rites, and symbols which have been the object of study in different schools throughout the world (see Evans 2006; Jackson 1968; McLaren 1986). This similarity is related to the origins of schooling, which, according to some authors, is linked to the creation of a European model of national society (Ramirez and Boli 1987). Indeed, as in many other countries, the foundation of the first schools in Chile was partly motivated by the political project of modern nation-states (see Peña 2015; Serrano et al. 2012; Tiramonti 2005). This project rested on a "developmental", "progressive", or "evolutionary" conception of culture. This idea was part of the Enlightenment tale according to which all cultures "could be ranked or placed in stages, from low to high, from savage to civilized, from primitive to modern, from backward to advanced, culminating in the way of life of the English, the French, or the Germans" (Shweder 2002, p. 118). The modern school was meant to carry out this civilizing project in the emerging democracies of the eighteenth and nineteenth centuries (see Butts 1967; Díaz Arce and Druker 2007; Dubet 2006; Peim 2001; Ramirez and Boli 1987; Tiramonti 2005). Mainly through disciplinary practices, formal education had to prepare citizens for the new social order—or, as Peim (2001) put it, to "transform the unregulated human material of the urban population into the trained and self-disciplined citizen of modernity" (p. 182).

---

[9]This, of course, is a very particular way of construing inclusion, given that none of the several accounts of inclusive education one can find in the literature describes it in these terms. Actually, inclusive schools are usually conceived of as being open to *all* students and as having relatively high expectations about their capacity to learn. This is why (genuine) inclusive pedagogy focuses on school practices, cultures, and policies rather on students' alleged deficits or special needs (see Ainscow 1995; Booth and Ainscow 2000; Florian and Kershner 2009; UNESCO 2004).

It is not surprising, then, that one of the first measures of the Chilean state just after its constitution in 1810 was to start an educational project, which, in the words of its intellectual author, was intended to "create, confer political existence and opinion to a nation that has never had it" (Serrano et al. 2012, p. 63; see also Díaz Arce and Druker 2007; Egaña Baraona 2000; Peña 2015). A year later the *Instituto Nacional*—the first public school—was founded in order to educate the governing class. As for the education of the governed class, another institution, the *Escuela Normal de Preceptores*, was created by Sarmiento in 1842, with the understanding that the "savage" population had to be "civilized" (Serrano et al. 2012, p. 78; see also Egaña Baraona 2000). Its purpose was to prepare "preceptors" to take the popular classes out of the primitive, barbarian state they were supposed to be in—a task that its own foundational decree conceived of as "the basis of intellectual progress" (Serrano et al. 2012, p. 83).

However, beyond the crucial differences between these two early schools, one teaching "to govern the republic", and the other "to govern the poor" (Serrano et al. 2012, p. 83), both of them, and in fact all of the public schools founded during the following decades in the country, had the aim of developing the moral character required to produce a nation under the Enlightenment's progressive notion of culture. Whether students attended schools to govern or to be governed, all of them were expected to become citizens in the modern sense of the word, by acquiring a common set of values and principles that would make them feel that they were all Chilean. The nation had to be built, and one of the main goals of the school was to do so through the implementation of the civilizing project inherited from Europe (see Díaz Arce and Druker 2007). The project involved bodily training and the deployment of civic rites to transmit discipline and order (Serrano et al. 2012). Certain "school habits" are created, such as to "raise one's hand before speaking, form a line to enter and leave the classroom, address the teacher as 'Sir' and the students by their surnames, sit straight, refrain from talking during the lesson, etc." (Díaz Arce and Druker 2007, p. 67). This followed closely the modern European model of school work, in which students learn how to control their bodies and their more instinctive life through "the repetition of exercises presented like many other formal rites: learn by rote, recite, copy, form a line, answer when spoken to" (Dubet 2006, p. 51). In the next section, we focus on two dimensions of the social practice studied in Coigue School and Alerce School, which show how the civilizing project is still in place: body control and recruitment for national citizenship, which also encompasses the transmission of cognitive and operational skills. These dimensions are deeply interconnected, the first one, body control, is particularly crucial. What nineteenth-century thinkers called "morality", one of the main aims of education, is achieved mainly through ruling the body, which is also necessary to express attachment to national symbols and values (e.g., singing the national anthem) and to show the right disposition to develop cognitive skills (e.g., sitting quietly and paying attention to the teacher).

7.5.1 The Enactment of the Civilizing Project

Body control encompasses several aspects and is manifested in different forms. The education of the body requires, in the first place, appropriating the distinction between private and public spaces so that body expressions are regulated accordingly. Usually, in schools, there are no private spaces for children, except for the bathroom. Bathrooms are separated by gender and are provided with a common area and an individual area. In the latter basic necessities can be met, while not being seen by other people. Even if the common area is not completely private, entering it allows certain behavior that is not permitted outside. The bathroom door, therefore, establishes a first limit between different regimes of body control, and the toilet door establishes a new one. This means that, albeit different, a normativity is established for each space. In Coigue and Alerce schools, the bathroom is seen as both the place where bodies can be totally unruly, because of its private nature, and as the appropriate setting for restoration and recovery. The supervisor (inspector), the figure in charge of behavior and order in schools, is usually the person who normalizes the use of the bathroom.

> You girls, why don't you stop arguing? Can't you see that, apart from making me scold you, it is bad that you fight with each other? Moreover, you are messy. You'd better go to the bathroom, sort it out and clean up.

The supervisor of Coigue School continued, explaining the rationale behind the intervention: "Some girls have a more developed body; therefore they must be *señoritas* [ladies] and behave accordingly."

In Alerce School, one particular situation demonstrated how the bathroom can also be a risky place. A girl came out of the bathroom with wet hair and clothes. The supervisor asked her why she had that appearance and the girl answered that she was hot. The supervisor told her to take off her apron and hang it on a tree to let it dry. After a while, another girl came out of the bathroom, also very wet. The supervisor tried to get into the bathroom but the door was closed. She knocked firmly on the door, asking for it to be opened. Since nobody answered, she took the keys from her pocket and reproached the girls, ordering them to get out. "If you behaved as a *señorita*, this would not happen to you", she said to one of the girls as she left the bathroom.

Being a key component of body control, a neat appearance is valued very highly within the school apparatus. It implies looking clean, well combed, with the body appropriately covered and clothes properly worn, and avoiding any bad smells. For this reason, in Coigue School, after Physical Education, Year 8 boys are sent to the bathroom to wash their armpits and apply deodorant. The school uniform is a key element of the neat appearance that is expected for the body. Wearing the uniform is a sign of adhesion to the educational project and, particularly, to the educational project of a specific school, because in Chile every school has its own uniform, where the school name and logo are embroidered on one side. Therefore, the uniform is a sign of distinction and belonging and, at the same time, imposes a standardization and order and gives account of the massive recruitment into the educational enterprise. This fact is clearly revealed by the reaction in Alerce School to the idea (proposed by one teacher) to abolish the school uniform, given that it was scarcely worn by students. Unanimously, it was argued that, despite the norm that it was, in practice, not followed, its mere existence contributes to order and control. However, what this episode actually seems to show is that a rule that imposes standardization and homogenization, where the difference is the norm, has a relieving effect on staff, somehow counteracting the general lack of order and normality that they experience in the school.

As a complement to the uniform, in the demonstration of recruitment and submission, the formation activity is another important component of the performativity of schooling. Every day, before getting into the classroom, or at the end of the school day, before leaving the building, children are recalled by means of a resounding bell to gather and position themselves in lines, besides their course teacher (*formación, formarse*). The teacher assumes an authoritative tone, reinforcing what seems to be trying to emulate a military parade, as the following extract from Alerce School shows:

Teacher 1: Line up! Line up! [¡*A formarse!* ¡*A formarse!*]

Teacher 2: Girls of that course must come out! [Pointing. They get out.]

Sebastián: Come here and line up!!

Teacher 3: Let's see, Year 5 is in line. Okay. Goodbye.

Teacher 2: Come and line up, come and line up.

Child 1: We want to take the ball!

Teacher 2: No! There's only one owner of the ball.

Teacher 1: García! García! Come out walking! What are you doing there? See you! Year 8 girls! Out! Year 8 girls! Out! Come out orderly!

There are fewer children inside the school. Many of them have not lined up and are hanging around. Laura, from Year 4 or 6, is waiting behind a post.[10]

Formarse or lining up, like the uniform, is charged with meaning. It is a rite whereby students are reminded of their belonging to the school as an institution and also to a particular school. Like making the sign of the cross before leaving a church or ending a prayer, *formarse* is an act of underpinning adhesion to a set of beliefs and ideology just before moving into a space and time where that adhesion could be less evident. So, before crossing the school limits to go home, children are required to corroborate their recruitment to the civilizing project. They do it by temporarily submitting their bodies to new restrictions (of movements) before freeing them from school norms and exposing them to an area outside the school's control.

If moral neatness is demonstrated through a clean and tidy physical appearance, language is another important expression of it, especially for women. Again, the supervisor in Coigue School commented on the importance of girls having a proper language: "They must speak properly and not swear so people of a better status may want to interact with them." It seems evident that language acquisition, more than a

---

[10]Fieldnote extract.

tool for understanding the world or for social mobility, is seen rather as a presentation card that opens possibilities of social acceptance from other, more valuable, social classes.

While all the forms of body control described above are applied to all the children (despite often being stricter for women), particular measures are designed for certain kinds of students. In Alerce School, medication is an established practice favored by the school to regulate systematic and more "extreme" expressions of antisocial behavior. Medication is used when children are deemed unable to be part of the school space because their way of being is a "danger" to other children. Medication is not provided by the school, but the school requires parents to give it to their children regularly; otherwise, they cannot go to school. Pedro was formally banned from school since he was not taking his medicine, having been diagnosed with neurological disorders; therefore, he had missed 25 days of school. This case was addressed in a teachers' meeting, where the principal expressed her concerns since children's prolonged absences affect the voucher scheme that the school benefits from. However, despite the dilemma that this kind of case places the school in, accepting the prolonged absence is preferred to the eventuality of having a "decompensated" (as it is called) body out of control within the school space. Other devices are less invasive and designed for more occasional decompensation: the pushing ball and the trampoline, which are, as previously mentioned, innovative strategies adopted by Alerce School to help some kinds of special needs children, and which are also meant to govern imbalanced bodies.

Recruitment for national citizenship, the second dimension of the civilizing project that we looked at, is expressed, in the first instance, through submission to school institutionality. Being governed by a set of norms and by a group of people who are invested in particular faculties by virtue of their role is the basic condition for belonging to the national project. For this reason, children are constantly expected to demonstrate their acceptance of, or subordination to, rules and adult roles through situations such as lining up similarly to a military parade, but also, and more frequently, through small gestures of recognition of adult authorities and of the formality of the school space. Taking one's hat off the head, standing up when the teacher enters the classroom, among other signs imposed on children in daily school life, are meant to remind them of the official and institutional character of the place they inhabit at all times. Obedience is the first virtue that children are expected to show as evidence of their belonging to the nation-state community.

However, the sense of national belonging is also cultivated through the circulation of specific symbols associated with the nation-state, such as exhibiting the flag and singing the national anthem. Even during the Latin American Festival in Coigue School, which may be considered the most emblematic event of the school in terms of endorsing multiculturalism, the Chilean flag is exhibited much more prominently than the other Latin American flags, and the national anthem begins the celebration. The exaltation of national identity above other feelings of belonging is made explicit through the words of the teacher who leads the Festival celebration: "Nationalities do not matter. Let's show we are all Chilean. This is the real integration in Coigue School!" Furthermore, as previously mentioned, history classes that approach controversial relationships among Latin American countries show that the last word always goes to the Chilean perspective.

Finally, the training of cognitive skills is the primary objective around which school activities are organized. Children spend most of their school time in the class-rooms where that training is expected to take place. It has previously been discussed how the transmission of what was considered crucial knowledge to integrating the labor market and exerting political rights was one of the basic tenets of mass school-ing during the eighteenth century. This basic function of schooling is clearly still valid since, beyond the permanent emphasis on the different kinds of body performance related to recruitment, most of the time children are expected to do cognitive work: listening, answering, writing, reading, and reasoning around a given academic sub-ject. However, class participation in the Alerce and Coigue schools does not account for teachers' real concern with the fact that children develop certain abilities or mas-ter particular subjects. Children, with the exception of a few, are mostly disengaged from academic activities and do not follow teachers' instructions; and, for their part, teachers do not seem to make an authentic effort to engage them. Shouting, calling for attention, and censuring inappropriate behavior occupy most of the class time and seem to be oriented toward supervising children's disposition to learn rather than ensuring effective learning. The following scene from a class in Coigue School illustrates this point:

> The teacher asks the children to stand up. "But we said hello already in the morning," a student says. "But now we have a guest, so we need to do it again," the teacher orders. The children say hello with a total lack of enthusiasm. The teacher starts a speech about them having to work harder, as many of them are failing that course subject—and not only because of their low grades but also because some have too many absences. She asks one of the girls, "How is it that you can get such good grades?" "She takes drugs!" says another student, and everybody laughs. The teacher continues with her speech on the need to try harder. Some listen to her, whereas others quickly lose interest and get distracted. Their body posture begins to decline. They slide down in their seats. The teacher says that all of the content is in the textbook and that they must study from it. One student complains that some of the content is not in the book. Another one, from the back of the room, makes comments and weird noises from time to time. Some children frequently laugh at the teacher. She talks about the scholarships they can win for entering educational programs for good students, which could eventually allow them the possibility to go to university when they finish their secondary studies. One girl replies that she is no longer allowed to apply, because she is older than 14 years old. The teacher ignores her, showing confusion. Then she starts reprimanding the children: "Sit up right! Open your notebooks! Shout out! Take off that cap! Write this down!" She orders a boy to open his notebook. "I didn't bring it," he answers. "Use a sheet of paper, then," she says; and he replies, "I didn't bring any." She says, "Then, look at the board!" The boy: "I can't see." "That's not my problem! Listen, then!" she answers.[11]

The teacher's discourse sought to motivate the children to improve their attainment in order to prepare them for higher education, which may be accessible through scholarships. However, the students did not take her words seriously. They reacted with jokes and laughter, and showed a lack of interest through their body postures. The teacher became impatient with the children's reactions and ended up shouting

---

[11] Fieldnote extract.

that it is not her problem that a child does not have the proper conditions to participate in academic activities, thus revealing her lack of interest in the children's learning.

During class time teachers resort to several technical devices to deploy their teaching role and intent: they write the objective of the lesson on the board, ask questions to elicit previous knowledge, call for attention to be paid to the subject, provide explanations, and so on. However, all of these actions demonstrate their concern with performing as a teacher rather than with teaching. Students, for their part, pay little attention to the teachers' instructions. They make noises, interfere with academic interactions, do not take out their notebooks and do not write anything in them, even tending to escape the classroom, as is frequently the case in Alerce School. They seem to perceive that teachers' actions have a merely performative function as if they were simulating teaching, without a real expectation of achieving academic learning. However, for the civilizing purpose academic learning is not what matters. The teachers' performance seems sufficient for transmitting very basic skills to the majority of children since children will eventually leave school managing to decode written information and do basic mathematical operations, which is everything they need to obtain academic certification and thereby to be recruited into national society.

However, students are mostly reluctant about recruitment. This is not just evident in the classroom—in which, as shown in the previous extract, academic work is evaded and even resisted though jokes and sarcasm. It is also made explicit in the scarce use of the uniform and the unwillingness to line up and, generally, to obey and show respect to adults and follow rules. The lack of enthusiasm for singing the national anthem can also be read as a sign of disengagement from the recruitment mission of schooling.

7.6   Discussion

The two schools involved in our study have embraced a discourse of institutional acceptance and even a celebration of difference. In Alerce School, this discourse feeds from the conceptual framework of inclusive education, especially from what has been labeled *mainstreaming* (Artiles et al. 2006; Baker 2002; Graham and Slee 2008)—the idea that everybody can be educated in mainstream schools, including those who are described as having disabilities or special needs. In Coigue School, the acceptance discourse is couched in terms of multiculturalism and, more specifically, the idea that the presence of different cultures and nationalities can be a positive contribution to the school community. It does not define itself as a *multicultural school*, but their members openly recognize cultural rights and the value of the coexistence of different cultural ways of being, particularly when, by talking of "Latin American brotherhood", they exalt the cultural uniqueness of the different countries.

The official endorsement of diversity as something positive has different implications for each school. In Alerce School, being inclusive entails particular attitudes and expectations regarding children, focused on emotional containment, satisfaction of basic needs, and behavior control rather than academic achievement. This approach permeates daily school life, creating a particular community of practice whose members have learned to compromise on the common understanding of what a school is. On the contrary, Coigue's multiculturalism is not reflected in daily practice. Instead, it concerns particular events and situations during the year that have an impact on school activities (e.g., preparing and rehearsing performances) and school aesthetics (e.g., colorful representations of Latin America), without significantly altering or challenging the staff's modus operandi. In this sense, we would say that in Coigue School, there is a facade of multiculturalism.

Despite these differences in their discourses and in the extent of their daily engagement with them, both schools seem to praise the fact that they have a heterogeneous student population: both appear to endorse what we called earlier the diversity project. However, the ethnography illustrates the sheer contrast between certain members' discourses on, and practices around, diversity, on the one hand, and the expressions of their beliefs in daily life, on the other. In our view, such expressions reveal that these members are not only unconvinced about the advantages of diversity but are even quite uncomfortable with it.

Let us first note that, in both schools, the features that make their students diverse are in fact treated as aspects that must be *corrected*. In Alerce School, "decompensated" bodies are addressed through medication or other means that seek to make them as similar as possible to *normal* students. Some have described school practices like this even as a new form of eugenics (Baker 2002), insofar as they involve the development of "perfecting technologies" (Baker 2002, p. 675) designed to achieve a sort of quality control of the population. At any rate, a community in which diversity is something that subjects must be *cured* of (by medication or by any other means) is far from being diversity friendly. The very logic of the Program for Educational Integration is that people with special needs must receive special help and support in order to mitigate the differences between them and their normal peers. According to this view, the ideal classroom should reduce rather than foster heterogeneity.

In the same vein, Coigue School's alleged exaltation of cultural diversity is carried out by means of communitarian celebrations, which, ironically, start with the national anthem and have the slogan "We are all Chilean". The motto "Nationalities do not matter, let's show we are all Chilean!", which the master of ceremonies of the Latin American Festival declaims at the beginning of the event, seems intended to manifest a benevolent attitude toward foreigners: they are granted the privilege of integration into the nationalist spirit despite the fact they are immigrants. These practices reflect an assimilationist approach to cultural diversity, even within a context of official acclamation of cultural differences. Assimilationist intent camouflaged by acts, norms, and discourses of celebration of cultural specificities are part of the phenomenon called *neo-liberal multiculturalism* (Kymlicka 2013). This theory claims that, under the influence of a neo-liberal ideology, multiculturalism has become a form of governance that seeks to contain cultural rights through their legitimation (Hale 2005). By leaving space and even encouraging demands for cultural recognition, neo-liberal multiculturalism may trace the limits of its legitimacy and therefore keep the threats to the integrity of the political and economic order under control.

One mechanism for this is to include cultural differences as part of the national heritage (Boccara 2011). In this way, cultural specificity is acknowledged as valuable, not per se, but by virtue of its belonging to the dominant nation. Furthermore, stressing people's own cultural particularity, and profiting from it, fits into the neo-liberal scheme because it allows culture to be "marketized"—a phenomenon that Comaroff and Comaroff (2009) allude to by talking of "ethnicity, Inc".

All of these features of neo-liberal multiculturalism can be observed to some extent in Coigue School, where differences are minimized by celebrating them, insofar as their official recognition allocates them to nationalistic principles and values. An expression of this is the exhibition of the Chilean flag as a larger, more dominant symbol than the other national flags. Consider also the validation of the Chilean narrative as the ultimate version of Iquique Naval Combat, having admitted, however, that each country had its own motives. In this way, different forms of understanding history are allowed to circulate and are also justified; however, this does not lead to challenging the official version of that controversial fact. Instead, it seems to be the grounds for ratification of the *truth*—a nationalistic one—that stands as unquestionable above any other. However, keeping the multicultural label, even within a nationalist framework, serves the needs of a neo-liberal state, since with it the school seeks to gain appeal to compete in the market, attract students, and, consequently, receive more funding from the state.

It is important to remember that the diversity turn is not the result of a premeditated, conscious decision on the part of either school. As mentioned earlier, opening the school to a heterogeneous population was the result of the way the educational market works in Chile: students are excluded from entering other schools and those who are ready to receive them obtain economic incentives from the state. In a critical context in which many schools struggle to offer quality education for students and families who may have considered them as their last educational option, different or unconventional students may represent their only chance for the economic survival of institutional projects. One would expect that a school community harboring the conviction that diversity is desirable would be open to all kinds of students because of that conviction rather than because of the economic benefits of that openness—and indeed regardless of such benefits.

However, perhaps the clearest evidence that neither of the two schools is genuinely committed to the diversity project is the prevalence, in daily school life, of the civilizing project. Practices meant to discipline students' bodies and recruit them for national citizenship occupy most of the school's time. Beyond those declarations and practices in which difference or particularism is presented as a good thing, the majority of the things happening in the two schools bear the burden of standardizing people for civilization building and maintenance around the Chilean nation. This is simply at odds with the diversity project. Either people's psychological and national particularities are respected and valued or a standard is established to dissolve such particularities into a single manner of being a citizen. You cannot have it both ways.

This logical incompatibility between the civilizing project and the diversity project is perceived at some level by school members. In Coigue School, nationalizing immigrants makes no sense, even under the guise of recognition of the other (as in neoliberal multiculturalism). The struggle inherent in the process of making sense of the different nationalities becomes evident insofar as staff frequently manifest surprise at the presence of non-Chilean students, which is evident in various comments that point to it, either literally or sarcastically. For example, the sarcasm expressed at the championship prizes achieved by all non-Chilean students reveals disappointment and frustration, as attainment and triumphs in a school are more than an individual matter: they are a tribute to the nation and are therefore functional to recruitment for national citizenship. However, no real recruitment can be accomplished with non-Chilean people, so one of the primary functions of schooling—conceived in light of the civilizing project—is put into question. In other words, if the civilizing project challenges and constrains the display of multiculturalism and inclusion, the diversity turn and project undermine the enactment of the civilizing project. This is quite serious, insofar as abandoning such a project would modify the very meaning of schooling and, moreover, those who cannot think of citizenship beyond the nationalization of people can easily feel that the legitimacy of the school as a social institution is at risk (see Peña 2015).

In Alerce School, in turn, there is a sensation that the quantity and nature of cases to be submitted to normalization—or to civilization processes—overcome real possibilities of intervention and therefore put into question the viability of integration and civilization. As previously discussed, the recurrent idea of a *limit* in terms of school staff is evidence of the anguish of receiving non-educable students and of being just about leaving the school status and turning it into something else: a special school, a refuge, a center where basic humanitarian aid is provided rather than education or normalization. Alerce School is clearly failing to civilize children. The problematic case of the child who stayed at home for 25 days because his parents had not given him any medication is evidence of this failure.

However, as this ethnography shows, the failure of the civilizing project may not always be undoubtedly associated with the diversity project. The general disengagement of adults and children, and the weak responses of the latter to civilizing practices, suggest that the civilizing project has simply lost its drive. The audience who sing the national anthem unwillingly in Coigue School may be a sign of this. However, more generally, students in both schools directly resist normative practices and adults show a lack of commitment or enthusiasm, especially in their teaching, which looks more like a simulation than real activity. In this sense, the diversity project has provided the chance to give these schools a new thrust, since the civilizing project is no longer truly engaging and fails to give community members a sense of "joint enterprise", as Wenger (1998: 83) puts it. At the same time, building up the discourse about the acceptance and celebration of diversity seeks to present a praiseworthy image to outsiders resorting to officially validated multicultural and inclusive narratives. The problem is that, in line with what contemporary research tells us (see introduction), even teachers who have no ideological problem with welcoming diverse students feel they have not been prepared for teaching in these contexts, or that they lack the proper conditions to do so. The celebration of diversity finds not only ideological but also implementation and pragmatic barriers.

To conclude, in both schools, welcoming and celebrating diversity has a dual position. It pretends to save schools from two opposite threats: on the one hand, the social delegitimation provoked by the new heterogeneous school population, which makes it undesirable, compared to selective schools; and, on the other hand, the weakening of the civilizing project, which may leave school communities with no sense of identity. However, if we are right, the main reason that explains the discomfort that school members experience with the diversity project is the fact that, even when weakened, the civilizing project is still much enacted in schools, molding daily school practices. Therefore, despite inclusion and multiculturalism being a camouflage, school members resent the threat to the civilizing project, represented by the diversity turn and project. With the pragmatic failure of the civilizing project, school subjects are left in a vacuum of meaning, where disconcert, anguish and nostalgia of normality prevail.

References

Ainscow, M. (1995). Education for all: Making it happen. *Support for Learning, 10*(4), 147–155.
Apple, M. W., & Weis, L. (Eds.). (1983). *Ideology and practice in schooling*. Philadelphia: Temple University Press.
Artiles, A. J., Kozleski, E. B., Dorn, S., & Christensen, C. (2006). Learning in inclusive education research: Re-mediating theory and methods with a transformative agenda. *Review of Research in Education, 30*(1), 65–108. https://doi.org/10.3102/0091732X030001065.
Baker, B. (2002). The hunt for disability: The new eugenics and the normalization of school children. *Teachers College Record, 104*(4), 663–703.
Boccara, G. (2011). Le gouvernement des «Autres». Sur le multiculturalisme néolibéral en Amérique Latine. *Actuel Marx, 50*(2), 191. https://doi.org/10.3917/amx.050.0191.
Booth, T., & Ainscow, M. (2000). *Index for inclusion. Developing learning and participation in schools*. Manchester: Centre for Studies on Inclusive Education.
Bourdieu, P., & Passeron, J. C. (1977). *Reproduction in education, society, and culture*. London: Sage.
Butts, R. F. (1967). Civilization-building and the modernization process: A framework for the reinterpretation of the history of education. *History of Education Quarterly, 7*(2), 147. https://doi.org/10.2307/367558.
Comaroff, J. L., & Comaroff, J. (2009). *Ethnicity, Inc*. Chicago: University of Chicago Press.
Díaz Arce, T., & Druker, S. (2007). La democratización del espacio escolar: una construcción en y para la diversidad. *Estudios Pedagógicos (Valdivia), 33*(1), 63–77. https://doi.org/10.4067/S0718-07052007000100004.
Dubet, F. (2006). *El declive de la institución: Profesiones, sujetos e individuos en la modernidad*. Barcelona: Gedisa.
Egaña Baraona, M. L. (2000). *La educación primaria popular en el siglo XIX en Chile: una práctica de política estatal*. Santiago: Ediciones de la Dirección de Bibliotecas, Archivos y Museos.
Evans, G. (2006). *Educational failure and working class white children in Britain*. London: Palgrave Macmillan UK.
Everhart, R. (1983). *Reading, writing, and resistance: Adolescence and labor in a junior high school*. Boston: Routledge & Kegan Paul.
Florian, L., & Kershner, R. (2009). Inclusive pedagogy. In H. Daniels, H. Lauder, & J. Porter (Eds.), *Knowledge, values and educational policy: A critical perspective* (pp. 173–183). New York: Routledge.

Foley, D. E. (1990). *Learning capitalist culture: Deep in the heart of Tejas*. Philadelphia: University of Pennsylvania Press.

Gaete, A., & Gómez, V. (2019). Introduction. In A. Gaete & V. Gómez (Eds.), *Education & poverty*. Cambridge: Cambridge Scholars.

Gaete, A., Gómez, V., & Bascopé, M. (2016). ¿Qué le piden los profesores a la formación inicial docente en Chile? *Temas de la Agenda Pública, 11*(86), 1–18.

Giroux, H. (1983). Theories of reproduction and resistance in the new sociology of education: A critical analysis. *Harvard Educational Review, 53*(3), 257–293. https://doi.org/10.17763/haer.53.3.a67x4u33g7682734.

Gorski, P. C. (2016). Poverty and the ideological imperative: A call to unhook from deficit and grit ideology and to strive for structural ideology in teacher education. *Journal of Education for Teaching, 42*(4), 378–386. https://doi.org/10.1080/02607476.2016.1215546.

Graham, L. J., & Slee, R. (2008). An illusory interiority: Interrogating the discourse/s of inclusion. *Educational Philosophy and Theory, 40*(2), 277–293. https://doi.org/10.1111/j.1469-5812.2007.00331.x.

Hale, C. (2005). Neoliberal multiculturalism: The remaking of cultural rights and racial dominance in Central America. *Political and Legal Anthropology Review, 28*(1), 10–28.

Infante, M. (2010). Desafíos a la formación docente: inclusión educativa. *Estudios Pedagógicos, 36*(1), 287–297.

Jackson, P. W. (1968). *Life in classrooms*. New York: Teachers College Press.

Kymlicka, W. (2013). Neoliberal multiculturalism? In P. A. Hall & M. Lamont (Eds.), *Social resilience in the neo-liberal era* (pp. 99–126). Cambridge: Cambridge University Press. https://doi.org/10.1017/cbo9781139542425.007.

Levinson, B. (1996). Social difference and schooled identity at a Mexican secundaria. In B. A. Levinson, D. E. Foley, & D. C. Holland (Eds.), *The cultural production of the educated person: Critical ethnographies of schooling and local practice* (pp. 211–238). Albany, NY: State University of New York Press.

Levinson, B. A., Foley, D. E., & Holland, D. C. (Eds.). (1996). *The cultural production of the educated person: Critical ethnographies of schooling and local practice*. Albany: State University of New York Press.

Luna, L. (2015a). Cooperative learning and embodied accountability: An ethnographic analysis of classroom participation in an English school. *Education Policy Analysis Archives, 23*(99). https://doi.org/10.14507/epaa.v23.2050.

Luna, L. (2015b). Construyendo "la identidad del excluido": etnografía del aprendizaje situado de los niños en una escuela básica municipal de Chile. *Estudios Pedagógicos (Especial), 41*, 97–113.

Madrid, S. (2016). "Diversidad sin diversidad": Los colegios particulares pagados de elite y la formación de la clase dominante en una sociedad de mercado. In J. Corvalán, A. Carrasco, & J. E. García-Huidobro (Eds.), *Mercado escolar y oportunidad educacional: libertad, diversidad y desigualdad* (pp. 269–299). Santiago: Ediciones Universidad Católica de Chile.

Martinic, S., & Elacqua, G. M. (Eds.). (2010). *¿Fin de ciclo?: Cambios en la gobernanza del sistema educativo*. Organización de las Naciones Unidas para la Educación, la Ciencia y la Cultura. Pontificia Universidad Católica de Chile, Facultad de Educación.

McLaren, P. (1986). *Schooling as a ritual performance: Toward a political economy of educational symbols and gestures* (3rd ed.). Lanham: Rowman & Littlefield.

Meyer, J. (1977). The effects of education as an institution. *American Journal of Sociology, 83*(1), 55–77.

Ministerio de Desarrollo Social. (2016). Encuesta de caracterización socioeconómica nacional, CASEN 2015. Gobierno de Chile.

Paredes, R. (2016). El sistema de vouchers en la educación chilena. In J. Corvalán, A. Carrasco, & J. E. García-Huidobro (Eds.), *Mercado Escolar y Oportunidad Educacional: Libertad, Diversidad y Desigualdad* (pp. 57–79). Santiago: Ediciones Universidad Católica de Chile.

Peim, N. (2001). The history of the present: Towards a contemporary phenomenology of the school. *History of Education, 30*(2), 177–190. https://doi.org/10.1080/00467600010012454.

Peña, C. (2015). Escuela y vida cívica. In C. Cox & J. C. Castillo (Eds.), *Aprendizaje de la ciudadanía: Contextos, experiencias y resultados*. Santiago: Ediciones Universidad Católica de Chile.

Ramirez, F., & Boli, J. (1987). The political construction of mass schooling: European origins and worldwide institutionalization. *Sociology of Education, 60*, 2–17.

Serrano, S., Ponce de León, M., & Rengifo, F. (Eds.). (2012). *Historia de la educación en Chile Tomo II (1880–1930)*. Santiago: Taurus.

Shweder, R. (2002). On the return of the «civilizing project». *Daedalus, 131*(3), 117–121.

Tiramonti, G. (2005). La escuela en la encrucijada del cambio epocal. *Educação & Sociedade, 26*(92), 889–910.

UNESCO. (2004). *Temario abierto sobre educación inclusiva*. Oficina Regional de Educación de la UNESCO para América Latina y el Caribe: Santiago de Chile.

Valenzuela, J., Bellei, C., & De Los Ríos, D. (2010). Segregación escolar en Chile. In S. Martinic & G. M. Elacqua (Eds.), *¿Fin de ciclo?: cambios en la gobernanza del sistema educativo* (pp. 209–229). Organización de las Naciones Unidas para la Educación, la Ciencia y la Cultura. Pontificia Universidad Católica de Chile, Facultad de Educación.

Valenzuela, J., Villaroel, G., & Villalobos, C. (2013). Ley de Subvención Escolar Preferencial (SEP): algunos resultados preliminares de su implementación. *Revista Pensamiento Educativo, 50*(2), 113–131.

Vega, A. (2009). Integración de alumnos con necesidades educativas especiales: ¿existe coherencia entre el discurso y las prácticas pedagógicas ejercidas por los profesores básicos? *Estudios Pedagógicos (Valdivia), 35*(2), 189–202. https://doi.org/10.4067/S0718-07052009000200011.

Wenger, E. (1998). *Communities of practice: Learning, meaning, and identity*. Cambridge: Cambridge University Press.

Willis, P. E. (1977). *Learning to labor: How working class kids get working class jobs*. New York: Columbia University Press.

Chapter 8
Unpredictable Meanings

Claudia Matus

Abstract This chapter presents excerpts produced in the field arranged around themes. I organize this chapter rhizomatically rather than linearly to explore the political possibilities of meaning taking form *in* the relation between the reader and the scenes. The act of interpreting and getting *something* out of field notes interrupts the narrow idea of *expertise* through understanding field notes as already analyzed pieces of data. As such, the process promotes a more political, chaotic, and unpredictable usage of this material and forces the reader to question her/his own ways of perpetuating dominant understandings in the production of normal and deviant school identities.

8.1   Entering...

In this chapter, I present groups of excerpts produced in the school field arranged around themes. These themes show practices of *doing/being/feeling* within the field. As I organize this chapter rhizomatically rather than linearly, my intent is to explore the political possibilities of producing meaning out of pieces of field notes that have not been reduced to the production of the analytic writer. To accomplish this, I do not present an analysis (in its traditional understanding) of these pieces. My only intervention to the texts is directed to the selection and organization of the pieces around specific titles. More than a collection of accounts arranged around themes to produce an individual reading that fits the actual arrangement of the field notes, I expect the reader to be exposed to the singularity of the process of producing meaning. This process is always chaotic and unpredictable. I hope the following fieldnotes arrangements bring the reader to the very moment when we, as ethnographers, are exposed to *life itself* and make sense of it through observing and naming. As such, this chapter claims that representation, understood as the uncritical belief that words reflect a reality out there, becomes a tramp to define categories, causal relations, and strict possibilities to produce meaning.

C. Matus (✉)
Center for Educational Justice, Pontificia Universidad Católica de Chile, Santiago, Chile
e-mail: cmatusc@uc.cl

© Springer Nature Singapore Pte Ltd. 2019
C. Matus (ed.), *Ethnography and Education Policy*, Education Policy
& Social Inequality 3, https://doi.org/10.1007/978-981-13-8445-5_8

The coming excerpts illustrate to the reader to two critical conditions when producing meaning: the consideration of "jumping scales" (Smith 1992, p. 60) and "slow violence" (Nixon 2011, p. 2). To produce subjects in relation to categories, we jump scales of power (times, spaces, and matter) all the time. This means that we go back and forth to explain our own localities and the position of others in relation to power. Racism, xenophobia, homophobia, sexism, genderism, ableism, as "material-semiotic agencies" (Rosiek 2018, p. 415) respond to our research questions and interventions as transforming themselves into something else. They are resilient to the possibility to be *caught* and as such being problems to be solved and disappear. As assemblages of power, they take different forms and continue moving, taking different shapes to produce biological, social, and cultural hierarchies and as a result, racialized, sexualized, abled, gendered subjects continue being as real. As such, making meaning out of the coming excerpts *extends*, *moves* across different times, spaces, and materialities to continue acting as stable possibilities to know.

The coming stories reflect how "slow violence" (Nixon 2011, p. 2), as the invisible, out of sight affective relation to producing subjects, has delayed effects. These effects have come to be the unpredictable meanings we assign to the other. Violence is not visible in such a way that we cannot see the threads our knowledge about the other produce. As such, these excerpts are a rehearsal of the complex passage from ways of knowing—to feeling—to continue producing more or less rigid structures that dictate who we and others are. This critical passage shows how "thinking is more than the discrete final form it takes in language. To come to language is more than to finalize form. To come to language is to feel the form taking of concepts as they prearticulate thoughts/feelings" (Manning 2009, p. 5). A way of feeling (more or less rigid) about the other and his/her otherness is violent. How the body, performative acts of gender, classing processes, skin color take forms, happen is the final purpose of this chapter. These *happenings* are not reduced to the production of the analytic writer. They are the production of the spectator of these excerpts. These passages take form in the relation between the reader (as a speculative decoding of knowledge) and the scenes proposed for this rehearsal. These scenes may look disconnected, but they are actual moments, they are being produced in the *now*, they move, they transform themselves as they travel through different readers' matrices to know. They look independent and disconnected from one another, as they reflect the power to explain how scales and violence operate. These excerpts show the imperative of life to adjust bodies, experiences, and feelings to a lingering category to make it real. Movement and fraction get out of the possibility of becoming. As Manning (2009, p. 11) notes, "To locate identity as the point of departure of a body is to deny the complexity of the concurrent planes of thought, expression, conceptualization, articulation."

What you are about to read are common scenes of daily lives at schools but what matters is how different planes of producing meaning converge around the concepts that make them real. Deviance, nonconforming, lacking, contested, unspeakable are the common threads that guide teachers' possibilities to talk about who they are and who their students are. This is how we create space, time, and matter as assemblages of power.

The following are a collection of accounts from interactions with various school actors and observations from the schools.

8.2   Gendering and Sexualizing [Bodies]

When the situation [chaos within the classroom] was partially controlled, the school inspector positively reinforced the girls, they stayed where she had indicated: "you look very pretty there, obedient and still."

Observation of the ethnographer watching the exit of the morning shift students, All-Girls School, 2014, School X.

"You, why are you taking photographs? You cannot take photos without my authorization. Furthermore, this is an all-girls' school."

School inspector mentioning to the ethnographer the forbiddance of taking photos, All-Girls School, 2014, School X.

There's some noise within the classroom for which the head teacher noticeably lowers the tone of her voice and explains [to the counselor, who is also in the classroom] that since [the students] are young ladies and not animals, she will not shout at them.

Head teacher to the class, during an activity with the counselor, All-Girls School, 2014, School X.

The counselor comments to the students that, unfortunately in this world, not all people are good, and as girls, you do not know the intentions that people on the street may have when they see you in short skirts. Of course, we care for you and do not have bad intentions and if you go about with short skirts, nothing bad occurs with us, but outside is different. So, the school sets rules that you all may not like, but we do it for your wellbeing because we care about you and look after you.

Counselor emphasizing to students during an activity, All-Girls School, 2014, School X.

The teacher addresses one of the girls and says to her: "Yesterday I saw you with a dress on and you looked very beautiful." The girl listens to what the teacher is telling her, but with a certain nervousness. She does not give any response. She becomes uncomfortable and distances herself a little from us.

The teacher reiterates: "Really, I saw you with a dress on and you looked very beautiful."

Later, the teacher addresses it for the third time, but on this occasion, she addresses a teacher who is conversing with to us [team of ethnographers] why she made this remark. She justifies this comment as her way of affirming when the girls look pretty when they worry about being seen as delicate or young ladies. In addition, she adds that the girl she spoke to wears boots, which make her look rough and not very feminine.

Teacher talking to a student, All-Girls School, 2014, School X.

"If they allowed us to come with more of our own style, with something lighter that did not get [me] as hot, I would even like to come to school."
"If we are all equal, why can the teachers wear big earrings?"

Student conversing with a teacher, All-Girls School, 2014, School X.

Another situation is that of a girl who has trouble eating, because her older sisters urge her to eat less, so as not to gain weight. She [the head of the cafeteria] gives her the necessary time so she can eat.

Conversation between the head of the cafeteria and an ethnographer, All-Girls School, 2014, School X.

The custodian comments that girls are not very messy: "You are merely little girls, perhaps the little boys behave worse." Upon thinking about older girls, from ninth to twelfth grade, "I don't think they would be messier either, if they are just young ladies." A group of girls chat standing out of the way that they will behave badly during the school activities, referring to activities that the girls will do at school.

Conversation between the establishment's custodian and the ethnographer, All-Girls School, 2014, School X.

At the school's gala, each grade does two presentations and participation is mandatory: "what girl doesn't like to dance…" declares the theater teacher.

Conversation between the theater and dance teacher, All-Girls School, 2014, School X.

"I do not know how the [male] teacher addressed the topic of obesity or what the students have interpreted, but the thing is that three girls came to my office, the fattest ones [from the school], and they complained. Well, the one who complained was the roundest of them all (the principal makes a gesture with his hands and mouth, like an inflated balloon) and said that the teacher had called them overweight."

Conversation between the principal of the school and the ethnographers, All-Girls School, 2014, School X.

"The school has three fundamental tasks: educate proper girls, provide knowledge and strengthen skills, and lastly that the girls (sometimes he does not say girls, but rather 'children') achieve the possibility to continue their studies at the best schools in Chile." In answering the question about what is expected of the girls, the principal points out that the most important is that they are good mothers, concerned for their children, and that they form a family.

Interview with the principal, All-Girls School, 2014, School X.

One of the last topics addressed in the conversation with the school's principal is about the meaning of what the establishment indicates as "to be young ladies," to which the principal comments: "the recognition of gender is not the school's responsibility… At school, the girls are taught to be proper people, young ladies, misses. This means that they behave according to their gender: that they are polite, that they have good manners, flawless moral and good habits. That they do not spread their legs while sitting, that they are respectful, that they do not bite their nails. This is one of the strengths of our establishment: the education of young ladies."

Interview with the principal, All-Girls School, 2014, School X.

One of the kindergarten teachers recounts the moment when a guardian approached her because according to her daughter [the student], she [the teacher] had squeezed her belly. The teacher denies the event and argues, "Of course, they do not make Barbies like before."

Comment from a kindergarten teacher, All-Girls School, 2014, School X.

The [science] teacher explains to me the situation of "one of the Catalinas" [there are various students in the class with that name]. She tells me that her mother died when she was in third grade and that her sisters are the ones who take care of her today. She has two older sisters who also study at the school and are very good girls. The two are professional and are responsible for their sister. "Well, they live with the father, but he works, so it is them who come to the meetings, to the school presentations. If you could see them, participating, not missing an act, they are always there. If you have to make sopaipillas [a type of fried bread eaten in Chile], they immediately volunteer. There you see how this concern influences the girl's willingness. Catalina then is responsible, hard-working, and gets good grades…"

Regarding Sofia [another student in the same class], [the science teacher, a woman] explains something quite different. "You will not see her now because she was suspended three days ago. They caught her pushing a classmate." They say she is a smart-mouthed, defiant girl, who loves to call attention to herself, and that others are fixated on her all the time. She has bad manners, is sassy, and volatile. "See, if you have to keep up with her, it will take all the time in the world. Suppose that she arrives to classes late and is in a good mood, she enters the classroom, asks permission, and sits down calmly and quietly. But, if she is in a troublemaking mood, she enters the class without asking permission, greets only five classmates that are her friends, without saying good day to the others, very arrogantly. She is loud and greets others with a kiss, interrupting the class and you have to wait until she is finished greeting whomever she wants, one by one, to continue with the class. […] If you could see how disrespectful she is. I understand that she has a stance and does not want to sing the national anthem, but everyone understands that if you are in a ceremony, an act where they are singing the national anthem, but you don't want to sing, [you should] at the very least stay silent, out of respect. She does not do that, on the contrary, she dances during the anthem and clowns around for everyone to see, to make her classmates laugh, and she has that attitude the whole time. So I always have to be supervising how she behaves." Finally, the science teacher adds, "What are you going to ask of a girl if her mother is crazy? Here at school, we all know that she has mental problems and needs treatment. She even says it is okay to go to the protests and be aggressive towards the police. What can you hope for the daughter of a mother like that?"

Conversation with the science teacher, All-Girls School, 2014, School X.

"Look, I have a teaching assistant in my history class and he is an older man, more than 50 [years old] and the girls do not care, not even a little. They have thighs like this (she gestures with both hands in the form of an extended circle). They sit in whichever way; they do not care. Additionally, they are very forward and take advantage." (I ask her what they take advantage of.) "You should see the faces that they make to the [male] teachers (and she makes the gesture of batting her eyelashes and smiling). You should see how they throw themselves at them, how they fling themselves at some teachers and that just cannot happen."

Comment from the science teacher, All-Girls School, 2014, School X.

The teacher told me that she believes the [female] students are "very sexist". I ask why she thinks that and she tells me that they only pay attention to men. "Notice when we make them form [a line] to enter the classroom. If it is a woman that is at the front, they do not listen and act silly, as if they had not heard. But, if it is a man, they get quiet right away. It does not cost them a thing. The same [thing happens] in the classroom. I could spend a half hour trying to keep them quiet, to work, to pay attention, but if Don Pablo or another [male] teacher arrive, for example, right away they straighten out. Just today I told them off for this. I told them that they are very sexist and that when they are older, they would have their boyfriend inspecting their Facebook and telling them what to delete and what to keep [on it]. Why did he like your post? And you all will delete the 'like'. Why did you upload that photo? And you all will take down the photo, because your boyfriend tells you to, because you have already learned to obey men."

Conversation between teacher and ethnographer, All-Girls School, School X.

"Many things will change when the girls reach high school [a school that historically has been male and that has been integrating women for 7 years]. Everyone involved knows that the transformations will be profound. The school will not be the same and dating relationships will be an important part of human relations."

Teacher comments about a traditionally all-boys school that converted to a coed school, 2014, School Y.

"Boys: the hot season is beginning and you play a lot of soccer. So, out of respect for your teachers and classmates, [please] shower in the morning, wash your armpits, and use deodorant. If you don't, do not play."

School inspector to male students, Coed School, 2014, School Y.

The teacher comments about an announcement she saw in the television that said, "60% of men use body or face lotion versus the 30% of women." She laughs and points out that now men are more feminine than women.

Conversation between teachers in the teacher's lounge, Coed School, 2014, School Z.

The teacher puts the male and female students in a line, and then indicates that they should jog 3 laps around the court. She reaffirms various times that they jog and not run and that they do it like big kids [only hinting at the boys]. To the males, she calls them "champion" or "buddy", to the women she only says "girls".

Observation from a physical education class, Coed School, 2014, School Z.

A couple of the girls want to help the teacher [to lift some heavy materials], but the teacher stops them: "Let's leave it to the men, they are stronger."

Comments from a physical education class, Coed School, 2014, School Z.

While watching a boys' soccer match, a boy between sixth- and seventh-grade stands out. This boy has a rebellious attitude with the rest of his teammates. He speaks to a teammate in the match [signaling another player on the court] and tells him, "That fellow is gay, that's why he's never learned how to play soccer."

Observation from recess, Coed School, 2014, School Z.

At school, there is a mural where the girl and boy students write their dreams. There are plenty that want to be soccer players, police officers, runway models, and "to find the man of my dreams and get married." There are only some dreams that have to do with going to university.

Ethnographer's observation of the "dream mural", Coed School, 20154, School Z.

The school inspector told me that there was a child "of switched sex" before, and that spoke very well, for which the student was teased. She even told me that a teacher denied the student from entering her class and the student had to change. "It's that he spoke like this [she flaps her hands and sharpens her tone] and we told him not to do that, but to speak properly."

Conversation among school inspectors, Coed School, 2014, School Z.

One of the administrative secretaries of the establishment [without having seen or spoken to me beforehand] told me that the girls of this institution have many problems. Their parents are irresponsible and that there are girls with eating disorders. She points out that "the girls at this establishment are crazy. Since there are no men, they let loose."

Conversation between the administrative secretary and the ethnographer, All-Girls School, 2013, School A.

In a conversation with the institution's counselor, she tells me: "let us begin from the base that the students of this establishment are girls, and being girls, they are more jealous than boys, they are more gossipy. They are more big-mouthed than boys. For example, if a boy has a problem with another, he goes and tells him, hey what's your problem with me? And probably, they throw a punch and the problem is over. It's that they are more direct to resolve their conflicts." In the girls' case, they are always like "she looked at me badly, you know we don't get together with her, let's tell Juanita to not hang out with Carlita because Carlita looked at my boyfriend," etc. "They are much more gossipy, more manipulating, they are more... eh... how to say it? I don't know if it's the correct word that I want to say, but I feel that they are exhibitionists, that they liked to be looked at. Today I brushed my hair differently, look at me, I brought a different magazine, look at me, I am the center of attention, I have problems. So in this sense, I feel that their personalities clash between them, their egos."

Conversation between counselor and the ethnographer, All-Girls School, 2013, School A.

The teacher comments about the students' use of the internet and Facebook. She tells her students that the internet is a misrepresentation and that they should take care of themselves: "take care of your intimacy, show concern for your femininity, always be young ladies, be respectful […] I know that they are impulsive, but they should control themselves."

Teacher speaking to her students in class, All-Girls School, 2013, School A.
The teacher makes an intervention during the parent/guardian meeting, "You all
[parents and guardians] have the most special bond that one can have and that is the
love that your children feel for you. Therefore, the first love will always be that of the
family: mom and dad. You are the first role model. We [the teachers] are the second.
The students come to school to put into practice what they have learned at home."

Counselor at the parent/guardian meeting, Coed School, 2013, School B.

8.3 Classing [Affects]

The social worker indicated that this is a school where no great difficulties are presented, noting that [the environment] is "less complex" where there is less social
vulnerability and where there are fewer cases of those who should receive economic
benefits. She indicates that the problems [those that she has knowledge of] principally have to do with familial situations that affect the girls and that translates into
behavior problems. Generally, the girls that sit in the back [of the classroom], those
who do not take notes in their notebooks, those that talk during class and apparently
look good, those [students] have the most problems. And one wonders [signaling
the psychologist who is also in the meeting]: "Do you also have those problems?"
[alluding that there are girls who "hide" that they have problems].

Conversation between ethnographer and social assistant, All-Girls School, 2014,
School X.

In a conversation with a student, he highlights the opportunities that the school
gives to get to know "all types of people." For example, he explains, that during the
Olympics [an activity that the school organizes where students from other regions
of the country are invited] they appreciate that the visitors have to stay in homes of
families from the school. This allows them "to get to know different people," just
like what happens in volunteer work [another school organized activity where they
support families from other regions of Chile]. These activities [of getting to know
another type of person] help them in future interpersonal relationships they will have
upon entering university [points out the student].

Student's comments, traditionally all-boys school now passing to Coed, 2014,
School Y.

One interviewed student comments that they tease a classmate with the nickname
"big-shot." He says that this classmate laughs about his condition [as a student with
higher economic standing] and that he does not take it badly. Later, the interviewed
student points out, "[this is] because we are not going to call any classmate poor."
After, he comments that it is not the students that distinguish [each other] economically, rather that "the parents are those who make differences between people, for
the commune where one lives, for example." "I know of some classmates that live
in Las Condes [one of the affluent commune of Santiago, Chile] and their parents do
not let them go to other, less affluent neighborhoods."

Conversation between ethnographer and student, traditionally all-boys school now passing to Coed, 2014, School Y.

In a conversation with a teacher about the immigrant students of the institution, she indicates that there were differences between children of different countries: "I believe that the Peruvian students that are in school are less advantaged than the Colombians, the Venezuelans, and the Chinese. I think that all the teachers that have had Peruvian students in our courses have seen it, because one hears all the time, 'the Peruvians this and the Peruvians that.' I see that race also influences and influences a lot if you are dark-skinned. Now then you are screwed! I don't know what can be done to change that. The Peruvian girls, for example, apply a lot of makeup. For example, when there is a school event, they wear a lot of makeup to not appear as tan, but how cute they already are! I mean I find that they have pretty skin, but they really wear makeup to appear less dark-skinned."

Focus group among teachers, Coed School, 2014, School B.

8.4   Diagnosing [Protocols]

The board of teachers discusses disruptive students and one teacher from the group points out: "if from here on out there are no changes with these students, we are going to have to become responsible as a school, [and] face these pupils who at some moment we should have taken measures for, because they are without medication and we already know that having them in the classroom is a threat to all."

Board meeting for teachers and administration, Coed School, 2014, School B.

During a teacher's board meeting, they talk about one class in particular [tenth grade B, who's teacher asked for help from the ethnographer to understand some "complicated" cases]. The first commentary made in the meeting is that this course needs the support of the school counselor. The tenth-grade teacher points out: "I have almost 15 girls with serious problems: panic attacks, nervous breakdowns, abandoned by their mother, under extreme pressure. I think that you have to communicate and work with them. A counselor should have time to attend to such things."

Board meeting of high school teachers, All-Girls School, 2014, School A.

Mentioned in a conversation between teachers: "It takes a lot for the specialists [psychologists] to empathize with the school system and not only from their individual client-patient idea. For example, we do not know what the specialists like a psychologist or neurologist know about the problems we have in the classrooms. We have to go about guessing because there is not fluid communication between the specialists and us teachers. And for example, Francisca's family, like the other families, does not acknowledge the weight of the fact that we are the ones who deal with Francisca and her problems daily. Even worse, when the girls are attacked, they tend to take the aggressor's behavior and defend themselves attacking other children with that attitude."

Board meeting of high school teachers, All-Girls School, 2014, School A.

At the teacher's board meeting, one of the participants indicated that the majority of the problems with the girls are due to the lack of commitment from the families with the establishment's demands.

Teacher's board meeting at high school, All-Girls School, 2014, School A.

At the teacher's board meeting, they comment on the case of one [female] student and indicate that she lacks the abilities to develop well and get good grades, but that these abilities are specific skills that they should develop at and in the home. One of the teachers refers to this lack of ability as "child-rearing problems" and that she is not the only one in the classroom with these types of problems.

Teacher's board meeting at high school, All-Girls School, 2014, School A.

At the teacher's board meeting, Mónica, the fifth-grade language teacher, comments on the case of a girl who may have dwarfism, for which the others tease her about a little. In addition, she adds that the girl's mother is a "young girl" who seems like she could be her "friend," so "there's zero commitment from the family, especially on behalf of the mother."

Teacher's board meeting at high school, All-Girls School, 2014, School A.

At the teacher's board meeting, Manuela, a high school teacher, spoke in respect to the vulnerability of the [female] students. She comments that the greatest vulnerability she sees in her students is the affectionate, emotional part and [it is] not so much related to the socioeconomic standing of the girls.

Teacher's board meeting at high school, All-Girls School, 2014, School A.

Manuela, a high school teacher, mentions to me about some of the girls who attend the educational psychologist, saying: "She [pointing out the spot where one of the girls sits regularly] impedes the work of others. She is very easily distracted." Later [pointing at another seat] she says: "She is a stone, you have to activate her. It's all the contrary, reinforcement and support." Later, she adds: "All of the cases have been attended to and have improved with pills."

Conversation between ethnographer and teacher, All-Girls School, 2013, School A.

In the school's administrative team meeting with the Center for Diagnostics, they talk about the case of a girl who has been with irregular pharmacological treatment prescribed by a neurologist: "When she is without treatment [the girl] does not function […] It's that her mother is very irregular with her daughter's treatment, when she has been treated, she is fine." The specialist at the Center for Diagnostics says: "clearly she is a tormented little girl, since the beginning, the mother resisted giving her the medications." Everyone present makes sad faces due to the situation they are talking about. For them, it is a big problem that the mothers do not take their daughters to the neurologists, and if they do take them, that they do not follow the treatment that is prescribed. They comment that when the girls take their medication, they change positively and engage better in the classroom. One of the teachers says: "I think it would do her good to be held back [in school]," but the professionals from the Center for Diagnostics express their opposition, arguing: "Again? I do not think so; the solution is something else because…" Another teacher adds: "the girl engages well with the treatment." The professionals of the Center for Diagnostics respond:

"I think that we have to make a conditional [situation] for the girl, so that her mother takes her to the specialist and explains to her that the girl has a rough time without treatment."

Administrative meeting with the Center for Diagnostics, All-Girls School, 2013, School A.

In one of the Center for Diagnostics' team meetings, the professionals comment: "there are various students that should continue a pharmacological treatment for attention deficit and hyperactivity," to which one of the present teachers in the meeting replies: "What happens in these cases is that there are family matters (referring specifically to the separations between fathers and mothers and to mothers with depression)."

Administrative meeting with the Center for Diagnostics, All-Girls School, 2013, School A.

In a conversation between the educational psychologist and the ethnographer, we talk about the girls a little and how unfocused they are. The educational psychologist affirms that she has a very intense job, as it is already complicated to get the girls to pay attention and control themselves to work in the classroom. She also says that many are able to overcome their lack of concentration at the end of treatment and they can even out with the rest of their classmates, but the greatest difficulty is that many need medication and the parents do not take them to the specialist (neurologist).

Conversation between educational psychologist and ethnographer, All-Girls School, 2014, School A.

– "What grade are you in?"
– "First grade, but I was held back."
– "And what happened to you, that you were held back a year?"
– "It's that I have a lot of troubles, I don't have much of an attention span, and I only pay attention to my classmates."

Conversation between student and ethnographer, Coed School, 2014, School B.

The teacher also spoke to me about the medicated children. Many of the students use medications and the teacher informs that she has seen how the medication helps them.

Conversation between teacher and ethnographer, Coed School, 2014, School B.

"For the hyperactive child, I let him leave, run, return, and calm down. If he cannot, if it is too much, then I seek the mother's help. The other thing that concerns me is that everyone has their diagnosis. When I see that something happens to some child, I say: Ok! Can you evaluate this child?"

Conversation between teacher and ethnographer, Coed School, 2014, School B.

I [the ethnographer] ask where the guardians get the medications. She tells me that some are from the doctor's office, other parents buy them, because in the doctor's office they are given [for free], but "they do not give, for example, Aradix which is like the best [medication]. This medication is from another laboratory. They give you Ritalin. And although they are truthfully the same components, it does not have the same effect."

Conversation between teacher and ethnographer, Coed School, 2014, School B. The teacher recounts what has happened this year. "Now the majority of the students with behavior problems have been diagnosed. We even brought a specialist to the school." However, she adds that they still do not have pedagogical training to confront the problems, nor preparation to resolve behavior problems. "It is still insufficient. We have 55 students formally in the Scholar Inclusion Program and many times the teachers are not trained to face problems with them."

Conversation between teacher and ethnographer, Coed School, 2014, School B. The teacher talks to me about José and tells me that for 25 days he does not go to school due to a lack of medication. For some time, the school defined that a child who should be medicated and is not following the treatment indicated by the specialist, will be suspended from the establishment. The teacher adds, "I told his father, as a last resource: we are going to have to suspend your son until you buy him the medication or you come to the establishment so that we can solve the problem, assuming that for the parents it is a problem that their children cannot come to school. And nothing. José has not come for 25 days".

Conversation between teacher and ethnographer, Coed School, 2014, School B. The teacher points out that this is an inclusive school and obviously by being inclusive, there is diversity amongst the children, but the diversity expresses principally in the emotional, cognitive, and psychiatric aspects, which are the most difficult [aspects]. She points out "I feel that we need more specialists or more training for us to be able to manage the topic of inclusion because we are elementary teachers, those of us that are working. Although we have ideas of what happens and of the types of diagnosis that can be present, we are not specialists."

Conversation between teacher and ethnographer, Coed School, 2014, School B. The teacher, Carmen, writes a very large "Z" on the board. A girl says to her "Miss! I had sushi with my mom," and Carmen asks her if she liked it, to which the girl responds smiling with "Yes, [it was] tasty!" Now, Carmen looks at her watch and calls a girl to give her a pill. The girl listens, takes the pill, and returns to her spot. The "Z" activity consists of the girls drawing what the sentence is written on the board says.

First-grade Language Class, Teacher, All-Girls School, 2014, School X.

8.5 Common Sense [Lives as They Are]

The teacher tells me that these girls are different than those before, in regard to sexuality. "The girls talk about kisses, about adult couple relationships, about friends with benefits, they even say they have boyfriends and then the teacher responds to them, 'No! You guys are 5 and 6 years old, you have friends. Raise your hand those who have friends, raise your hand those who have boyfriends,' and various students raise their hands saying they have boyfriends."

Ethnographer: "And has any said that they have a girlfriend?"

Teacher: "One girl says she likes girls and that she gives them kisses in the bathroom." The teacher tells them, "that they shouldn't do that." The teacher recognizes what it does to tell them that they should not kiss between girls, and that she should not do that because it sounds homophobic, but from her conviction, she believes it is normal this way and for that reason, she tries to communicate it.

Ethnographer: "And the girl who feels things for the other girls, what place does she have?"

The teacher tells me that she does not think it is possible, that she has never seen a girl liking another girl very often. What she has seen a lot of is how the little girls live [their] sexuality, masturbating inside the classroom, rubbing themselves against tables or chairs, and that when she looks at them, they become embarrassed. She says that she is surprised that other colleagues do not see these things, that maybe they cannot see it because they do not accept it.

Conversation with kindergarten teacher, All-Girls School, 2014, School X.

After a while, the girls start to take their snack and sit in their places with a tray (this is the routine). Carmen (the teacher) sings a song so that the girls sit down and listen: "Very quiet I will stay,

and to the Miss I will listen,

I will sit up straight,

with my back against the chair" (etc.)

The girls sing in chorus while they go about the performance that dictates the song. Carmen tells them: "Eyes closed, one, two, three… begin" and the girls thank Jesus for the food and later sing a song, "about to eat… about to eat!" and when they finish, Carmen announces "now you may eat."

While they eat, the teaching assistant comments to the class that Ricky Martin came yesterday [to a concert in Santiago, Chile] and adds that she loves him. Many of the girls exclaim, "I love him," "I adore him," and one girl says to another, "but how? If you like Prince Roy… or Romeo Santos?" The teaching assistant asks, "What does Romeo Santos look like? Is he dark-skinned?" A girl says, "Yes, he is dark-skinned." And the teaching assistant responds, "Ah, then he's ugly, I don't like him. If he's dark-skinned, he's ugly." Another girl [Ecuadorian] intervenes, saying "but we are all dark-skinned." The teacher acts like she did not hear.

Kindergarten class, teacher, and teaching assistant, All-Girls School, 2014, School X.

The physical education teacher tells me that today is not for thinking a lot [alluding to the programmed conversation with the ethnographer] because there was a suicide attempt at school and she feels responsible and dirty, that she does not want to cry and adds that she would feel more dirty if she cries. I asked her what is wrong with crying and she says it is strange because she supposes that strong people do not cry and that she should demonstrate that to the girls and their peers. I ask her if that the strength she alludes to is because she is a teacher, because she is a woman, because she is young, and she responds saying it is for all those reasons. She adds that it is stranger for men to cry, that you can see a woman crying on the subway or on the street, but [to see] a man [crying] is strange. A father does not cry; on the contrary, he is brave and strong. I ask her why and she tells me she does not know where she got this [idea] that men and fathers should be this way, because her father is not that way.

Conversation with elementary school physical education teacher, All-Girls School, 2014, School X.

The history teacher tells me he feels that "little by little we are starting to be invaded by women, now that there is a woman president, woman mayor, woman president of the class." Later, there is a moment of distraction in the classroom and the teacher comes closer to me. He introduces a [female] student to me, he passes me her notebook and tells me that she is the class president, that she is Peruvian, and she likes Chilean history a lot. She tells me [the history of Chile]. It is remarkable.

(…)

Later, he tells me that the Haitian [student] that left the class a couple of minutes before is a child who does not like the class, because he is not liked by the others, because he is full of himself. He tells me that on a field trip, they went to a museum and this Haitian student asked permission to talk with some girls that were not part of the class and that he answered him that he could not, because it was not appropriate.

(…)

Finally, the teacher makes them draw a seaport. In the class, there is a Bolivian student, to whom the teacher teases, saying to him, "You should be very happy drawing a port, as you are Bolivian"[1] Later, the teacher tells me that the students are easily distracted and that the students who recently left the classroom for academic support are from Haiti and the Dominican Republic, pointing out that it is better that way, because if they are in the classroom, they distract the rest of the class.

Sixth-grade history class, Coed School, 2014, School Z

The ethnographer asks the group of teachers what they are referring to when they say the students are full of themselves. One of the teachers points out that it is because they use makeup and go about with cosmetics bags. Another teacher present at the meeting mentions that, "of course, they use make up, they talk about men [she lowers her tone of voice], they talk about sex. They talk about these things and they tell me. They are very into music, they even go to concerts…" Another teacher present at the meeting says "They are consumerists, very consumerist, because everything has to be expensive, from the backpack, all the backpack are 48 USD and up, backpacks are quite expensive, wheeled backpacks, cute lunch boxes that go with the backpack, the pencil cases are also all the best, the latest on the market, the ones that are most popular, those are what the [females] bring to school. A lot of them go about with impressive cell phones. I am not familiar with many of the brands and prices, but you see that sometimes one as a teacher has a more modest cell phone than the students have and when you have 'casual day,' the students from kindergarten to twelfth grade attend with the latest fashion…" [All of the teaching assistants take a seat at the meeting.] Another teacher comments that the students already come

---

[1]There is an implicit reference here to a historic geopolitical dispute over Bolivia's access to the ocean.

to school made up from their homes, that their very mothers allow them to come with eye shadow, lipstick on, and their hair down… also with their tight-fitting pants. Another teacher comments, "As a religion teacher, I feel that they are lacking a little bit of modesty. I think the girls from before had a little more modesty. I think that our mothers instilled more values within us, but now it is all the same if it is cold like it is today, it is all the same to go around with a t-shirt, crop top and a vest over it, taking off their coats. In other words, they are full of themselves." Another teacher comments about the dances and says, "One sees how they dance and even the littlest ones do the dances, no!… Some dances, very erotic dances."

Group interview with teachers, All-Girls School, 2014, School A.

In a conversation when asked about if the students date, one of the teachers commented "…Yes, they date a lot and from very young ages and I am talking about relationships much more serious than one would think. The boyfriend is the very opposite example of the prototype that one would want, for example, of a studious boy, a boy who complies with schedules, but no, all the contrary, these boyfriends are very inappropriate, very contrary to what one hopes as a mother, for example, he is no prince charming. They have earring gauges and go about with their sagging pants and tattoos."

Group interview with teachers, All-Girls School, 2014, School A.

We reached the classroom located on the first floor, at the end of the patio of the elementary school section. The teacher and the teaching assistant introduce me to the students: "She is Carmen and she will be with us during the class." That day, the class is about calligraphy and the students are working on exercises with the letters L, M, O, and P. Some students look at me and some others continue writing in their exercise books. The teacher moves a chair closer to me and asks me to have a seat. Carolina [the professional in charge of the Integration Project] gives some papers to the teacher and asks her if she has identified some students with learning difficulties to be evaluated. The teacher nods and in silence observes the students. Then she reaches to the teaching assistant and asks her if she has some students in mind who need to be evaluated and be sent to the Integration School Program. The teaching assistant stays beside the whiteboard and observes the students.

The teacher walks around the classroom, and touches one student's shoulder and looks at the teaching assistant. The teacher does not say a word. However, the teaching assistant says aloud: "yes, she can be, sometimes it is hard for her." Then the teacher continues walking and gets closer to another student. She looks at the teaching assistant again and asks: "and how about her?" The teaching assistant responds aloud "no, she is not interested, but she is good." Finally, the teacher points to another student with her finger and the teaching assistant says, "yes, she is got a deficit problem, because she gets distracted easily." While the teachers continued identifying students with learning problems, the students talked and continued working on their writing exercises.

Language class, All-Girls School, School A.

8.6 Afterthought

The implications of being an active force, as a reader, in creating meaning makes me wonder about how we give life to particular epistemological frames to reproduce and circulate ideas of the other. As we intra-act with the above excerpts we all are implicated in the iterative production of particular material, discursive, and affective boundaries among people. To experience this chapter is to think of gender, sexuality, ability, age, race, and social class not as bounded and ready to read identities but as relations or events in the making. In this sense, how I am implicated in particular reproductions of these power structures becomes important. In other words, how far away am I from traditional understandings of identities to produce a different research question or even to retell a story captured in a fieldwork? How evident are power structures to my own analytic experiences of school life? I hope this chapter provides a bit of the political and creative moment of producing meaning while school lives are happening at this very moment.

References

Manning, E. (2009). *Relationscapes. Movement, art, philosophy*. Cambridge: MIT Press.
Nixon, R. (2011). *Slow violence and the environmentalism of the poor*. Cambridge: Harvard University Press.
Rosiek, J. L. (2018). Agential realism and educational ethnography. Guidance for application from Karen Barad's new materialism and Charles Sanders Peirce's material semiotics. In D. Beach, C. Bagley, & S. Marques da Silva (Eds.), *The Wiley handbook of ethnography in education* (pp. 403–421). New Jersey: Wiley Blackwell.
Smith, N. (1992). Contours of a spatialized politics: Homeless vehicles and the production of geographical scale. *Social Text, 33,* 55–81.

Chapter 9
Disentanglements

Claudia Matus

Abstract This chapter argues that the production of ethnographies can be a critical source for informing policy design on issues of diversity and inclusion. Ethnography from a post-representational perspective and the implications for the ways we conceptualize and represent issues of difference in school contexts and policy-making are explored. In making sense of the possibilities ethnographic research practices afford for informing policy design, the chapter engages in the exploration of new ways of thinking and researching *inequalities*, and the possibilities of change and transformation they might bring. I contend that the regulation of subjectivities through specific meanings of normalcy and difference leaves no opening for active politics. This chapter intends to advance on more creative ways to achieve social transformation.

9.1 Introduction

In our research study on the production of normalcy in school spaces using post-representational ethnographies, we intended to expand our way of framing the study to collaborative work with policymakers in charge of the educational reform on issues of diversity. The articulation among policies (State), practices (Schools), and research (University) seemed particularly relevant to us if the purpose was to shake those normative framings that reproduce the problem of normalcy (Davis 2013; O'Connell 2015, 2016) as an ideal and difference as an essentialized status for people. Using post-representational ethnographies to produce information on the ways the concept of difference was produced in relation to an invisible and neutralized idea of normalcy challenged our research group in terms of how we had to organize our work with the State, and how to communicate this information to policymakers in charge of producing policies intended to regulate the school space. This task was particularly challenging because we anticipated that those participating policymakers were working from rationalist accounts on policy design. In this sense, to talk about the production of normalcy as an imaginary ideal that frames policies meant to intro-

C. Matus (✉)
Center for Educational Justice, Pontificia Universidad Católica de Chile, Santiago, Chile
e-mail: cmatusc@uc.cl

© Springer Nature Singapore Pte Ltd. 2019   151
C. Matus (ed.), *Ethnography and Education Policy*, Education Policy
& Social Inequality 3, https://doi.org/10.1007/978-981-13-8445-5_9

duce a new concept to policymakers who are used to seeing a difference as the target for policies. The rationality behind policy-making related to issues of diversity in schools emphasizes instrumentalism and rationalities of decision-making (Webb and Gulson 2015) which, for the purpose of our research study, reinforces the problems we tried to overcome. We started with the following question: In what ways do these policies designed under positivistic rationalities not allow for the transformation of the problem of difference? First of all, the re-inscription of categories as stable and immutable (immigrants, women, disabled) does not allow for the reorganization of society which is something we believed was key. Second, the problem they are solving is located in a single axis of identity as we showed in other chapters of this book. Instead, the problem of essentialized difference as a result of the articulation with imaginaries of the normal is incommensurable and belongs to different and always changing locations. As Rosiek (2018) states, difference, and normalcy as concepts have agency and purpose. As such, they always respond in different ways to different methodological practices; therefore, the question of what kind of research policies they are listening to is relevant. Third, the linear relation between *problem* and *solution* in which policies are based, reduces the problem of difference to solutions such as compensation and assimilation. The totalizing ways to understand categories, the linear processes expressed in policies as problem and solutions, and the identity segmentation to address issues of diversity were signals for us that the policy landscape we were entering to think about policies as more generative of transformation and change was a hard task.

I think of policy as a materiality that stabilizes the configuring of the regularizing framework of the normal and the different subject. In such a way, the challenge was not only to present the information generated in 2 years of working with five schools to those State agents but also to challenge their own possibilities to understand the produced information. In so many ways, we had to deal with the idea that even though policymakers, were very engaged in the idea of justice and democracy, they may have been reinforcing structures of power when designing their policies. Concepts, as they are active and purposed, may co-opt policymakers (Rosiek 2018). As I show in this chapter, to design policies from normative understandings of race, class, gender, sexuality, age, nation, and ableness is troubling because they activate processes of differentiation, homogenization, normalization, and common sense as unproblematized ways of knowing. To make these professionals move to a different framework to revisit their own assumptions about the problem of difference was challenging, creative, and critical work. In our work with state policy designers on issues of inclusion and diversity, we came to understand the importance of data as the source for policy designers in understanding the problem they were producing in the policy itself and the solutions state professionals were given as possibilities for change and transformation. As Pillow (2017) states, "Data theorization—including what counts as data and when data counts—are key to thinking about what and who is imagined and unimaginable in this context" (p. 135). This is particularly critical when I consider that data in the case of the production and proliferation of the rationale of normalcy and difference expressed in the policies addressing issues of diversity in Chile are referring to unquestionable values assigned to people.

These conclusions lean toward a critique of the ways in which aspirations for inclusion and recognition by the state are far from neutral, and more critical, that they re-create the matrices of power to disenfranchise subjects. As I will show in our work with policy designers on issues of diversity and inclusion during 2013 and 2015,

> normative inclusion entrenches notions of proper versus improper, natural versus normal, and normative versus abject. There is no such a thing as a movement for inclusion and citizenship for *some* that does not further the vulnerability and disenfranchisement of *others*. (Brandzel 2016 p. x, italics in original)

Therefore, we took the idea seriously that to work with theoretical frames to dismantle violent normativities and critique those systems that naturalize and use common sense as real and as the normative knowledge was a means to define and construct the real of the political (Brandzel 2016). As a result, the normative framework of policy regarding issues of difference is violent in several ways. If this normative framework is not challenged, difference continues to be known and felt as lacking, or something to be solved which means that people were seen as the problem. It allows for the proliferation of cultures of risk, compensation, recovery, and prevention as natural for policymakers. Assimilationist perspectives through its anti-intersectional dimensions continue separating and giving different statuses to subjects. The perpetual refusal of the mutuality and contingency of the production of subjects of regulation translate into simple, non-complex matrices from where subjects are deemed to be regulated. As Brandzel (2016) states, "...the term *citizen* is often used as if it were synonymous with being a 'good' or ethical participant in some form of social contract, therefore working to mark and produce proper—read, *normative*—behaviour" (p. 13, italics in original). We understood our work with State agents as a possibility to advance issues of justice and transformation.

9.2 Policies as Trajectories of Regulation

In the current legality framework in Chile, on issues of diversity, we find an interesting trajectory of laws. In particular, there are three policies of interest of our research study, namely the School Vulnerability Index (JUNAEB 2007), the Law for School Inclusion (MINEDUC 2015), and the School Community Law (MINEDUC 2011). These policies provide a framework to understand the new legal configuration to work on issues of diversity and difference in schools. These laws, even when speaking only from their objective of regulation and sanction of practices considered outside the law, also have an effect that for the case of our investigation was crucial. By this, I mean that these laws are not only regulatory texts of institutional behaviors and practices, but they also shape the cultural and social production of schools, highlighting the daily discriminatory practices of subjects that until now have been located in the space of the common sense of people, resulting in the fact that the community must learn to recognize, name, and denounce what in many moments have seemed habitual ways of relating.

The invitation to our research team to work and support the Ministry of Education in formulating policies and documents regarding educational reform on inclusion issues was interesting since these laws were implemented in a social and cultural context that works with installed and accepted ways of racism, classism, xenophobia, sexism, homophobia, etc. For example, at the beginning of our research work, the available statistics documented the high rates of discrimination in school establishments in relation to physical characteristics, personal appearance, physical or intellectual disability, gender identity, sexual orientation, nationality, problems of health (HIV, among others) with the adults being the most discriminating actors in school spaces (INJUV 2013). This is a relevant data for the understanding of the contexts in which these laws are installed, and it is also relevant because it tells us about the forms that laws should take in order to promote a transformation in the ways in which subjects understand and value democratic and fair coexistence. In other words, if laws are aimed at sanctioning and penalizing discriminatory acts, then we should also think about how we educate to name situations in which one is the object of discrimination.

It is in this complex scenario, in terms of how school agents and State institutions live inclusion and exclusion in everyday life, that our research suggests that it is necessary to delve into the relationship between the type of research, how this type of research is communicated to policymakers, and how this information is channeled into the language of the policy. In other words, our efforts to work articulately with policymakers on these issues were characterized by guiding our work based on what they call inclusion to questions such as: What is the problem that the policy tries to solve? Who does it sanction? Who does it defend? What is the order that is implicitly and explicitly naturalized in the policy? (nuclear family, whiteness, middle class, Western culture, hegemonic femininity and masculinity, ableness, etc.). With these questions as a basis for our work with the State, we aimed not to lose the horizon raised from the research: to complicate the production of the biological, social, and cultural difference that the law resolves, and thus to advance in the gaps of these regulations and their operationalization. All of this in order to reorient and redesign aspects related to the ways of categorizing and hierarchizing discriminatory practices, to define what the regulations are supporting and to provide new orientations for thinking about school spaces outside of the sanction and penalization of discriminatory practices.

9.3 Assimilation and Compensation as Natural Processes of Policy

It is important to emphasize how school organization has historically been involved in the devaluation of identities that are thought of as distinct, marginal, vulnerable, or minority (Ahmed 2012; Youdell 2006, 2010). For example, this can be examined in the language used by the compensation policies that require the definition of those students who for any reason are defined as unfit, slow, deficient, culturally diverse, emotionally complex, etc., in order to become worthy of state support. Looking at this further, these policies have a component or rather an orientation to *assimilate* these groups to the *dominant culture* of the school through the production of moralities by installing hegemonic ideas about capacity to learn, valuing certain types of confirmation of family groups or ways of organizing intimate life, valuing certain leisure activities, etc. This is all based on the assumption that policies are neutral and that they only have a positive impact on school communities. However, for these compensation policies to be put into operation, they require that those attributes and specific provisions of the vulnerable groups that are the focus of the State's action be defined. This subtly establishes the idea that there are first and second class subjects in school communities.

Another important problem to consider about the ways in which we have generated a legal culture on issues of inclusion and diversity has to do with the fact that there is a generalized perception that these laws are exclusively for homosexuals, immigrants, the disabled, women, the vulnerable, etc. In many ways, this is a way in which the policy has been translated into society as a legal instrument that resolves issues of those who have *a problem*. For example, in the case of xenophobia or homophobia, immigrant or homosexual students, they are not the only ones who are harmed by these practices in school spaces. Children with immigrant family members or friends, the same children who bully, or children who are not immigrants but whose skin color or some other trait can be characterized as *immigrant* or *indio*, or students who are not or do not identify as homosexuals but do not exhibit the characteristics indicated by gender norms (e.g., look, act, speak like *a real man*) are also damaged. It is this group of students and community that most people belong to and perhaps, the most important point that we should pay attention to is the fact that it reminds us that all students live the pressures of presenting themselves in certain ways in order to avoid being made fun of, punished, socially penalized, or discriminated against. For example, cases that seem so innocent or subtle when students shout "fag", or affirm that "men don't cry", or claim that a student is "weird" because they walk with their hand on their waist, or complain about those girls who shout or are very restless and that this is an indication that they do not behave like "little girls", shows us how sexism and homophobia permanently monitor the limits of what is acceptable in relation to the identification of gender and sexual orientation for all students, not only for those who define themselves as homosexuals (Kimmel and Mahler 2003). This indicates that the problem is not only homophobia, sexism, xenophobia, and misogyny, but also the norms that are monitored and guaranteed by these practices, for example, heterosexuality, the valuing of hegemonic masculinity and femininity, the privileging of white culture, the progress associated with Western culture, etc. Questioning, visualizing, and exposing these norms is often complex because they are difficult to see, as they are often hidden in a language of what is "natural", "normal", "appropriate", and "moral".

In the case of the research proposal documented in this book, moving from observing and examining only the practices and actions that harm some groups of students to those norms and practices that harm and affect the entire community also redirects the types of questions that educational reforms and policies on the subject should make. We could go from thinking of a policy that only protects students who for some reason are thought of and defined as "different", "distinct", or "vulnerable" to some questions that are oriented to protect all students, practices that privilege particular notions of normality in the color of the skin, ways of speaking, sexual and gender practices, etc., in this sense, a policy that monitors and regulates the practices of differentiation, homogenization, normalization, and the use of common sense to get to know the students, would help.

Concretely, a policy considering these issues should frame itself in critical politics of knowing. For instance, we might think of policies answering and reporting questions about their processes of being produced. Let's imagine policies responding to these questions: (1) how policy prevents itself from seeing differences as essences (how policies achieve the categories they use; what are the consequence of using such categories in this manner (e.g., immigrants, women); (2) to report on what type of data the policy uses to produce what it sees as a problem to solve; and what type of data is missing or not considered and for what reasons; (3) what biological, social, and cultural orders the policy promotes and validates; which groups continue to be entitled and which groups continue to be seen as marginalized and for what purposes. A policy capable of answering these questions offers possibilities for transformation. Transformation itself starts when policies do not see themselves as neutral productions.

So, the challenge is how to advance in a policy design that does not promote assimilationist practices nor that puts the actions of the State in taking care of or improving the experience of those defined as lacking, but generating a policy that implies both what is thought of as lacking and who is thought of as privileged and how both groups are currently learning to think about some groups as advantaged and others as disadvantaged. An important contribution to this proposal is given by Yoshino (2007) who points out that society often measures its levels of progress through the ways in which the State regulates forms of discrimination and the degree to which it sanctions or penalizes them, legally and culturally. This is how a society can be considered to be *progressing*, when it goes from a discourse of thinking about differences as something to be *converted* or *changed*, to demanding that these differences be *recognized*. This way of thinking about progress in terms of the legality of differences and how marginalized groups are legally incorporated into institutional life has some problems. First, it establishes a hierarchy among the identities that must be assimilated in school establishments. For example, in the case of inclusion policies in Chile, the emphasis has been on disability and educational needs where it is stated that today it is believed that disability is the great problem of *diversity* that must be resolved in schools. This has generated the idea that we recognize the student with a disability more easily than the immigrant student. In the second case, groups that are *visibly* different have been thought of as the groups most in need of legal protection and specific institutional practices for pedagogical work. This legal protection means that there are equally discriminated groups but that unlike *the obvious* of disability, other "marginal" or "minority" groups may *change* or *hide* their differences and therefore not be subject to discriminatory acts. In these cases, legal protection falls within the scope of "good argumentation and/or justification" to produce "the case". Of course, the distinction between groups that are *visibly marked by difference* and those that are not is not always completely clear. For example, racial or gender differences are not always evident, as those students, for example, who are "foreigners (Peruvians) but look white" or those homosexual students "that you can't tell [are homosexual]."

For example, there may be a tendency to think that there are differences that can be qualified or that are expected to change (losing an accent, speaking more *cuico* ("high class" attitude) and less *flaite* (trashy), wearing only certain types of clothes, using certain hairstyles, behaving within the hegemonic parameters of the genre, etc.). Expanding on what the policy intends means that it must be understood that it does two things. On the one hand, it protects citizens from social and cultural demands that ask them to be something else, and at the same time fail to protect subjects against the practices of "hiding yourself so that they cannot see what you really are." While more subtle forms of discrimination may be seen as less severe practices, they impact on the sense of the self of the subjects (Roberts 2011). By failing to protect what people can change about themselves, particularly those characteristics that mark them as different, antidiscrimination laws indirectly require that differences be assimilated, since with assimilation, people can avoid discrimination.

Rather what is required is a change in the ways in which differences are thought about, that is, articulated to the idea of normality that underlies the demands we make of those differences, and the complicity with discourses and assimilationist practices should be transformed. Then the question would be in regard to the practice of the laws that regulate discriminatory acts in school spaces: To whom do they refer as the subject that has to change? The homosexual student or the homophobic student, teacher, administrator? The woman or the sexist? The racial minorities or racist? (Yoshino 2007). In this sense, it is not difficult to find examples of how schools demand the assimilation of difference through different school practices: formal and informal curriculum, didactics, extracurricular activities, school culture, school relations with the community, school organization, administration, discipline, etc., to name a few.

9.4 Resilient Concepts

In what follows, I want to consider three concepts that travel across those policies that were of interest in our research study. Vulnerability, healthy coexistence, and inclusion have proven to be independent of analysis and critique. Their adaptability and capacity (Rosiek 2018) to resist critique is something that I have to highlight.

9.4.1 Vulnerability

The Chilean policy landscape is particulary interesting since the ways policies produce deficit and disadvantage is, to say the least, shameless. This is the case of the School Vulnerability Index, in which the aim is to produce a measure to sort students into "degrees of vulnerability". Once students are assigned a percentage of vulnerability, the school they belong to receives monetary support for those targeted students. What is interesting to me is the type of questions this instrument uses to produce a vulnerable student. It is worth mentioning that this survey is intended for early childhood education, the first grade in elementary school, and the first year in high school (freshman). Also, this survey is mandatory for every school except for those belonging to private administrations (8% of the total number of schools in Chile). This survey produces information about family history, asking for the number of people who live with the children, who is defined as the head of the household, and the parents' school levels and current occupations. In a different set of questions, we find home information such as if the child sleeps alone, if there is a defined space for the child to study, or if the home is near recreational places or hospitals, and, finally, who cares for and does homework with the child. Another group of questions is oriented to find out about the student's health, asking how problematic the child has been in performing different cognitive tasks, and if he or she has visual, learning, or behavioral control problems, or suffers from any diagnosis of a chronic illness. In addition, the survey presents a set of questions regarding relevant aspects of early childhood upbringing. Here, questions seek to learn about the mother's age at the time of the child's birth, the child's birth weight, if he/she was premature, the type of lactation received, the type of schooling, early childhood stimulation, and finally, if the father was physically or economically present during the child's upbringing. Lastly and more disturbing, is a group of questions concerning lifestyles, characteristics, and expectations about the student. Parents are asked about the student's emotions, attitudes, and behaviors, as well as the parents' educational expectations about the student's performances. Once this information is registered, students are allocated to different priority levels according to their vulnerability percentage. This particular policy, which I understand as a state-funded production of discriminatory practices, reveals a particular orientation of policies in Chile. There are practices to regulate and sanction those who do not perform or exhibit the ideals of a normative family or ideal behaviors or capacities.

The imaginaries these types of policies have created, supported by specific kinds of research, have become popular knowledge which is critical (Bacchi 1999, 2014; Scheurich 1994; Shore and Wright 1997). If the Chilean educational system has been long recognized for its success in segregating students based on social class and merit, then these types of policies only reinforce and justify the difference they produce about subjects. Without a doubt, the future for students and families is produced by these policies that lock subjects and communities into an inescapable circle of disadvantage. At the same time, the classed and gendered deficit assumptions embedded in these policies come from research that perpetuates these assumptions where causal relations between single-parent homes or teen pregnancy and school success are not problematized or simply are produced as relational causes. "Data shows" or "studies state" is not enough to inform a policy whose intention is to overcome inequalities. We need to question data and the ways it reproduces stigmatization about particular groups. To work on issues of inequalities we need to question how understandings of data shape policies (Pillow 2017) and as a consequence, possibilities for subjects and new futures are possible.

9.4.2 Healthy Coexistence

Another policy of interest is "Discrimination in educational contexts. Orientations to promote an inclusive school" (2013), which details those categories through which students might be discriminated against in schools: race-ethnicity, nationality, socioeconomic situation, language, political ideology and opinion, religion or beliefs, unions or the participation in labor union organizations or the lack of them, sex, sexual orientation, gender identity, marital status, age, affiliation, personal appearance, sickness or disability (p. 9). This particular document reinforces a rationality of identification that "seeks to definitely identify bodies, to place them in categories delineated by race, gender, or ability status, and then to validate that placement through a verifiable, biological mark of identity" (Samuels 2014, p. 2). This list is intended to raise awareness (and at the same time it establishes the idea that we require "evidence" to justify the status of subjects and communities) for school agents to detect and prepare the school space for any discriminatory practice that may arise. In so many ways this list is a claim that "identity is fixed, measurable, and intrinsically connected to social worth and citizenship" (Samuels 2014, p. 20). Nonetheless, when our research team was working with those in charge of designing this policy (nearly 30 professionals), the questions we raised to start complicating the policy itself, was: What is the problem this policy intends to solve?; Who can be excluded from this list?; and in what ways does this policy continue to perpetuate the stigma of certain groups through specific categories and at the same time reinforce the idea that the normal subject exists somewhere out of this policy? Our concern was that at the time you mention those categories from which one can be discriminated for with no reference to what is the opposite category for the production of them, the idea of the normal subject becomes neutralized with important political consequences. It was after these questions were presented to the policymakers that ethnographic excerpts played a key role. We asked: Does what you see in these excerpts similar to what you stated as a school problem in your policies? In what ways are they different? What kind of research do we need in order to establish, more substantially, policies on issues of diversity or inclusion? The crisis or shock the State agents reported after confronting the problem they produced in policies for the same schools we were working with and their confirmation that the problem was somewhere else, was one of the most rewarding moments for our research team. Ethnography from a post-representational framework was key to advance our work with policymakers. In our work with policy designers, our intention was to make strange their naturalization of the normative dimension of their policies even though they were oriented to critically address issues of discrimination.

One other question we might ask in regard to this particular policy is: Who is the expert dictating how to make the distinction among people subjected to these categories? As Samuels (2014) notes "…fantasies of identification stubbornly persist, despite being disproved, undermined, or contradicted, and this persistence provokes resistance and disidentifications from subjects attempting to escape the fantasy's totalizing imposition of identity" (p. 3). Therefore, if we think that these categories embrace the whole spectrum of our biological, social, and cultural lives, then who is the one who is discriminating? We must use the issue of privilege associated with the idea of unquestioned normality as a relevant point to begin to think about how and why discriminatory practices are possible.

Even though there is an intention to think of everyone as equal, in practice the production of images and meanings about *different* students are based on a consensual common sense centered around ideas learned, for example, about hegemonic practices of being a woman or a man, the ideas of economic progress and cultural status associated with the skin color and the origins of people, the cultural and social attributes and dispositions assigned to students depending on the communes they live in, the normative idea of the *able* body, etc. We propose that these ideas and ways of knowing *the other* are sustained in policies, in school dynamics, and in the classrooms, causing inequalities to persist (Matus 2015; Matus and Haye 2015; Matus and Infante 2011; Matus and McCarthy 2003; Matus and Rojas 2015, 2018). Obviously, we are not saying that this is an apprenticeship that occurs only at school or from policies; on the contrary, numerous social institutions assure and encourage that these ways of thinking about *the differences* are and seem to be evident.

The state's normativizing project to identify, differentiate, and assign statuses to different categories makes the messiness of identity incomprehensible (Brandzel 2016).

9.4.3   Inclusion

As of 2015, the State has decided to face the challenge of improving the equity and quality of education through the processing and implementation of what has been called the School Inclusion Law (Law Number 20,845). This law is based on three main guidelines: (1) the end of profit; (2) the end to the copayment in educational systems financed with public resources; and (3) nonarbitrary discrimination and inclusion. In order to do this, some of the normative bodies that govern our current education system have been modified: the General Education Law, the Subsidies Law, the Quality Assurance Law, and the Preferential School Subsidy Law. Specifically, the School Inclusion Law is operationalized by restricting educational establishments from selecting students and demanding extra fees when dealing with establishments that are financed with public resources. This is intended to reduce existing barriers so that all students can enter the schools they wish and choose. The complexity of the implementation of this reform, imposed by law, means that it will bring several consequences associated with the promotion of diversity in schools: (1) schools will be more heterogeneous which will highlight cultural expectations unquestioned that circulate in school communities about specific groups, which probably do not coincide with the imaginary ones so far constructed: *other families and communities, other types of children*, etc., will be integrated into the establishments; (2) mismanagement of this heterogeneity can lead to discriminatory practices within schools and between students; (3) *Diversity* may again be the object of identification of the *other* students (of subjects, groups, families, establishments, etc.) from which new or other forms of exclusion and unequal distribution of learning that were less obvious could be produced; (4) new hierarchies between the schools and between teachers will be produced, associated with the management of these changes in the school population. In this context, both at the level of schools, teachers' organizations, institutions that evaluate, supervise, and support the schools as well as at the level of different organisms of civil society, it has been advised that the proposal of change that the reform entails should: (i) contemplate substantive transformations in relation to school cultural structures in order to adapt to the new diversity scenario (in particular in regard to the ways of conceptualizing quality) and (ii) incorporate mechanisms that support teachers in the approach to the consequences associated with this change in school culture and organization. On the other hand, the current educational reform challenges the establishments and school agents to the extent that they do not make reference, for example, to specific sociocultural contexts (for example, the situation of all-boys or all-girls schools, of communes, regions, and cities with a high density of indigenous or immigrant populations, etc.). In regard to these laws implemented and in the process of being progressively implemented, it became evident that school access policies themselves are insufficient to influence the achievement of greater opportunities for all, particularly in regard to the quality of learning and inclusive practices.

This law, unlike the previous processes of addressing diversity, no longer tries to act on disadvantaged groups, but at the level of the educational system structure, and by questioning and challenging those discursive and material systems of school life that uphold the privileges of certain groups and subjects. Now, from our work done with the Ministry of Education, our proposal was to see how the dominant discourses about the ordering of identities prevail and/or lead to reinterpretations of the law that reinforce the sanction and punishment processes.

Our concern, which stems from our research, is that, as this law proposes, when insisting on the issue of access with a strong component of nonarbitrary discrimination, the idea of what to do once all the students are inside the school establishment is ignored. For our research team, the unequal distribution of quality and inclusion is due to the complex articulation of divisions and sociocultural values existing in the common sense of the community associated among others with social class, gender, race and ethnic origin (Ahmed 2012; Matus and Haye 2015; Youdell 2006, 2010) also present in the policies presented.

9.5 Moving Beyond Representation in Ethnography and Policy

It is through the daily life activities of schools (possible to record through post-representational ethnographies) that essentialist and naturalized knowledge (ideas) about who are the valued student identities and who are thought of as lacking, marginal, or in condition of repair solidify. This has particular relevance when the objective is to understand the effects of the implementation of laws, in particular, those that are oriented to inclusion issues, especially because what is sought is to transform school cultures in relation to inclusion, diversity, and difference. The knowledge derived from ethnographic work has significant value because it accounts for the particularities of how institutional processes can be optimized for other establishments that enter into implementation dynamics.

Among our ways of problematizing what laws *do*, we should question at least two of the principles that they are based on neutrality and stability of concepts, and the culture of diagnosis and risk.

Neutrality and stability of concepts need to be addressed when referring to issues of difference. Those laws that seek to regulate issues of diversity are based on neutrality. These laws are thought of by defining categories for topics of inclusion in schools, such as race, gender, sexuality, etc. This is how laws refer to universal values rather than explicit references to how power issues related to the inclusion of students are understood. This translates into adherence to legality and protocols, the incorporation of lawyers for the preparation of manuals, the delimitation of the types of problems that will be addressed, which allows us to understand that the neutralization of processes and actions is a strategy to be able to face the extra work that addressing issues of inclusion in the school space implies. When regulation is under the concept of protocolization or the vision of new professionals (such as lawyers) entering the regulation field of discriminatory actions, the sanction is transformed into the way of taking charge of these issues, disassociating pedagogical processes from practices dealing with the management of students.

The culture of diagnosis and risk is the second concept that needs to be questioned. New rationalities to segment students have come to operate as relevant to work with students. Making a diagnosis comes to be an institutionalized practice which allows for the possibility to find more differences to be named, and therefore, to enter the circle of medication. Along with this, behaviors, emotions, and attitudes that never were considered problems are now symptoms to be treated with medication, and they have become an important resource to label students. Along with connecting the idea of diagnosis with obtaining more resources (which is extremely complex in itself), this institutional practice makes it possible to establish a logic of individualization and visibility of difference, which has tended to medicalize cultural and social practices. In other words, I am referring to behavioral issues (interrupting in the classroom, not sitting still in the chair) as *symptoms* or characteristics of the students that can lead to a psychological diagnosis (with the consequence of eventual medication).

Policies as practices of differentiation, homogenization, normalization, and installation of common sense focus on the installation of sanction and punishment norms in order to identify deficit identities. This should cause us to ask ourselves about the type of work that should be done before approaching the subject of sanction and punishment. Addressing the issues of difference and diversity with practices oriented toward tolerance and respect *for the different* does not modify structures of how difference is reasoned. Rather, tolerance is a way of regulating aversion to this difference (Brown 2006) and, therefore, generates other types of discrimination. This idea can be supported by national studies that indicate that Chilean society is moving from manifest forms of prejudice toward more subtle ones (Cárdenas and Barrientos 2008). What I propose as a problem is that to the extent that the policy does not reflect the knowledge that has to do with the effects of essentializing and naturalizing knowledge, people, communities, and the construction of difference will continue to be the dominant framework for building school subjects. These practices install the production of marked subjects to be tolerated, which for our investigation, was understood as part of the problem if the idea is to build more democratic societies. The discourses of tolerance, position the marked individuals as deviant, marginal, or undesirable by what they are by virtue being tolerated for, which inevitably brings with it the exercise of superiority, not problematized, by those who are trained to tolerate. For example, Brown (2006) explains that tolerance discourses simultaneously promote three actions: (1) intensify the regulatory effects of essentialized identities; (2) ideologically, constitute a *difference* outside a system of subordination or inequity; and (3) strengthen the hegemony of the unmarked or dominant identity. For example, when policies promote that school communities must tolerate the race, ethnicity, culture, religion, or sexual orientation of their students, there is no suggestion of how these differences or identities are produced or how they have been historically and culturally constructed. In fact, these policies fail to show that these differences themselves are the effect of power and of the hegemonic norms of social and cultural organization; instead, the difference itself is what school institutions must learn to tolerate. The logic of sanction and punishment, in addition to the discourses about tolerance and respect for the *different* that occupy much of the official discourses of educational establishments today, promote ways to organize normality and difference as unquestionable, and as a consequence, reproduce unequal systems. Undoubtedly, current times demand more sophisticated proposals to think about the problem of policies in terms of difference. One proposal is to design policies that monitor and regulate the practices of differentiation, homogenization, normalization, and common sense as a way of knowing. These habits of mind (Barad 2003) must be the problem of policies if we intend to overcome inequalities as we know them today.

References

Ahmed, S. (2012). *On being included. Racism and diversity in institutional life*. Durham: Duke University Press.

Barad, K. (2003). Posthumanist performativity: Toward an understanding of how matter comes to matter. *Signs, 28*(3), 801–831.

Bacchi, C. (1999). *Women, policy, and politics. The construction of policy problems*. London: Sage.

Bacchi, C. (2014). *Analysing policy: What's the problem represented to be?*. Australia: Pearson.

Brandzel, A. L. (2016). *Against citizenship. The violence of the normative*. Chicago: University of Illinois Press.

Brown, W. (2006). *Regulating aversion. Tolerance in the age of identity and empire*. Princeton: Princeton University Press.

Cárdenas, M., & Barrientos, J. (2008). Actitudes explícitas e implícitas hacia los homosexuales en Chile. *Psykhe, 17*(2), 17–25.

Davis, L. (2013). *The end of normal. Identity in a biocultural era*. Ann Arbor: The University of Michigan Press.

INJUV. (2013). Experiencias y percepciones en torno a la discriminación. Jòvenes entre 15 y 29 años. Retrieved from http://www.injuv.gob.cl/storage/docs/Libro_Octava_Encuesta_Nacional_de_Juventud.pdf.

JUNAEB. (2007). Indice vulnerabilidad escolar. Retrieved from http://junaebabierta.junaeb.cl/catalogo-de-datos/indicadores-de-vulnerabilidad/.

Kimmel, M. S., & Mahler, M. (2003). Adolescence masculinity, homophobia, and violence: Random school shootings, 1982–2001. *American Behavioral Scientist, 46*(10), 1439–1458.

Matus, C. (2015). The uses of affect in education: Chilean government policies. *Discourse: Studies in the Cultural Politics of Education, 38*(2), 235–248. https://doi.org/10.1080/01596306.2015.1087678.

Matus, C., & Haye, A. (2015). Normalidad y diferencia en la escuela: diseño de un proyecto de investigación social desde el dilema político-epistemológico. *Estudios Pedagógicos, 41*, 135–146.

Matus, C., & Infante, M. (2011). Undoing diversity: Knowledge and neoliberal discourses in colleges of education. *Discourse: Studies in the Cultural Politics of Education, 32*(3), 294–330.

Matus, C., & McCarthy, C. (2003). The triumph of multiplicity and the carnival of difference: Curriculum dilemmas in the age of postcolonialism and globalization. In W. Pinar (Ed.), *International handbook of curriculum research* (pp. 73–82). New Jersey: Lawrence Erlbaum Associates.

Matus, C., & Rojas, C. (2015). Normalidad y diferencia en nuestras escuelas: a propósito de la Ley de Inclusión Escolar. *Revista Docencia, 56*, 47–56.

Matus, C., & Rojas, C. (2018). Ethnography of the normal. In J. Assael & A. Valdivia (Eds.), *Lo cotidiano en la escuela. 40 años de etnografía escolar en Chile* (pp. 254–290). Santiago: Editorial Universitaria.

Ministerio de Educación. (2011). Ley de Convivencia Escolar. Retrieved from https://www.mineducacion.gov.co/1759/w3-article-322486.html.

Ministerio de Educación. (2015). Ley de Inclusión Escolar. Retrieved from https://leyinclusion.mineduc.cl/.

O'Connell, K. (2015). Bad boys' brains: Law, neuroscience and the gender of "aggressive" behavior. In S. Schmitz & G. Hoppner (Eds.), *Gendered neurocultures: Feminist and queer perspectives on current brain discourses*. Retrieved from https://ssrn.com/abstract=2581322.

O'Connell, K. (2016). Unequal brains: Disability discrimination laws and children with challenging behaviour. *Medical Law Review, 24*(1), 76–98.

Pillow, W. (2017). Imagining policy [data] differently. In S. Parker, K. Gulson, & T. Gale (Eds.), *Policy and inequality in education* (pp. 1–5). Singapore: Springer.

Roberts, D. (2011). *Fatal invention: How science, politics, and big business re-create race in the twenty-first century*. New York: New Press.

Rosiek, J. L. (2018). Agential realism and educational ethnography. Guidance for application from Karen Barad's new materialism and Charles Sanders Peirce's material semiotics. In D. Beach,

C. Bagley, & S. Marques da Silva (Eds.), *The Wiley handbook of ethnography in education* (pp. 403–421). New Jersey: Wiley Blackwell.

Samuels, E. (2014). *Fantasies of identification. Disability, gender, race.* New York: New York University Press.

Scheurich, J. J. (1994). Policy archaeology: A new policy studies methodology. *Journal of Education Policy, 9,* 297–316.

Shore, C., & Wright, S. (1997). Policy: A new field of anthropology. In C. Shore & S. Wright (Eds.), *Anthropology of policy* (pp. 3–42). New York: Routledge.

Superintendencia de Educación. (2013). *Discriminación en el context escolar. Orientaciones para promover la escuela inclusiva.* Retrieved from https://www.supereduc.cl/resguardo-de-derechos/nueva-guia-para-la-no-discriminacion-en-el-contexto-escolar/.

Webb, P. T., & Gulson, K. N. (2015). Policy scientificity 3.0: Theory and policy analysis in-and-for this world and other-worlds. *Critical Studies in Education, 56*(1), 161–174.

Yoshino, K. (2007). *Covering. The hidden assault on our civil rights.* New York: Random House Trade Paperbacks.

Youdell, D. (2006). Impossible bodies, impossible selves. Exclusions and students subjectivities. Netherlands: Springer.

Youdell, D. (2010). *School trouble. Identity, power, and politics in education.* New York: Routledge.

Chapter 10
Future Thoughts

Claudia Matus

Abstract In this final chapter I argue that social transformation and educational justice, as part of our concerns and motivations to pursue the writing of this book to report our research study, cannot be talked about out of the neoliberal frame of the policy landscape in Chile. The active production of diversity and inclusion discourses in Chile since 2012 represents an effort to undo the pervasive effects of school privatization practices driven by the neoliberal agenda. Since school privatization is highly supported and promoted by not only neoliberal but also neoconservative ideologies, policies, and political projects, the current discussion on public education and diversity provides a rich context to discuss the possibilities and challenges new reforms offer to transform segregated educational systems worldwide.

In this book, we have covered the political, theoretical, and methodological trajectory of a critical research study implemented in a conservative political and cultural time for policies on inclusion and diversity in Chile.

Social transformation and educational justice, as part of our concerns and motivations to pursue this research study, cannot be talked about out of the neoliberal frame of the policy landscape in Chile. The active production of diversity and inclusion discourses in Chile since 2012 represents an effort to undo the pervasive effects of school privatization practices driven by the neoliberal agenda. Since school privatization is highly supported and promoted by not only neoliberal but also neoconservative ideologies, policies, and political projects, the current discussion on public education provides a rich context to discuss the possibilities and challenges new reforms offer to transform our segregated educational system. Therefore, in our research project, presented in this book, we question the economic, cultural, and political practices engrained in the privatized model in Chile (Carrasco and Gunter 2019; Carrasco et al. 2019). As the educational system in Chile is recognized as a successful testing ground for neoliberal policies in education, it also provides a critical context to explore the possibilities and challenges to the reinstallation of the notion of public education. Those discussions on how public can public education be after the long

C. Matus (✉)
Center for Educational Justice, Pontificia Universidad Católica de Chile, Santiago, Chile
e-mail: cmatusc@uc.cl

© Springer Nature Singapore Pte Ltd. 2019
C. Matus (ed.), *Ethnography and Education Policy*, Education Policy
& Social Inequality 3, https://doi.org/10.1007/978-981-13-8445-5_10

history of privatization in Chile, once again neutralizes discussions on how school segregation is grounded in uneven social and cultural relations where race, social class, gender, sexuality, ability, age, and ethnicity play a significant role on how to understand the ways in which the educational system thinks of students' differences and gives reasons on why they should be divided.

As we have shown through the different claims and discussions presented in these chapters we, as researchers, have an obligation to rethink the ways we have been used to thinking about problems related to discriminatory practices and the ways we have been trained to study and report them. To continue using ideas such as: "gender gap," "inequality as a problem of access," or "meritocracy as a positive and fair approach" does not recognize the uneven starting point for subjects and the ways we position them to explain issues of inequalities. This is a research question in itself: the ways we produce and reproduce knowledge about inequality itself. This, as we have shown in this book, is an urgent request for researchers interested in social transformation.

Our research study has shown that it is possible to produce a research question, objects of study, and research practices without using the colonialist trap of deficiency imposed on those who have been historically defined as minorities, marginalized or vulnerable identities and communities. The colonialist model of normalcy, as has been the focus of our inquiry activity, has proven to be adaptable to those approaches of critical thinking. In fact, an important moment for discussion while producing those ethnographic studies was to deal with the fact that we might be producing those very normative structures we were questioning. In other words, even though we trust in our political positionings to address these issues we had to surveil ourselves constantly in order not to get caught in those naturalized ways of producing normative ways of thinking about difference.

This was a major challenge and learning experience. Our methodological stance always pointed to the idea that to document *the problem of difference*, we need to problematize our own ways of knowing about difference, being that this is usually located in the unquestioned ideas of the *normal*. Part of this positioning was to be critical about the ways common sense has become a regular way of knowing and privileging conservative thinking. The colonial models we have been pressed to put to work unquestionably in our research help us to think critically about how research practices themselves (e.g., qualitative research) insists on the production of particular knowledge, and consequent maintenance of particular truths (Denzin et al. 2008).

In this sense, our effort has been to think of postrepresentational frames to think about ethnography as a possibility to advance a critique on Eurocentric research practices and colonial ways of producing normative frames of positioning us/other; normal/abnormal. As we moved out of thinking and describing the other or the abnormal or the stranger and focused on researching on the one imagined as the normal identity or community, we question the traditional models of thinking and doing research about difference. Therefore, our postrepresentational and posthumanist orientations, as possibilities to escape humanist, colonialist, and rationalist frames of thinking, provide a rich possibility for political and intellectual advancements. For instance, for us to advance on issues of dismantling illnesses such as racism, genderism, ableism, homophobia, and xenophobia, we need to go back to the naturalized dichotomy of nature/culture (Barad 2007; Keller 2010; Kirby 2011) and question our-selves on how that separation has given us a particular way of understanding what we know and what for. To problematize and update the complex relationships between the biological, social, and cultural spheres and the effects their relations have for the production of subjects, objects, and affects is part of the problems that require attention.

For the research study presented in this book, we seek to rethink not only objects of research and methodological practices but also their relationships, thus allowing the production of new problems and the exploration of their potential for change. Posthumanist and postrepresentational approaches provide us with a political frame to question the natural separation of the subject who knows from what she knows as a problematic *habit* for the production of what we have come to believe as truths. In other words, I might claim that the imaginations we have created about those named as minorities, vulnerable populations, or discriminated groups are based on humanist assumptions such as that nature and culture are two separate realms that affect or influence one another, and feed the persistent ideal relation between humans as biological categories, objects representing and belonging to particular cultures, space, and subjectivities as corresponding, time as a predictable sequence, etc. Nature and culture, as two distinctive realms, produce particular systems to reason that perpetuate ideas of separation, linearity, and causality to explain and justify issues of power in our daily lives. For instance, temporal sequencing in school practices refers to the idea that there is a biological reality that determines cognitive, emotional, attitudinal, and physiological developments (Seaton 2012). On the other hand, the production of the body and its disciplining (Wagener 1998) has been used as evidence or essential idea (Seaton 2012) to proliferate all kinds of ideologies. Therefore, the body is seen as a *natural material*, independent from social influences, and the ideas of the human and the nonhuman are embedded in this distinction. From here, we have been taught to produce ideas of who we are and who the others are not only from a semiotic production of a binarism but also from the production of relations required to conduct our daily lives, accordingly.

We hope our theoretical, methodological, and political exercise (presented in this book) dislocates some of the processes involved in doing research.

References

Barad, K. (2007). *Meeting the universe halfway: Quantum physics and the entanglement of matter and meaning*. Durham: Duke University Press.

Carrasco, A., Bonilla, A., & Rasse, A. (2019). El futuro del sector particular subvencionado después de las reformas: ¿cuentan con capacidades para transformar su calidad? In Carrasco, A. y Flores, L. (Eds.), *De la reforma a la transformación. Capacidades, innovación y regulación de la educación chilena*. Santiago: Ediciones UC.

Carrasco, A., & Gunter, H. M. (2019). The "private" in the privatisation of schools: The case of Chile. *Educational Review, 71*, 67–80. https://doi.org/10.1080/00131911.2019.1522035.

Denzin, N. K., Lincoln, Y. S., & Smith, L. T. (Eds.). (2008). *Handbook of critical and indigenous methodologies*. Thousand Oaks, CA: Sage Publications.

Keller, F. E. (2010). *The mirage of space. Between nature and culture*. Durham: Duke University Press.

Kirby, V. (2011). *Quantum anthropologies. Life at large*. Durham: Duke University Press.

Seaton, E. (2012). Biology/nature. In N. Lesko & S. Talburt (Eds.), *Keywords in youth studies: Tracing affects, movements, knowledges* (pp. 24–29). New York: Routledge.

Wagener, J. R. (1998). The construction of the body through sex education. In T. Popkewitz & M. Brennan (Eds.), *Foucault's challenge. Discourse, knowledge, and power in education* (pp. 144–169). New York: Teachers College Press.

Printed by Printforce, United Kingdom